James B. Adamson studied at the University of Edinburgh and in 1954 was awarded the Ph.D. degree from Cambridge University for a thesis on the Epistle of James. He is a Presbyterian minister in Santa Rosa, California.

The New International Commentary on the New Testament

F. F. BRUCE, *General Editor*

THE EPISTLE OF
JAMES

by

JAMES B. ADAMSON, M.A., Ph.D.

WILLIAM B. EERDMANS PUBLISHING COMPANY

Copyright © 1976 by William B. Eerdmans Publishing Co.
255 Jefferson Ave. S.E., Grand Rapids, Mich. 49502

Printed in the United States of America

Library of Congress Cataloging in Publication Data

Adamson, James B
    The Epistle of James.

    (The New International Commentary on the New
Testament)
    "Text, Exposition, and Notes": p. 47.
    Bibliography: p. 40.
    Includes indexes.
    1. Bible. N.T. James—Commentaries.
I. Bible. N. T. James. 1976. II. Title.
III. Series.
BS2785.3.A3   227'.91'07   76-9840
ISBN 0-8028-2377-7

TO
P. B. R. FORBES
ΕΥΧΑΡΙΣΤΗΡΙΟΝ

CONTENTS

CONTENTS

EDITOR'S PREFACE

With this volume on the Epistle of James the New International Commentary on the New Testament enters on a fresh phase of its existence. Standard series of commentaries on the Old and New Testaments, especially on the European Continent but also in the English-speaking world, have been kept up to date over the years through the replacement of earlier volumes by new ones. We think in this regard of the Meyer series and the Lietzmann *Handbuch zum Neuen Testament* in Germany, of the *Commentaire du Nouveau Testament* in the French-speaking world, and now of the International Critical Commentary among ourselves. There is good reason for the New International Commentary to follow the same policy, now that it is a quarter century old.

The volume on *The Epistles of James and John* by the late Professor Alexander Ross, first published in 1954, has served its generation worthily; but the intervening years have seen the emergence of new problems relating to this group of New Testament documents, and it has been decided to replace that volume by two, written by different scholars, each of whom has paid special attention to the text with which he is to deal.

Another new departure relates to the English version used as the basis for the commentary. The basic version hitherto has been the American Standard Version of 1901 (apart from the late Norval Geldenhuys' commentary on Luke, for which the British Revised Version of 1881 was used). For the second edition of the series it is proposed to invite the commentator to construct his own English version, and this has been done in the present volume.

Dr. James B. Adamson, the author of this commentary, is a graduate of the Universities of Edinburgh and Cambridge. By the latter University he was awarded the Ph.D. degree in 1954 for a thesis entitled "An Inductive

9

Approach to the Epistle of James: Materials for a Fresh Study.'' He has put these materials to good use in this commentary.

Dr. Adamson is now a Presbyterian minister in Santa Rosa, California.

1976   F.F.B.

AUTHOR'S PREFACE

My interest in the Epistle of James was first developed in my studies under Professor C. H. Dodd at Cambridge, then under Professor C. F. D. Moule, and with his generous guidance for some years afterward, and more recently under the stimulating encouragement of Professor F. F. Bruce, without which this effort could scarcely ever have been completed. I am greatly indebted also to one of my former Edinburgh teachers and warm friend, Mr. P. B. R. Forbes, of whose constant interest, help, advice, and inspiration I record my deepest appreciation. To him I dedicate this book with gratitude and affection. My special thanks are due to my wife, Jean, who read the proofs, and indeed to all the family, Fiona, Jennifer and Wendy, whose love and care, in the midst of the busy pastorate, made this book possible.

Among books on the Epistle of James I have found three that are indispensable: J. B. Mayor, *The Epistle of St. James* (1913); F. J. A. Hort, *The Epistle of James* (1909); and J. H. Ropes, *A Critical and Exegetical Commentary on the Epistle of St. James* (The International Critical Commentary, 1916).

One of the chief aims of this book is to combat what I consider a fatal error made already by Luther and now in far too many modern commentaries on James: his Epistle is generally regarded as completely lacking any cohesion of thought or design. Thus C. Leslie Mitton: "There is in fact no discernible plan in the epistle"; B. S. Easton: "While the entire work undoubtedly possesses a certain unity, it lacks any formal plan—not only as a whole, but in its separate parts"; and William Barclay: "It is difficult, if not impossible, to extract from James, a continuous and coherent plan or scheme." This point will receive attention in due course.

The vindication of its structure will be seen to strengthen our belief in the date and authorship of the Epistle, as do also (*inter alia*) the style and structure of 5:1–8. Here the strong Old Testament and Jewish element is obvious, especially in the verb "howl," in 5:1, which occurs here alone in

11

the New Testament and, as we were bound to expect, in a passage of prophetic, not evangelical character: the rich here denounced need not be taken to be present in the listening congregations any more than the nations and people are present in Isa. 34:1. James thus takes us back to the technique of the Old Testament and the synagogue, comforting the afflicted in the Hebrew manner with a prediction of the fall of their enemies and oppressors, in the same way as, for example, the comprehensive curse of Isa. 34 upon the evil is immediately followed by the next chapter's sublime comfort for their victims.

J. B. A.

ABBREVIATIONS

AG	[W. Bauer's] *Greek-English Lexicon of the New Testament*, trans. and adapted by W. F. Arndt and F. W. Gingrich (1957)
ATR	*Anglican Theological Review*
b.	Babylonian Talmud
BDB	Brown-Driver-Briggs, *A Hebrew-English Lexicon of the Old Testament* (1906)
Bl.-D.	F. Blass-A. DeBrunner, *A Greek Grammar of the New Testament and Other Early Christian Literature* (E.T. by R. W. Funk, 1961)
ERE	*Encyclopaedia of Religion and Ethics*, ed. J. Hastings (1908)
E.T.	English Translation
EVV	English Versions
ExT	*Expository Times*
HTR	*Harvard Theological Review*
ICC	International Critical Commentary
JBL	*Journal of Biblical Literature*
JE	*Jewish Encyclopaedia*
JTS	*Journal of Theological Studies*
KEK	Kritisch-exegetischer Kommentar über das Neue Testament (founded by H. A. W. Meyer)
KJV	King James Version, 1611 (Authorized Version)
LS	H. G. Liddell and R. Scott, *Greek-English Lexicon*, revised by H. S. Jones (1940)
M.	Mishnah
MM	J. H. Moulton and G. Milligan, *Vocabulary of the Greek Testament* (1930)
NEB	New English Bible
NICNT	New International Commentary on the New Testament
NTS	*New Testament Studies*
R	Rabba (Midrash Rabba)
RSV	Revised Standard Version

RV	Revised Version
SB	H. L. Strack and P. Billerbeck, *Kommentar zum Neuen Testament aus Talmud und Midrasch* (1922–28)
TDNT	*Theological Dictionary of the New Testament,* ed. G. Kittel and G. Friedrich (E.T. by G. W. Bromiley, 1964ff.)
TR	Received Text
Vulg.	Latin Vulgate version
WH	B. F. Westcott and F. J. A. Hort, *The New Testament in Greek* (1881)
ZNW	*Zeitschrift für die neutestamentliche Wissenschaft*

THE EPISTLE OF JAMES, A SHORT SUMMARY

1:1	James, to all Christian Jews.
1:2–4	Welcome *peirasmos;* it consummates discipleship by forcing you to exercise in practice what you have learned in Christ.
1:5	But if you still have something to learn in discipleship, ask God for illumination.
1:6–8	But ask in faith—not, "O God, if there be a God."
1:9–11	(And you are not alone in your difficulties.) In the society of Christian brotherhood, let the slave, for example, rejoice in his new-found equality of manhood, and let the rich rejoice in openly putting off the false rank of wealth and in descending, as the world would say, to the common level, which, being brotherhood in Christ, is the only true dignity of man.
1:12–18	And in *peirasmos* remember the reward of endurance comes, and is sure to come, from God: *peirasmos* comes, not from God but from natural lusts. Make no mistake about this: God is the source of all good, and of nothing but good, with absolute consistency. Of his own mere motion and special grace he regenerated us, by the gospel, to be the first-ripened fruits of his creation, perfected by that word of truth in spite of the world's temptations.
1:19–20	So endure with patience,
1:21	and pure living, and open your minds to the saving truth, which he implants within man.
1:22–25	But such opening means not only hearing the word of truth in the gospel, but also doing it,
1:26	by careful speech,
1:27	and by pure living, and by acts of love, e.g., to the bereaved,
2:1–4	with brotherly love, remember, not with snobbish respect of persons: that is inconsistent with the law of love.
2:5–11	If, by discrimination against the nonrich, you break the royal law, and truckle to oppressors and blasphemers, (a) by breaking one law you are reprobated by the law as a whole, and (b) by breaking that particular law, the law of love, you are not only condemned under all, according to (a), but you are also by your own

15

action excluded from the benefit of mercy (an aspect of love) which otherwise may win pardon for sinners.

2:12–13   For the law of freedom, which frees us in Christ, by faith, from the condemnation prescribed (subject only to God's mercy, as at work even in the OT) under the law before Christ came, is a law of love, and obviously is not available to those who palpably reject it by loving, not their neighbor, i.e., their fellow man, but only the rich; and in truth snobbery, even within its own circle, is only a false show of love.

2:14–26   (I said, you must be doers, 1:22–25.) Faith cannot live except by bearing fruit in deeds.

3:1   The risks and responsibilities of being a teacher:

3:2–12   he is sure to say many things to offend many people. If he can avoid that, he can do anything, in act no less than in word, that is needed for perfected discipleship.

3:13–16   So let the teacher lead a good life, with a wisdom untainted with pride, not with the vainglory of academic strife and envy, which are a devilish denial of the gospel truth and foment disorder and evil.

3:17–18   True wisdom is the opposite of that: its chief mark is purity and peace.

4:1–5   (I have said that strife is the companion of sin, ch. 3 *ad fin.*) Strife arises from worldly, carnal lusts, which war, within our bodies, against God

4:6–10   and the grace he offers, if we are meek enough to accept it, instead of relying on ourselves and living the life of pleasure.

4:11–12   (I said, meek enough.) But it must be true humility; censorious backbiting slander is the reverse of humility; for it is "sitting in judgment" on your fellows. A Christian believes the best as long as he can, i.e., till the contrary is convincingly proved true: and then he condemns only the sin, not the sinner. The sinner he leaves to the judgment, and mercy, of God: anything else would be a sin of pride.

4:13–16   So is vain boasting of the morrow, in the pursuit of riches, as in the Parable of the Rich Fool.

4:17   So remember (as I said at the beginning of this chapter) the responsibilities of knowing the gospel; you cannot plead ignorance, which sometimes at least excuses the sinner.

5:1–6   And pride is not the only mark of the rich: so are its fruits [of which there is a mention in 4:13–16. Now follows a fuller denunciation of the martyrdom of man by the insolent profligacy

5:7–8   of the rich and their oppression of the poor]. Under such oppression we Christians must patiently endure: but [now James adds, for comfort] the time will not be long.

5:9   But do not take to blaming one another. Do not be caught in that frame of mind. As the captain might say to the crew, "The race is next week," so I say to you, The coming of the Lord is nearly upon us; don't let him find us grumbling and growling at one another.

5:10–11   Rather, endure like the prophets of old. [Again he adds for comfort]: The Lord is full of feeling for men in distress.

16

5:12   But when these oppressors drag you to court (as in 2:6), do not seek to maintain your case, however honest, by the oath of purgation; you may be held to countenance or even believe in heathen gods, for your governors are mostly pagans; and in any case, an oath, which must express or necessarily imply a curse on a defect of truth, leaves no room for honest error or failure of memory. And the same applies to nonlitigious assertions, if any, with an oath.

5:13–18   (At the beginning of my Epistle I spoke of your difficulties.) In all the vicissitudes of life, in joy or sorrow, have God always before you, in health or sickness or shortcomings, with praise and prayer. And do not rely on your own efforts: as I reminded you when speaking of temptations and the need for learning (1:9–11), you are a brotherhood; so tell your troubles to the others, and their prayers will help you: remember the power of Elijah's prayers.

5:19–20   Correspondingly, do not grudge your help to a man in need of instruction. Again I come back to where I began (1:5): God is the giver of wisdom; and a man who corrects error by teaching truth is doing a Godlike act, which will counterbalance many a sin that he (the teacher) may have committed.

          [So joining the end of his Epistle to its beginning, after logically developing all the aspects of his chosen theme, James gives his work the (characteristically Greek) beauty of the completed circle.]

INTRODUCTION

I. AUTHOR

We must realize that this Epistle is alive with the personality of its author and other influences of which we here name only these—the Galilean background, the home bond between James and Jesus, the gospel of Jesus, his Christian mandate to the disciples, the pastoral passion of James for the people of Israel (matching that of Paul for the Gentiles), and the essential condition of the gospel as preached by both: "Refuse all substitutes" (see Jas.1:1).

The personality of James is to be felt at once in his choice of words: of the 570 words in the vocabulary of the Epistle about 73 do not occur elsewhere in the NT—about ten more than in the parallel case of 1 Peter, which is of approximately the same length. Of these 73 words 46 occur in the Greek Septuagint, with which James was obviously familiar; and one of the not more than three quotations that he expressly introduces with "The Scripture says" (Jas. 4:5) is neither in the Scriptures nor traceable anywhere else at all.

The authorities are so divided on the identification of his Hebraisms that for these no figures can here usefully be given. His actual Hebraisms are certainly few, but his familiarity with both the Greek Septuagint and the Hebrew OT gives a definite biblical character to his style. Idiomatic Hebraisms are apparent in such (fairly frequent) locutions as "hearer of forgetfulness"[1] for "forgetful hearer" (1:25). There are also many phrases peculiar to Biblical Greek, for example, "Cleanse your hands"[2] meaning "Give up sinning" (4:8). "Plenteous-in-compassion" (one word),[3] a compound of two ordinary Greek words, occurs only in Jas. 5:11, and the number of such found by the authorities in James varies from seven to seventeen. Amid

[1] ἀκροατὴς ἐπιλησμονῆς.
[2] καθαρίσατε χεῖρας.
[3] πολύσπλαγχνος.

18

varying opinions it seems certain that in the Epistle at least ten words were used for the first time, and these with the power of the expert craftsman in language.

J. H. Ropes, in his commentary (p. 24), gives special praise to the writer's command of well-chosen and expressive figures. "The vivacity, simple directness, and general attractiveness of the style are conspicuous even in the English version." It is obvious also in the Council's Letter in Acts 15:24, in the drafting of which James must have taken at least a large part: the importance of his position and his importance in it can scarcely be disputed (see, e.g., Gal. 1:19; 2:9).

A certain Greek compound verb means (fundamentally) "to furnish with gear,"[4] and the opposite compound of the same verb has a meaning like that in our "displenishment,"[5] as (at least formerly) used of the sale when a man was giving up farming or the like. The choice of that word by James in Acts 15:24, here only in the NT, to signify the disturbance that had been created in the minds of Gentile Christians, is highly characteristic of the style of James as seen also in the Epistle, and so is the characteristic intensification of the already forceful term in the picture, "troubling,"[6] with the still stronger "upsetting."[7]

The same background and the same quality of style are obvious in the marine analogy in Jas. 1:6, where the picture of the wavering doubter is probably drawn from the Sea of Galilee, a surface of waves driven this way and that with every change of the wind. Ropes actually writes, "The sentence is made less forcible through the excessive elaboration of the figure" (commentary, p. 142); others would call the art of the figure here not excessive but appropriate and highly effective.

II. PURPOSE

Among our NT Epistles that of James is unique, a distinction which too often has led to its disparagement. The quality and diversity of the contents of his Epistle have nevertheless been recognized by some commentators. D. A. Hayes,[8] for example, rightly aligns him in substance and authority with Elijah and Moses, and in style and diction with some of the best qualities of the Psalms and the Prophets: his earnestness is seen in his use of over 50 imperatives in the 108 verses of the Epistle, which from beginning to end

[4]κατασκευάζω (cf., e.g., Heb. 3:3f.; 9:2, 6; 1 Pet. 3:20).
[5]ἀνασκευάζω.
[6]ἐτάραξαν (from ταράσσω).
[7]ἀνασκευάζοντες.
[8]"James, Epistle of," *The International Standard Bible Encyclopedia* (1939), III, p. 1562.

19

burns with the passion of a sincerely Jewish Christianity. James may well be called "the Amos of the new covenant."[8a]

In our opinion, the Epistle of James is a quasi-prophetic letter of pastoral encouragement, and, no less, of pastoral rebuke, proceeding from an unquestioned right of pastoral vocation and authority. It was most natural that James, as first "Bishop" (or whatever we may style him) of Jerusalem,[8b] should address his charges, not only in Palestine but also in their many and great centers elsewhere; and if he was, as we believe, the author of the missive in Acts 15:23ff., it shows his skill in letter-writing. We have too long been hampered by two misconceptions, first that James lacks unity and coherence, and second that James's concept of Christianity is peculiar and unorthodox. First, the sustained unity of its structure is, we believe, indisputable,[9] and so is the sustained unity of its style: and, besides the author's distinctively powerful choice and use of language, no less impressive is the unity of personal character and Christian thought conspicuous throughout the Epistle. Second, it does seem truly characteristic of James to put the sum of his message into his exordium and then repeat it, elaborating and confirming it every time it recurs. In Jas. 1:3,4 we have the first statement of the whole theme of his religion, and of his Epistle—"faith," "endurance," "work," leading to perfection, to approbation, and to the final reward.

We should not be surprised that the Epistle of James does not even seek to outline all the essential doctrine comprised in the Christian faith. Like Paul in his Epistles, James is addressing people who are supposed to know the rudiments of Christianity; and his aim, as in the Sermon on the Mount, is to set forth the theonomic life in its essentials, that is, life lived according to God's Law. James's task, like Paul's in his Epistles, is mainly practical, to help the sincere to live up to their faith, and very often to correct errors, misunderstandings, and backslidings resulting in conduct unworthy of the Christian faith. There is indeed more *theology* in Paul and others than in James or in the gospel preached by Jesus, but essentially they all hold the same *religion,* the same as James preached in short but full simplicity.[9a] James should not, and cannot, be understood in isolation, but is to be read in the whole context of the NT.

The main difference between James and Paul is that, whereas the

---

[8a]A. M. Hunter, *Introducing the NT* (1945), p. 98.
[8b]Cf. F. V. Filson, *Pioneers of the Primitive Church* (1940), p. 171.
[9]For an excellent discussion, see the notable article by P. B. R. Forbes, "The Structure of the Epistle of James," *Evangelical Quarterly* 44/3 (1972), pp. 147–153; also F. O. Francis, "The Form and Function of the Opening and Closing Paragraphs of James and I John," *ZNW* 61 (1970), pp. 110–126.
[9a]Cf. E. Thurneysen: "James proclaims Jesus Christ, his cross and his resurrection, the power of forgiveness and the obedience of faith, and nothing else. He proclaims that but in his own way," *Der Brief des Jakobus* (1941), p. 5.

latter usually keys his letters to the specific weaknesses and worse in the particular congregations addressed, James is more catholic in the scope of his Epistle, comprising, for example, the nature of God and man, the evils of lust, pride, wealth, and so forth, which try the Christian, the virtues of hope and faith which inspire him, and the endurance and love in which that hope and faith work in the Christian life. James was well aware of the importance of Christian doctrine, including the truth that faith without action is dead (2:26) and action without faith has nothing to steer it. As Paul never tires of insisting that right knowledge is the sure guide to right behavior, so the emphasis on this truth in Col. 1:9–14 is no less conspicuous in James, in the extensive prelude to the same subject (3:1–12), in the vehemence with which Gnostic teachers and their "devilish" doctrines and their own temper are denounced (3:14–16), and in the comprehensive contrast to be seen in the true Christian *wisdom* and *peace* (3:17–18, and ch. 4; see the Commentary, especially the headnote on ch. 3, for a deeper treatment).

The Epistle of James comes from the center and head of the Christianity of its day, and speaks with all the pastoral authority of its source. It is necessary, however, to recognize not only that pastoral quality: all the NT Epistles are undeniably pastoral in their intention; that of James is uniquely rich in the compressed wealth of its contents. With few exceptions, we are sure, there is nothing in the Epistle of James that is not thoroughly applicable and relevant to today. The one important exception is the intense apocalyptic expectancy of an almost immediate end to the present world. The author of the Epistle of James definitely assumes that his days are the last days, and that the "first generation" of Christians, the Apostolic Age, is also to be the last: see, too, for example, Rom. 8:22–25; Heb. 10:36,37; 11:39,40; 13:20,21. In fact, in spite of all difficulties and obscurities, we submit that the Epistle of James, rightly approached and understood, takes us better than any other NT book back to the infancy of the Christian Church, to the purple dawn of Christian enthusiasm and the first glow of Christian love.

III. SYNOPTIC RELATION

In subject matter nearly all the commentators have been struck by the strong affinity between the Epistle of James and the Gospels of Matthew, Mark, and Luke; thus Hort writes: "the style is especially remarkable for constant hidden allusions to our Lord's sayings, such as we find in the first three Gospels" (p. xxxiii). We ourselves believe that this is at least mainly due not merely to James's early sharing some of the oral and written evidence to which those Gospels sooner or later were indebted, but to his own personal witness of the life and teaching of Jesus—a conclusion in harmony with the

21

fact that the groundwork of the Epistle is the same as that of the Sermon on the Mount, and with the other evidence and probability that the Epistle is by James, the Lord's brother. Noting the clear link between James and Matthew, especially in the Sermon on the Mount, R. R. Williams wrote: "What is more important than the exact literary history of the two documents is the fact that James has a *point of view* so similar to that which marks the teaching of Jesus *during his lifetime*. Much of James reads like the gospel *of* Jesus rather than the gospel *about* Jesus."[10] C. F. Schmid observed: "James not only agrees in numerous passages with Matthew's Gospel, which appear to be but the echo of the discourses of Jesus. . . , but also with that great body of precepts which Matthew gives as a whole, the Sermon on the Mount, which in its whole spirit may be looked upon as the model of the Epistle of James."[11] W. L. Knox also cited the curious, and perhaps significant, structural similarity between the Epistle and the Sermon on the Plain in Luke's Gospel, pointing out that the initial beatitudes and final exhortation in the Epistle show a form identical to those found in the Lukan version of the Sermon.[12]

These and many other congruences between the Epistle and the sayings of Jesus are not confined to the "Sermon," and one thing is clear: they are not so close as to warrant the assumption that they are direct quotations from the Gospels. The commonest conjecture from our leading commentators (e.g., Mayor, p. xliv) is that they are from early reminiscences of an eyewitness or from an early written version of the "Sermon," perhaps Ebionite; we would ascribe them to the recollections and purposes of James, the Lord's brother, in composing the Epistle. There is nothing in the thought of the Epistle that contradicts that hypothesis, and in the language there is much that takes us quite as far back as anything in the oldest features and elements of our New Testament.

IV. TEACHING

1. GOD: FATHER AND SON

a. Father

For James, as for the Jews before him, God is good, nothing but good, the sole source of good and of nothing but good (1:16,17). Man's temptations to

---

[10]*The Letters of John and James.* Cambridge Bible Commentary on the NEB (1965), p. 86. Cf. Ropes (p. 39): "James was in religious ideas nearer to the men who collected the sayings of Jesus than to the authors of the Gospels, but his religious interests are not identical with those of either group."

[11]*Biblical Theology of the NT* (E.T. 1870), p. 364.

[12]"The Epistle of St. James," *JTS* 46 (1945), p. 16.

evil come never from God but from an element—a desire for evil—in man's fallen nature, to combat which God has created in man a desire for good. In all God's goodness a Hebrew most emphasizes his love of mankind, especially as shown in the gift of his Law as the guide offered for each man's regeneration and salvation. "Good" is often applied in a redemptive sense to Torah.[13]

The thought of God both as Creator of the world (including man) and as Creator of its physical and spiritual light had already pervaded the whole of Jewish religion (see Ps. 27:1), and it forthwith passed into Christianity; see F. F. Bruce on Col. 1:13: "The statement of an ethical antithesis in terms of light and darkness . . . is too widespread for us to assume in such a reference as this the influence of any one system of thought in which these terms played a prominent part. . . . There is good Biblical precedent for their use, going back to the separation of light and darkness in the creation story of Gen. 1:4."[14] "Father of lights" implies God's constancy, for, unlike those heavenly lights, he does not change:

> Great is Thy faithfulness, O God my Father,
> There is no shadow of turning with Thee.

The license that God for the time being allows to sin is a fact James does not seek to explain but only to combat with his message of constancy in endurance.

b. Son

The Christology of James is implicit, not formally expounded, in his Epistle. The name Christ occurs only in 1:1 and 2:1, and we may be tempted to think that for James Christian ethics eclipsed all interest in the theological meaning of the incarnate Being of Christ: hence A. M. Fairbairn's understandable but mistaken observation of "the poverty of James's Christology."[15] But evidence such as that from the Dead Sea and Nag Hammadi has almost miraculously revealed or confirmed not only the state of first-century non-Christian Jewish theology but the continuity preserved in the distinctive Jewish character, thought, and language of early Christian theology. We can now see that the Jewish first Christians had grown up in a wealth of ancient but lively tradition of messianic Christology, so that James, writing to Jewish converts who had accepted the Christian message, "This is he," was able to give most of his Christian letter not to Christian theology but to Christianity in everyday life.

Early Jewish Christian theology was "almost exclusively Christol-

[13]See SB I, p. 809; III, p. 238; also 1:17, 18, and our notes on "Law" and "Wisdom," pp. 31 and 38.
[14]NICNT (1958), pp. 188f.
[15]The Place of Christ in Modern Theology (1893), p. 238.

ogy";[16] Matthew, John's Gospel, Hebrews, James, the Johannine Letters, 1 (and perhaps 2) Peter, and Jude "have closer ideological and conceptual affinities with a sectarian Judaism of the type seen at Qumran than to any other contemporary feature known to date,"[17] and are Jewish Christian writings reflecting a Jewish background and addressed to Jewish Christians, or to potentially interested Jews of Palestine-Syria or the wider Diaspora.

The Jews expected one or more than one great prophet to come in the Messianic Age (see 1 Macc. 4:46; 14:41; 2 Esdras 6:26; 7:28), "like unto Moses."[18] Nevertheless, though the Jewish Christians emphasized this line of thought, Paul in his mission to the Gentiles understandably exalts not Moses the giver of their law, but Abraham, the human father of their race. Such a prophet, however, was only to be the precursor of the Messiah (see Matt. 17:10–13; Mal. 4:5). The use of the Greek *Christos* as a title of Jesus and as the source of the adjective distinguishing his religion shows how basic Messiahship was in early Judaic Christianity, as in previous OT and other early Jewish literature. In Isa. 41:5 the Hebrew term is applied even to Cyrus as doing a specific task for God; and in (and perhaps before) the first century B.C. the word was a *terminus technicus* for the Anointed One who was to be the Jewish national and political deliverer in the last days (see Dan. 9:25f.). To this idea was wedded the title "Son of David," and in Jesus' day that notion of Messiahship was dominant.

In Acts, Messiahship is prominent in the early presentation of Jesus: thus Peter in 2:31; 3:18 (see 2:36; 3:20); so others (5:32; 4:26); Philip to Samaritans (8:5); Paul to Jews at Damascus (9:22), Thessalonica (17:5), and Corinth (18:5), and Apollos at Corinth (18:28). In Acts the term "Christ," alone or with "Jesus," occurs not as a proper name but always as an appellative, and always in address to a Jewish audience, except possibly by Philip to Samaritans, and by Paul before Agrippa II.

So it is elsewhere in the NT; thus in Matthew, except perhaps in 1:1,18, so also in all the Johannine writings it is used only as the theological designation equivalent, *Christos*. Paul shows awareness of the earlier force of the title, but more often he applies it as a personal name.

The designation of Jesus as *Lord* (*Kyrios*) was inspired by the Resurrection: to the Jews God had long signified the union of power and love, in blessing and in pity for mankind. In the two places where the NT transliterates "Sabaoth" (Rom. 9:29; Jas. 5:4) Paul and James are speaking of God's *kindness:* even in Isa. 1 there is mercy in vv. 16–19 and 26f.; and in

[16]O. Cullmann, *The Christology of the NT* (E.T. 1959), p. 3.
[17]R. N. Longenecker, *The Christology of Early Jewish Christianity.* Studies in Biblical Theology, Second Series (1970), p. 18.
[18]See Deut. 18:15–19; 4:7, 25f., 29; the Gospel of Matthew (esp. chs. 5–7; 17:1–13) and John (esp. 6:14; 7:40); Hebrews (esp. 3:1ff.); and the first part of Acts (esp. 3:22; 7:37).

the celestial overture of John's Gospel, 1:1–5 is a prelude to v. 6, "There was a man sent from God, whose name was John." The early Jewish Christians never lost their sense of God's love in the redemption of the world by their Lord Jesus Christ. So also when, for instance, James (1:1) calls himself "servant" of God and the Lord Jesus Christ, he does so in the zeal of devotion and love.

Another feature of the Christology of the Epistle of James is seen in 2:1, in the title word "Glory," read and interpreted as suggested in our commentary, "The Lord Jesus Christ, our Glory," the "Glory" being taken in the sense of the Shechinah, the Divine Presence. In the NT "glory" is used not merely in thought of the *impression* flowing from Christ, both in the past and the present and henceforth until his Second Coming, but in recognition of his *essential* nature. James's exalted Christology, like John's, is firmly rooted in the OT, especially in the idea of "the glory of Yahweh." In this use, the primary meaning of "glory" is the radiance of God's invisible splendor as shown in the divine character and deeds, especially in the character and deeds of "our Lord Jesus Christ."

"In the Lord Jesus Christ," notes Warfield, "James sees the fulfilment of these [OT] promises: He is Jehovah come to be with His people; and, as He has tabernacled among them, they have seen His glory. He is, in a word, the Glory of God, the *Shechinah,* God manifest to men."[19] According to James, therefore, God's "glory" was revealed supremely in "our Lord Jesus Christ," in what he was, in the events of his earthly life and death and resurrection, in his promised Second Coming, *and in his Church,* which is the extension of his Incarnation, revealing his glory as the glory of God was seen, for example, in the return of the exiles from Babylon: "The wilderness and the solitary place shall be glad for them. . . . They shall see the glory of the LORD. . . . *And sorrow and sighing shall flee away.*" But with the Christian promise and the Christian hope comes the Christian duty. By God's grace we all must strive, so far as we can, to "realize" the Incarnation in *our* lives, too; and that sets us the ethical duties on which, as we have often noticed, James ever insists.

2. THE ADVERSARY AND THE WAY OF VICTORY

a. Sin

James has a strong and typically Jewish sense of sin as a barrier between man and God and consequently between man and man. Of Satan and the historical origin of sin he gives no account. He distinguishes between sin as a

[19]B. B. Warfield, *The Lord of Glory* (1907), p. 243.

principle and sin as an act, and he dwells on the psychological origin, development, and issue of various cases; but his paramount aim is practical, and to this the rest of his study, however necessary, is a subordinate preliminary.

He ascribes sin to *desire* (in Greek, *epithymia*), assuming that his readers, being Jews, would understand what was familiar in Hebrew: the *yetser* is often found at Qumran and in rabbinic theology generally. The "desire" is not necessarily sinful in every case, but in itself desire is undiscriminating, as, for example, between a good appetite and gluttony. Of the origin of sin James says only that it does not come from God, nor is it hereditary and so antecedent to choice. Like Jesus, James was more concerned about the exodus of sin than its genesis. In his thought on this subject James is fundamentally as little Jewish and as nearly Greek as anyone in the NT. "The background of James's use [of the term *epithymia*, "desire"] is current popularised conceptions of Hellenistic philosophy. The Stoic discussion of the word in Stobaeus ii, 7 (Wachsmuth's ed., pp. 87–91) is instructive in this respect. See also on Jas. 4:1f." (Ropes, p. 156). The whole logic of Christian moral theology is that acceptance of the Word imposes the duty, and the gift of grace provides the means, to resist our appetites if and when right so requires: in Jas. 4:7 the choice between the Captains of Good and Evil is plain and imperative.

b. Regeneration

A few commentators, without denying the Christian origin of this Epistle, nevertheless maintain that in 1:18 "begetting" means not Christian regeneration but the creation of man as described in Genesis; the principal reasons adduced are these three: (1) the omission of the article with *word* and *truth;* (2) the use of a final noun in this verse that can, it is alleged, be properly used only of the material world, not of mankind, (3) an allegation that the contents of vv. 12–17 have no features identifying them with Gentile or Judaic Christianity, as—it is alleged—the usual Christian interpretation of the verse would require.

On (1), C. F. D. Moule's explanation is convincing.[20] On (2), the objection is without foundation: see 1 Cor. 11:9, where, as here in Jas. 1:18, the word is apt, being quite normally associated with the creation of the old man but inspired with the new meaning when applied to the new. On (3), we suggest that until the first verse of the Epistle is proved spurious the Christian intention of the rest of this chapter, not to mention the others, holds good, and needs no further specific attestation such as Hort desiderates in 1:12–17.

[20]*An Idiom Book of NT Greek* (1953), pp. 115, 177.

Ropes (p. 166) is right in emphasizing as "decisive" that "the figure of begetting was not used for creation (Gen. 1:26 does not cover this), whereas it came early into use with reference to the Christians, who deemed themselves 'sons of God.' The idea of a divine begetting and of the entrance into Christian life as a new birth has its roots in Greek not in Jewish thought."

c. Parousia and Judgment

James's eschatology may well be considered under the Parousia and the Last Judgment.

i. *The Parousia.* The belief of some that the parousia is a hidden cataclysmic event in the invisible spiritual world is clearly not that of James (see 5:7ff.), nor is it that of Justin, who also takes parousia literally, contrasting the Second Parousia with the First Parousia, the Incarnation. The Epistle of James, as G. Kittel remarks, is distinguished from the later NT writings by its expectancy of an almost immediate, not indefinitely delayed, parousia, in his age, not in some age to come;[21] and James shows no fear of delay, or anxiety about the interim state of the dead.

If, in fact, he mistimed the Second Advent, we must adapt ourselves, and his teaching, to the delay; but on his relation to the truth involved we must remember how much of messianic prophecy James had seen fulfilled, in the birth and resurrection of Christ. By a skillful turn, as Plummer shows (p. 290), James "makes the unconscious impatience of primitive Christianity a basis for his exhortation to conscious patience": that is the most important aspect of James's eschatology.

ii. *Judgment.* The parousia is closely associated with judgment, an idea that indeed pervades the Epistle. The judgment, we are warned, will divide men into two categories, the believing and the unbelieving. The unbelieving rich of 1:10f. will perish like grass scorched by the sun: this warning reaches its climax in 5:1ff., where James rivals the prophets in his invective. As for the judgment of believers, this theme is anticipated in 1:12, which links up with 1:2: the reward is eternal life, and a spiritual crown, eternally transcending those which many peoples gave victors after an athletic contest. James's concept of the crown, as at 2:5, imports the ideas of kingship and the joy of immortality in the heaven to come, the reward of Christian faith, meaning—far beyond any tenets of doctrine—the service, and hope, of the loyal Christian.

---

[21]"Der geschichtliche Ort des Jakobusbriefes," *ZNW* 41 (1942), p. 83.

3. THE CHRISTIAN LIFE

a. Trial and Temptation

The noun *peirasmos* occurs four times or thereabouts in secular Greek, with meanings varying from doctors' experiments with drugs to something like that in Hesiod *Works and Days* 101: "The earth is full of ills, of ills the sea."[22] The verb is commoner, sometimes meaning simply "to make trial of something or somebody," just to know the result, as when men used to tap the barometer, but sometimes indicating a devilish effort to get a result which the other party will in fact deplore, i.e., to *tempt* or *allure,* as at Jas. 1:12f., where the term is reinforced with two vivid synonyms of beguilement in v. 14. In the NT God's making trial of men, as of Abraham or Job, is presented as essentially, even if not *prima facie,* benevolent, not, as parents sometimes see in children, selfish, and not, like Satan's efforts, malicious.

In Jas. 1:2 commentators have generally confined the meaning to "adversities" or "afflictions" or the like: Oesterley and Parry are distinguished exceptions. The unity of the passage 1:2–21 must be fully recognized. Certainly blindness, for example, or disease tests a man; but so, for example, does sexual or other lust, or greed, or temper, or pride of wealth, strength, or beauty. In the former category we may use the term "affliction" or "adversity," but in the latter both our friends and we ourselves are much more apt to speak and think of "temptation" than of "adversity" or "affliction": the caution expressed in vv. 3f. is not directed only to the sick and similar sufferers, nor is the "perfection" of v. 4 only the absence of the (undeniable) moral inroads of (for example) physical disease and similar misfortunes: the very next point to arise (as it does in the next verse) is "wisdom."

In the not always well-perceived unity of this passage (1:2–15), the deliberate use of the adjective "diverse" (*poikilos*) in v. 2 opens the way for the ultimate prominence given to "lust" (*epithymia*) in 1:13–15, and for the final epitome of blessing in vv. 16–18, and the consequent moral duty in vv. 19–21. It is characteristic of James that here he powerfully uses *peirasmos* for both the pleasant allurements of Satan and the painful afflictions of the body: both are apt to lead men to sin. "Dost thou still retain thine integrity? Curse God, and die," said Job's wife to him in his affliction (see Job 2:9); but in this chapter our thoughts turn, from the opening of the message in 1:2, not only to sufferers like Job but also to the dangerous allurements of the flesh.

---

[22]πλείη μὲν γὰρ γαῖα κακῶν, πλείη δὲ θάλασσα.

b. Rich and Poor

In our Commentary on 1:9–11 we observe how James specially warns the rich, as he will throughout his Epistle. So it is in 2:1–13, especially in vv. 5–7, and, in a climax, 5:1–6, again in James's thoughts of Judgment Day. By NT times the social problem had become a religious issue,[23] poverty and piety, wealth and wickedness having become almost synonymous. Inevitably the Epistle of James was influenced by the OT "patriarchal-pietistic ethics of poverty."[24] Most of his readers were apparently drawn from the "poor," whose affinities were with the *anawim*.[25] James, however, does not teach that poverty in itself is a virtue. Nor does he regard wealth in itself as evil: what he does condemn is avarice and exploitation.

In seeking to understand the attitude of Christ and the early Christian teachers toward the rich we must not confine our attention to such passages as those on the Rich Young Ruler, Mt. 19:16–22, the Rich Fool, Lk. 12:16–22, the Camel, Mt. 19:24, or other such warnings as those in the Epistle of James. Christ and the disciples never held that all the rich were bound to be ungodly men, irreparably doomed to damnation.[26]

We must therefore be prepared to distinguish what we may fairly say James regards as the typical rich man and the recognizable exceptions, that is, those of the rich that are not possessed by their wealth. The typical rich are depicted in 2:1–13 and 5:1–6; 1:9 is addressed to the comparatively poor Christian brother who, amid the "diverse temptations" of 1:2 and 1:12ff., is exposed to the temptations of wealth—that is to say, sheer greed, for it has sometimes driven people to sin (see 4:1–3, 13ff. and Prov. 1:10–19). It is important to note that here, as in 1:9 and 4:10, 15, James urges the Christian to salutary and corrective "humility," signifying not a calamity from without, such as bankruptcy, or expulsion from his club, but a sane mental condition free (or, if there was need, freed) from pride. We believe that here in 1:10, with a thought parallel to the passages in ch. 4, James means that the rich Christian must seek joy not in spiritually insignificant worldly calamity

---

[23]See G. F. Moore, *Judaism* II, p. 156.
[24]See M. Dibelius, *Der Brief des Jakobus*. KEK (1964), pp. 37ff.
[25]On the development of the Hebrew word for "poor" (*'ani*), see Dibelius, *ibid.*; S. R. Driver, *s.v.* "Poverty," Hastings' *Dictionary of the Bible* (1908).
[26]We need not have recourse to Sir. 13:24, "Wealth is good, if sin has not tainted it"; Sir. 44:6: "Rich men furnished with ability"; and v. 10: "These were merciful men, whose righteousness has not been forgotten," though we may well note that here Sirach coincides with Jas. 1:13, in reckoning mercy an essential and leading element of righteousness in life. The nobleman in the parable of Lk. 19:11–28, and the Lord of the vineyard in Luke 20:9–19, are exemplars of justice; Joseph of Arimathaea, Matt. 25:27, was "a rich man, . . . who also himself was Jesus' disciple"; and Zacchaeus, Luke 19:2–10, "was the chief among the publicans, and he was rich."

to himself but in *humbling himself* with the temporally chastening but eternally saving realization that wealth *per se,* besides being a grave temptation to sin, is *worthless* for his salvation, and that the rich man, if he is nothing better than rich, will be condemned in the day of judgment.

In 1:10, we believe, the rich man is of the Christian brotherhood and is here warned of the danger that threatens him and all the rich. In 1:11 "the rich man" is a generic term, meaning any rich man, not necessarily a Christian. In 2:1–9 the rich incomer and the poor incomer *may* not be Christians but only visitors, serious or aimless; but we cannot positively assert, with Ropes, that apparently the rich visitor is not a Christian. Moreover, if we must conjecture, the serious warning in vv. 5–13 may not refer to visitors but to a regular habit in some churches of making class distinctions in the placing of the congregation, footstools and all. Obviously the "management" in this example was of the richer rather than of the poorer class, and this is evidence of an element of well-to-do people in the apostolic churches; the ideal of Jas. 1:27 was not presented to a flock consisting only of mendicants. There were also some not unreasonably called rich (Acts 4:34f.; 5:1–11); James, too, shows that he found some prevaricators among them, but the denunciation in 2:6f. is patently of non-Christians, blasphemers of the name of Christ, and the explicit aim of these verses is to give proof that it is un-Christian to worship such sinners (the rich) by "respect of persons." There is no difficulty about having Christian visitors or members of the congregation in 2:2 and non-Christian rich in 2:6f.; in 1:10f., in our view, we begin with a rich Christian exhorted to "humility" and pass on to the fate of the typical rich.

Chapter 4, a chapter on greed, includes, *inter alia,* murders and other such sins of worldly-minded lusts and pride, but, as is mentioned in the note on 1:9f., the theme in ch. 4 is sin in the pursuit, not in the mere possession, of wealth. To this latter theme James proceeds in ch. 5. Even in translation the change in style is startling, and is the key to understanding this passage. The rich in 1:11 and 2:6f. are not necessarily Christians; they merely represent the typical rich man. They are used as an argument (1:10f.) to turn a sincere rich Christian to humbleness, and (2:13) in admonishing Christians for toadying, virtually as accessories, to the rich. We must not assume that the rich visitor was in fact typical of his class: he was not a blasphemer of Christ, obviously, and need not have been an oppressor, like those of vv. 7 and 6 respectively; the sin of the Christians here is their deference to wealth *per se,* without regard to character or anything else. In ch. 4 the pride and lusts of Christian pursuers of gain at all costs are denounced, and these sinners, like those of 2:1–13, are exhorted to repent: ch. 5:1–6 is unique in the Epistle of James.

Verses 1–6 apostrophize the rich, not as Christians but as a class, with ruthless condemnation: the sequel (vv. 7–11) contains no rebuke for the Christian, no "Do not ye likewise." Even its one verse of caution (v. 9) is an aspect of the encouragement that rings through vv. 7–11, addressed to striving Christians, not to the hardened sinners of vv. 1–6. The thought, like the style, of vv. 1–6 is that of the prophets or of some of the Psalms, especially Ps. 58; exactly so does James, after his confident indictment of the rich, close the theme with no less confident comfort of his patient brethren.

The prophetic passage shows how in skill, power, and versatility James's Greek is unsurpassed in the NT. He is by no means the only biblical writer on worldly wealth, but we do not think any approaches him in the persistence, passion, and vehemence of his campaign against the sins of the rich. This should not seem strange to those of us who believe that the author of this Epistle was actually James, the Lord's brother; he would have good cause for his attitude to the wicked among the rich, knowing, as he must have known, the part money had in securing the trial and condemnation of Jesus.

In conclusion, James notably and consistently condemns not a few of the sins of the rich, including injustice amounting to social oppression. Jas. 2:1ff. is directed not so much against the rich themselves as against the church functionaries who succumb to the temptation to pander to them with escort to good seats and other subservient attentions. Later, however, those rich who have been so adulated in church are shown in their true light. They turn on the poor Christian, drag him into court and legally persecute him (2:5ff.). Chapter 5 is a vehement denunciation of the social sins of the wealthy, including nonpayment of the workers' earned wages, and there is no defect in James's theory or practice of Christianity that would justify any critic in representing James unfairly as merely aware of the rich being possessed by their riches, or otherwise indifferent to the poor.

c. Law

Let us here consider the basis of the conflict that history has long witnessed between Judaism and the gospel of Christ.

As among many—probably most—peoples, many of the oldest features of Jewish law have their origin in custom, in the customs of the Hebrew tribes, dating from their fight for physical and economic survival among the larger tribes of the desert and in their struggles to settle in Southern and Eastern Palestine, about 2000–1500 B.C., that is, roughly, from the period of Abraham to that of Moses. Behind that are also traces of folk memory and thought going back to prehistoric times, with primitive awareness of a divine love of mankind, and of some divine law in the universe. With Abraham begins the history of the Jews as God's own people, and with Moses that of their law as God's own law.

The effective difference between the Mosaic law and the Christian "law of liberty" is not really in character and content: for example, both condemn, among other things, adultery, stealing, murder and perjury, and each is a law of love, for example, in charity of word and deed. In matters of ceremonial and similar observances, such as circumcision or sabbaths or other holy rites and days, there are considerable differences, but the root difference between Judaism and Christianity is not in their "law" of life and worship but in their conception of the *nature* of that law, in that the Jews went even further than the Romans from the primitive notion of custom. "We turn naturally to the world's greatest legal system," says C. K. Allen, "for guidance concerning the rise and scope of custom; but here Roman jurisprudence is singularly indistinct." [27] On the other hand it is clear that for the Greeks the root of law was custom: they even use the same word (*nomos*) quite regularly for "custom" and sometimes for "law."

In human life habits are apt to be taken for facts of nature: like certain Scythians and Greeks on discovering the others' mode of disposing of the dead, by eating and burning them respectively, men are frequently shocked to find that besides their own there is another way of doing things. It was from this notion of a particular way as "the right way" that the Greek philosophers went on to elaborate the idea of justice as Nature's perfect way: it is no accident that Euripides includes it in his picture of a reversal of natural law: "Upward are flowing the pure rivers from their springs, and Justice (*dikē*) and all things are reversed." [28]

The difference between Judaism and Christianity is that, whereas both Christian and Jew believe the OT, the Jew goes further. The Jews' view of their laws as emanating from a divine revelation creates no insuperable difficulty; but the Jews therefore regarded those rules as teachings permanently true, established eternally. "The law of the Bible," says Maimonides, "suffers not any correction, addition or subtraction." Without pressing any doctrinal partiality for either side of this divergence, we hope we may be allowed to say that, as the Jewish conservative attitude has effectively preserved their religion from Abraham till now, so equally it has also excluded the possibility of any doctrinal basis on which the creed of James and that of Judaism might have met. The Jews went further than the Romans; they both regarded law as command, not custom; but for the Jews their law was God's immutable command.

[27]*Law in the Making* (1972), p. 74.
[28]ἄνω ποταμῶν ἱερῶν χωροῦσι παγαί,/καὶ δίκα καὶ πάντα πάλιν στρέφεται (*Medea* 410f.).

For perfect results, however, even a divinely given law would require an impossible perfection in all its human administration. Here we may well study the difference between the attitude of the Pharisee and doctor of the law, Gamaliel, in Acts 5:34–39, and that of the high priest, the chief priests, and others in (for example) John 18:14, 25; 19:6, 7, 11, 12, and often elsewhere in the Gospels, and in Acts 4:1–18.

After this very brief outline of the basis of Jewish law we must now turn to that of the Christian faith. The "law of liberty" is an idea prominent in Plato and in Stoicism; it is found also in later Jewish writings, including Qumran, and Philo makes considerable use of the Stoic term *empsychos nomos* ("ensouled law"), and its underlying concept of law as necessary to freedom in the life of man: indeed the same idea is familiar to the OT and the rabbis. From the first it is fundamental to Christianity, in the teaching of both Christ and his disciples, and conspicuously in that of James and Paul: thus, for example, Jas. 2:8 offers men the grace of *sonship* in the kingdom of Christ, by virtue (1:18) of the *regenerating* word of truth. This creates in the Christian a new positive norm, not of God's command only but of his love, not less but more inspiring than before the Incarnation.

God's mercy was already part of the Jewish faith. The Talmud says: "Be it my will that my mercy overpower my justice"; but since the Incarnation that mercy has abounded as not before. Clearly James in 1:18–21 is thinking of Christ as the incarnation of the law of liberty: cf. "he begot us" (1:21, with Gal. 4:4–7 and Rom. 8:19–25). James mentions the name of Jesus only in 1:1 and in 2:1, immediately after the climax in 1:16–26.

On the athetizers of the Epistle of James and the alleged disparity between James and Paul on Law see G. Kittel,[29] and Dibelius, p. 112: "We fall too easily into the error—supported by the manner of the primitive Christian tradition—that Paul has influenced all streams of primitive Christianity." After the death of James and the extinction of his Palestinian Church, the Gentile tradition did much to suppress all memory of him and his brief administration.

The combination of law and liberty presents an ideal like that of the Greeks, free from much mischievous rigidity, but not without the sanctions of law. Jas. 2:9–11 actually gives the Torah as part of the foundations on which sovereign law (v. 8) and the law of liberty (v. 12) can be built.

James says nothing about ceremonial law, not because he did not believe in the value and necessity of ceremony in a religious life, but because in addressing Jews, who scarcely needed much incitement to ceremony in religion, he evidently thought it right to concentrate on the paramount

[29]*Art. cit.*, pp. 71–105.

importance of the spirit, without which ceremony is apt to be worse than worthless.

Law, for James, is not "natural law" nor is it confined to Mosaic law and the traditions: it is "sovereign law," the law of liberty, a moral not merely a literal code of life. The Jews themselves had long cherished a faith that the Messiah would come and bring a new interpretation of the law, which in fact they called the "Torah of the Messiah,"[29a] the coming of which was a possibility that Gamaliel clearly had in mind in Acts 5:38f. Jesus in his life and his death had realized the ideal to which the law had long looked forward—an ideal of righteousness and love—and had established the meaning of the perfect law. Clearly that is what James has in mind when he speaks of "the perfect law of liberty."

All these considerations strengthen the view that the Epistle of James is a very early document, belonging to the period of the Jerusalem Church. Advocates of a later date cite as evidence what they allege to be its attitude to law, and the omission of reference to the Temple, to the Judaizing controversy, or to other great topics of interest to primitive Gentile Christianity. The Judaizing view, however, was pressed only by a minority, "certain of the sect of the Pharisees who believed" (Acts 15:5), not by James and Peter, the leaders of the Jewish Christians: both these leaders were chiefly concerned with the ethical content of the Christian law, not the entire Torah, so dear to the Pharisees. As we have noticed also, there was a tendency among Gentile Christians to minimize the importance, and even the history, of James and his Jerusalem Church. Of course, the early Christian Church at Jerusalem had at first no more inclination than Christ had had to separate from Judaism, and the salvation of the Jews was for a time the paramount immediate practical problem, as, on the whole, it had been in the ministry of Jesus. Yet from this period dates the inescapable fact that Christianity, a way of life and a standard of conduct, is a gift of the Jew to his Gentlle fellow Christian.

The Epistle of James is a document of the earliest Christianity. Jesus is the promised Messiah, the giver of the promised perfect law to Israel, and his teaching is the ethic to match that law. Ideally, his gospel would have been consummated in the merger of the Mosaic tradition with the Christian revelation: but the human difficulties have not yet been resolved.

d. Faith and Works

The Epistle of James has long been prejudiced by the stigma of Luther's condemnation. He admits that "there is many a good saying in it," and he

---

[29a]Cf. W. D. Davies, *Torah in the Messianic Age* (1952).

acknowledges its value in laying much stress on the Law of God, but he denies it the authority of apostolic authorship or endorsement, alleging that "it contradicts St. Paul and all other Scripture in giving righteousness to works."

We must therefore consider what the doctrine of James on faith and works really is. Faith, in order and in importance, is the first consideration of the Epistle, beginning (1:2–4) with the Christian's duty of striving for the perfection of his faith by steadfastness under the trials of life. (In the Epistle the noun *pistis*, "faith," occurs 15 times, 14 of them in chs. 1 and 2: the rest of the Epistle is rather full of anxiety over some backsliding types of Christian.) Then at once, 1:5–8, James adds that faith is an essential in effective prayer, and presently, in vv. 14, 17, 20, 24, and 26, he emphasizes that true Christian faith must find expression in Christian conduct, and conduct that is to have Christian quality must be rooted in Christian faith, for example, in Christian wisdom, endurance, or prayer: the thought of firm and unwavering faith animates the whole of the Epistle of James.

Faith is paramount: why then do both James and Paul insist on works? The obvious answer is, "Who wouldn't?" But for the Jew, as for the Roman, "law" primarily meant "command," and "faith" meant "loyal obedience." In Judaism national faith and loyal obedience appeared with Abraham, and only later came the more formal notion of law in the Mosaic Decalog. The Mosaic regime inevitably learned to look for consummated obedience, and not merely countermand and promise, in the incident of Gen. 22. Obedience of the will is part of the essence of genuine *de facto* obedience, and evidently in course of time the rabbis, in order to leave no anomaly in their scheme of Law, exalted Abraham's agreement to slay Isaac into the status of loyal operational intellectual obedience; but the notion of offering or even giving obedience to God's will or wishes is older than either Moses or Abraham, and the rabbinic sophistication of the unique case of Abraham is scarcely parallel to that of the ordinary struggling follower of Jesus.

James maintains that a faith not followed by a genuine effort to live up to it is itself not genuine. (He is not here concerned with abnormal cases like deathbed conversions.) In v. 14, "Can faith save a man?" means "faith without works"; and in v. 24, "by works, not by faith only," means "by works implementing faith and not by faith unfulfilled by works": see Ropes (p. 223) on the necessity of both faith and works together for the desired result (cf. 1:25 or 27, or 2:14–17 or 20). So in 2:21 "by works" indisputably does not mean "by works alone, without faith," but means "by works taking effect in conjunction with faith," as the next verse explicitly says, "Do you see that faith shared in his works, and by his works faith was consummated?" So in 2:26, "Faith without works is dead" certainly does not mean that works without faith are effective for salvation, but that as regards salvation, as Ropes says (p. 203), "Faith, if it does not lead to good works, is impotent to save."

For James faith is no less important than it is for Paul: in Jas. 1:19–27 the very root of reformed conduct is the act of faith: "With meekness accept the implanted word." James is too often hastily dismissed as "no theologian": in fact, here James, with his Galilean eye, sees no less clearly than Paul (in 1 Thess. 2:13) that the *logos* is both a message and a living and life-giving spirit, "with power to save your souls" (Jas. 1:21), unless men kill the good seed by poison (vv. 21, 26) or neglect (v. 23).

A word (e.g., "love") can only be an inadequate, and often misleading, clue to a thought; and this applies very forcibly to the word "work," in English and in its NT Greek cognate (*ergon*), and to the corresponding (unrelated) Hebrew equivalent (*ma'aśeh*). "By good *works* are to be understood all manner of duties inward and outward, thoughts as well as words and actions, toward God or man, which are commanded in the law of God, and proceed from a pure heart and faith unfeigned, and are referred unto God's glory."[30] But it would be folly to assume that this connotation springs readily to the mind of every hearer of the word so used in this sense. The word "duty" can also (though less easily) be almost emptied of moral meaning, as when we speak of a wife's "duty" (it may be) of washing up dishes, or a husband's, say, of locking doors at night, which—like religious performances sometimes—may be little more than a mindless routine; but the word "duty" is at least less dangerously ambiguous than "work" in a discussion or definition of our human duty to God.

The word long proved to be misleading among some non-Christian Jews, and it has long been so in some Christian theology, notably in that of Luther Theology gets its strength not from human logic but from human experience; and Luther's logic was, if possible, further obfuscated by his slavery to words—those of James and Paul—without understanding them: only so could he, or any man, have said that the Epistle of James "contradicts St. Paul and all other Scripture in giving righteousness to works." The real antithesis for Paul was not between ceremony and morality, nor indeed even between faith and the expression of it in our life—a controversy which, as T. W. Manson showed, obtained "an undue emphasis through our reading of Paul in the light of the soul-strivings of Luther"[31]—but rather between a salvation by God's grace, which needs only to be recognized and, however late, accepted in faith.

[30]A. Cruden, *Cruden's Complete Concordance to the Old and New Testaments* (1736), *s.v.* "Work."
[31]In E. I. J. Rosenthal, ed., *Law and Religion. Judaism and Christianity* III (1938), p. 139.

Paul's own history in religion (Acts 22:19f.) was bound to make him acutely conscious of the relative importance of faith as a governing factor in religion and life: indeed any normal person might well concede that the faith to which "works" give expression is greater than the expression itself, as the love is greater than the kiss. James's use of the same word "save" of both the Christian faith and Christian "works" does not prove that he did not give faith precedence in status as well as priority in time. Paul also applies "save" to both, and James coincides with Paul in maintaining that faith must be the first step on the path to salvation; Paul likewise agrees with James in holding that genuine faith must (in a normal life) produce "works." The difference between James and Paul is that, while each insists on the need for both faith and "works," Paul no less passionately insists that "works," though a concomitant token and fruit of genuine Christian faith, add nothing to the already complete efficacy of faith as the sole key to the door of salvation: their (normally) necessary presence as fruit of faith does not, in Paul's analysis of the operation, make "works" a *productive factor* in the salvation of the soul. James seems to teach, says John Baillie, citing Jas. 2:18–26, "that some acquisition of holiness is not merely a necessary consequence of justification but even an essential part of it. . . . It is probable that, just as the divergency of thought on this point between St. Paul and St. James cannot be entirely smoothed out, so we ourselves should avoid all one-sided extremes and be content with a never-completely resolved 'tension' between the two opposite truths that have here to be kept in mind. Only thus perhaps can we have assurance without complacency."[31a] In our opinion, the difference between James and Paul in this matter is not one of fact but of apperception: when in a lawcourt a man accused of a traffic offense "proves" that he was in bed in the hospital all that week, James would have said the man "proved his innocence"; Paul would say the man "tendered proof," and that what "saved him" was the court's acceptance thereof. So James would say action is (normally) inseparable from living faith, as breathing is from human life; Paul would say that the possible genuineness of a paralytic's faith proves that action is not categorically indispensable to salvation by faith.

This difference is very obvious in their notions of "justification." Paul confines the term to God's definitive *acceptance* of a soul into a certain status, as a court of law definitively accepts (or rejects) a man's plea of innocence.

Both in the LXX and Hebrew the word translated "righteousness" connotes "vindication of rightness in the matter under question," rather than "habitual morality in life." Paul's use of the word is primarily though

[31a]*Invitation to Pilgrimage* (1944), pp. 70, 71.

not exclusively forensic, keyed (not surprisingly) to the crisis of his acceptance and conversion on the road to Damascus. James, however, gives much more emphasis to the moral implications of the term. The example of Abraham well illustrates what James means by justification. By virtue of the covenant relation Abraham is "righteous" (*tsaddiq*): the sole condition of the covenant was obedience; i.e., "claim" (*Recht*) is linked with "obligation" (*Pflicht*). "That Abraham was justified and saved was of course recognised by all," says Ropes (p. 218); "that his justification depended not merely on the initial act of faith, but also on his confirmatory manifestation of this faith under trial is the contention of James." Abraham's willingness to sacrifice Isaac proved the genuineness of his faith, causing God again to confirm the covenant (Gen. 22:15ff.) and to "justify" his servant. For James, then, Abraham offered a perfect example of the relationship between faith and works: they are as inseparable as *Recht* and *Pflicht*. Abraham's conduct showed that he is righteous: he is justified by works as an expression of faith. Faith and works are not antithetical but complementary—cause and effect: both are necessary and inseparable (2:24). Faith is the inspiration of works, and works are the proof of faith.

e. Wisdom

Any serious evangelist may have to adapt his approach differently to the more and the less rich before him: so it is with James in his Epistle. In the first half, though aware of both classes (see 1:9f.), he gives little attention to the rich among his readers or hearers; the second, chs. 3–5, is largely, though not quite entirely, devoted to castigation and counsel for the rich. That is why, after the early mention of wisdom in 1:5, James says little more about wisdom until he comes to the second half of the Epistle, denouncing the characteristic pride and the other vices then prevalent among the wealthy, sins which are indeed described at some length in 2:1–9, but mainly by way of expressly deterring the common sort from sycophantic "respect of persons": exhortations to wisdom are not so appositely addressed by evangelists to people toiling for their food as they are to men being spoiled by the temptations of wealth.

One may venture to say that a Christian life can flow only from a Christian psychology: we avoid the terms mind, or faith, or heart, or hope, or even love, because they are too apt to be misunderstood, too narrowly applied. To James wisdom is not just some fraction or fractions but the whole power of God's inspiration and guidance active in a human life—what Paul calls faith, Peter hope, John love, and (we think) a devout pre-Christian Jew, the Torah. "If any of you is lacking *knowledge* (of God's way and will), let him ask of God."

James 3:17 and Wisdom 7:22–24 both voice the same diction and the same thought; but it was the Hebrew OT that inspired and instructed James in his presentation of "wisdom" in the Christian life. In that presentation there was not, and could not be, the later identification of Wisdom with the Holy Spirit. In James Wisdom is not personified, is not, as for Paul, the pre-incarnate Spirit of Christ, both Wisdom and Word. James's condemnation of conceited disputatious wisdom in no way implies a date too late for this Epistle to have been written by him.

f. Meekness and Endurance

In Jas. 1:19–21 the keynote is struck in v. 19, " . . . let every man be swift *to give ear*"; and then in v. 21 the same note is repeated: " . . . *lay apart* . . . and *accept* . . . with submission the *implanting* of the Word, which has power to *save* (your souls) *outright.*" In the Greek the contrast is clear between "eternally has power"[32] and "forthwith and instanter give ear,"[33] etc. The gift that follows submission is also immediate, as is clear in the Greek.

In v. 21 "endurance," like "salvation" and a host of comparable words, may connote an effort of mind or body or both, or the successful completion of that effort. NT Greek does not use the common classical Greek noun *karteria* or the (no less common) verb *kartereō* or its compounds, except in Heb. 11:27, in a passage appropriately full of activity, not only impregnability or invincibility against trials and suffering. Compare Jas. 1:4, "Let your effort of endurance seek (all the time) for consummated realization," that is, seek to carry it through to success.[34]

V. HISTORY

There is no definite evidence of knowledge of the Epistle of James or even its name till 180; and the Western Church, with the sole exception of Hilary of Poitiers (d. 366), shows no knowledge of it until Jerome's Vulgate (c.383), after which on Augustine's insistence it was admitted into the Roman canon. The Syrian Church was a generation later in overcoming her reserve. There is no evidence of any Syriac translation of any of the Catholic Epistles until the Peshitta (early 5th century A.D.). In Alexandria, Origen (185–254) is the first to champion the genuineness of the Epistle of James, to quote it as current scripture, and to name the author as (an unspecified) James, whom

[32]τὸν δυνάμενον (present tense).
[33]ἀκοῦσαι (aorist).
[34]See P. B. R. Forbes, "The Structure of the Epistle of James," *Evangelical Quarterly* 44 (1972), pp. 147ff.

he sometimes calls "apostle" (Ropes, pp. 92f.). The Epistle's place in the canon is now assured, the only point in dispute being the order of the Catholic Epistles; and this was settled by Athanasius in his Easter Festal Letter (A.D. 367). In Asia Minor Gregory of Nazianzus (c.390) and Basil the Great, following the Alexandrian canon, set their own to verse with the Catholic Epistles in this order: James, 1, 2 Peter, 1, 2, 3 John, Jude. In Palestine Origen's example inspired Eusebius to urge the "disputed" Epistle's inclusion in the canon.

After its recognition by the early Church Councils, the status of the Epistle of James remained unchallenged until the Reformation. While John Calvin accepted it with little question, Luther's hostility, both notorious and ill-founded, has influenced most commentators since. The Council of Trent (8 April, 1546), by *decretum de canonicis* officially declared the Epistle of James "Holy Scripture."

VI. SELECT BIBLIOGRAPHY

I. COMMENTARIES AND MONOGRAPHS ON JAMES

H. Alford, *The Greek Testament* IV, Part 1 (1864).

J. M. S. Baljon, *Commentaar op de Katholieken Brieven* (1904).

W. Barclay, *Letters of James and Peter*. Daily Study Bible (1961).

F. T. Bassett, *The Catholic Epistle of St. James* (1876).

G. R. Beasley-Murray, *The General Epistles*. Bible Guides (1965).

W. H. Bennett, *The General Epistles*. Century Bible (1900).

W. Beyschlag, *Der Jakobusbrief*. KEK (1888).

E. C. Blackman, *The Epistle of James*. Torch Bible Commentary (1957).

J. Blanchard, *Not Hearers Only*, 3 volumes (1971–73).

A. T. Cadoux, *The Thought of St. James* (1944).

J. Calvin, *Commentaries on the Catholic Epistles* (1551; E.T. 1855).

J. Chaine, *L'Épître de Saint Jacques*. Études bibliques (1927).

C. E. B. Cranfield, *The Epistle of James: Four Studies* (SCM pamphlet, n.d.).

W. M. L. De Wette, *Kurzgefasstes exegetisches Handbuch zum NT,* 3 volumes (1841–48).

M. Dibelius, *Der Brief des Jakobus,* 11. Auflage, ergänzt von H. Greeven. KEK (1964).

M. Dibelius and H. Greeven, *The Epistle of James,* E.T. (1975).

B. S. Easton, *The Epistle of James*. Interpreter's Bible (1957).

L. E. Elliott-Binns, *Galilean Christianity* (1956).

G. Estius, *Absolutissima in omnes beati Pauli et septem catholicas apostolorum epistolas commentaria* (1631).

P. Feine, *Der Jakobusbrief* (1893).

A. R. Gebser, *Der Jakobusbrief* (1828).

H. Grotius, *Annotationes in Novum Testamentum,* 3 volumes (1646).

F. Hauck, *Der Brief des Jakobus* (1926).

H. Heisen, *Novae Hypotheses interpretandae felicius Epistolae Jacobi* (1739).

J. C. K. von Hofmann, *Der Brief Jakobi* (1876).

G. Hollmann, *Der Jakobusbrief* (1907).

F. J. A. Hort, *The Epistle of St. James,* i.1–iv.7 (1909).

J. E. Huther, *James and John* (1882).

F. H. Kern, *Der Brief Jacobi* (1838).

R. J. Knowling, *The Epistle of St. James.* Westminster Commentaries (1904).

R. A. Knox, *A NT Commentary,* 3 volumes (1955).

J. Laurentius, *S. Apostoli Jacobi epistola catholica* (1635).

T. Manton, *A Practical Commentary on the Epistle of James* (1651; repr. 1962).

J. Marty, *L'Épître de Jacques, Étude critique* (1935).

J. L. Martyn, *Notes for Use in Studying the Letter of James* (1962).

J. B. Mayor, *The Epistle of St. James* (³1913).

M. Meinertz, *Der Jakobusbrief und sein Verfasser in Schrift und Überlieferung* (1905).

A. Meyer, *Das Rätsel des Jakobusbriefes* (1930).

C. L. Mitton, *The Epistle of James* (1966).

J. Moffatt, *The General Epistles.* Moffatt New Testament Commentary (1945).

J. A. Motyer, *The Tests of Faith* (1970).

F. Mussner, *Der Jakobusbrief.* Herders Theologische Kommentar zum NT (1964).

W. O. E. Oesterley, *The General Epistle of James.* Expositor's Greek Testament IV (1910).

R. St. J. Parry, *A Discussion of the General Epistle of St. James* (1903).

W. Patrick, *James the Lord's Brother* (1906).

A. Plummer, *The General Epistles of St. James and St. Jude.* Expositor's Bible (1891).

E. H. Plumptre, *Epistle of St. James.* Cambridge Bible for Schools and Colleges (1878).

D. J. Pott, *Epistolae Catholicae Graece* (1810–16).

B. Reicke, *The Epistles of James, Peter and Jude.* Anchor Bible (1964).

G. H. Rendall, *The Epistle of St. James and Judaic Christianity* (1927).

J. H. Ropes, *The Epistle of St. James.* ICC (1916).

A. Ross, *The Epistles of James and John.* NICNT (1954).

H. Schammberger, *Die Einheitlichkeit des Jakobusbriefes im antignostischen Kampf* (1936).

A. Schlatter, *Der Brief des Jakobus* (1932).

W. Schmidt, *Lehrgehalt des Jakobus-Briefes* (1869).

E. M. Sidebottom, *James, Jude and 2 Peter*. The Century Bible (1967).

H. von Soden, *Die Briefe des Petrus, Jakobus, Judas*. Hand-Commentar (1891).

F. Spitta, *Der Brief des Jakobus* (1896).

H. L. Strack and P. Billerbeck, *Kommentar zum NT aus Talmud und Midrasch* III (1926).

W. Stringfellow, *Count It All Joy* (1967).

R. V. G. Tasker, *The General Epistle of James*. Tyndale NT Commentary (1956).

B. Weiss, *Die Katholischen Briefe*. KEK (⁶1900).

J. J. Wettstein, *Hē Kainē Diathēkē* (1752).

R. R. Williams, *The Letters of John and James*. Cambridge Bible Commentary on the NEB (1965).

H. Windisch, *Die Katholischen Briefe*, 3. Auflage, neubearbeitet von H. Preisker. Handbuch zum NT (1951).

II. OTHER LITERATURE

J. Abelson, *The Immanence of God in Rabbinical Literature* (1912).

Idem, Jewish Mysticism (1913).

I. Abrahams, *Studies in Pharisaism and the Gospels*, 2 volumes (1917, 1924).

C. K. Allen, *Law in the Making* (1927).

W. Bacher, "Synagogue," *JE* XI (1908), pp. 619–643.

J. Baillie, *Our Knowledge of God* (1939).

Idem, Invitation to Pilgrimage (1942).

E. F. F. Bishop, *Apostles of Palestine* (1958).

A. Buechler, *Studies in Sin and Atonement* (1928).

S. J. Case, ed., *Studies in Early Christianity* (1928).

F. H. Chase, *The Lord's Prayer in the Early Church* (1891).

F. B. Clogg, *The Christian Character in the Early Church* (1944).

L. Coenen, C. Brown, *et al.*, eds., *New International Dictionary of NT Theology*, 3 volumes (E.T. 1975ff.).

A. Cohen, *Everyman's Talmud* (1932).

S. A. Cook, *The Law of Moses and the Laws of Hammurabi* (1903).

Idem, The Religion of Ancient Palestine in the Light of Archaeology, Schweich Lectures (1930).

O. Cullmann, *The Christology of the NT* (E.T. 1959).

G. H. Dalman, *The Words of Jesus* (E.T. 1902).

Idem, Jesus-Jeshua (E.T. 1929).

H. Danby, *The Mishnah* (1933).

D. Daube, *The NT and Rabbinic Judaism* (1956).

W. D. Davies, *Paul and Rabbinic Judaism* (1948).

Idem, Torah in the Messianic Age (1952).

G. A. Deissmann, *Bible Studies* (E.T. ²1909).

Idem, Light from the Ancient East (E.T. 1927).

C. H. Dodd, *The Bible and the Greeks* (1935).

P. J. DuPlessis, *Teleios: The Idea of Perfection in the NT* (1959).

W. Eichrodt, *Theology of the OT*, 2 volumes (E.T. 1961–67).

A. M. Fairbairn, *The Place of Christ in Modern Theology* (1893).

F. Fenner, *Die Krankheit im NT* (1930).

F. Field, *Notes on the Translation of the NT* (1899).

G. Fohrer, *Elia* (1957).

T. H. Gaster, *The Scriptures of the Dead Sea Sect* (1957).

E. J. Goodspeed, *Problems of NT Translation* (1945).

E. Hatch, *Essays in Biblical Greek* (1889).

W. Heitmüller, *Im Namen Jesu* (1903).

W. Hirsch, *Rabbinic Psychology* (1947).

A. M. Hunter, *Introducing the NT* (1945).

Idem, Paul and His Predecessors (1961).

A. G. Ikin, *New Concepts of Healing* (1955).

F. J. F. Jackson and K. Lake, eds., *The Beginnings of Christianity* I–V (1920–1933).

J. Jeremias, *Jerusalem in the Time of Jesus* (E. T. 1969).

M. Kadushin, *The Rabbinic Mind* (^{2}1965).

Idem, Worship and Ethics: A Study in Rabbinic Judaism (1964).

E. Käsemann, *Leib und Leib Christi* (1933).

R. H. Kennett, "The Contribution of the OT to the Religious Development of Mankind," in *The People and the Book*, ed. A. S. Peake (1925), pp. 383–402.

G. Kittel, *Die Probleme des palästinischen Spätjudentums und das Urchristentum* (1926).

J. Klausner, *The Messianic Idea in Israel* (E.T. 1956).

W. L. Knox, *St. Paul and the Church of Jerusalem* (1925).

Idem, Some Hellenistic Elements in Primitive Christianity (1944).

E. Langton, *Essentials of Demonology* (1949).

J. B. Lightfoot, *On a Fresh Revision of the NT* (^{3}1891).

R. N. Longenecker, *The Christology of Early Jewish Christianity* (1970).

A. H. McNeile, *Introduction to the Study of the NT*, ed. C. S. C. Williams (1953).

T. W. Manson, "Jesus, Paul and the Law," in *Law and Religion, Judaism and Christianity*, ed. E. I. J. Rosenthal, III (1938).

Idem, The Sayings of Jesus (1949).

Idem, The Teaching of Jesus (^{2}1935).

A. Marmorstein, *The Old Rabbinic Doctrine of God*, 2 volumes (1927, 1937).

L. H. Marshall, *The Challenge of NT Ethics* (1946).

B. Meistermann, *Capharnaüm et Bethsaïde* (1921).

K. Menninger, *Whatever Became of Sin?* (1973).

P. Minear, *The Commands of Christ* (1972).

Idem, Images of the Church in the NT (1961).

C. G. Montefiore, *Rabbinic Literature and Gospel Teachings* (1930).

C. G. Montefiore and H. Loewe, *A Rabbinic Anthology* (1938).

G. F. Moore, *Judaism in the First Centuries of the Christian Era*, 3 volumes (1927–1930).

C. F. D. Moule, *An Idiom Book of NT Greek* (1953).

J. H. Moulton and G. Milligan, *The Vocabulary of the Greek Testament* (1930).

G. Orfali, *Capharnaüm et ses Ruines* (1922).

J. Pedersen, *Israel* I–II (1926), III–IV (1940).

E. Peterson, ΕΙΣ ΘΕΟΣ (1926).

O. Pfleiderer, *Primitive Christianity*, 4 volumes (E.T. 1906–1911).

F. W. Puller, *The Anointing of the Sick in Scripture and Tradition* (1904).

A. M. Ramsey, *The Glory of God and the Transfiguration of Christ* (1949).

R. Reitzenstein, *Die hellenistischen Mysterienreligionen* (1910).

A. Resch, *Agrapha* (1906).

A. Richardson, ed., *A Theological Word Book of the Bible* (1950).

S. Schechter, *Some Aspects of Rabbinic Theology* (1909).

Idem, Studies in Judaism, 3 volumes (1945).

C. F. Schmid, *Biblical Theology of the NT* (E.T. 1870).

W. Schmithals, *Paul and James* (E.T. 1965).

C. A. A. Scott, *Christianity according to St. Paul* (1927).

E. H. T. Snell, *Principles of Equity* ([27]1973).

G. Surenhusius, *Biblos Katallagēs* (1713).

A. E. Taylor, *The Problem of Conduct* (1901).

H. St. J. Thackeray, *Grammar of the OT in Greek* I (1909).

C. C. Torrey, *The Apocryphal Literature* (1945).

C. C. Torrey, ed., *Lives of the Prophets* (1946).

J. Trachtenberg, *Jewish Magic and Superstition* (1939).

M. R. Vincent, *Word Studies in the NT* (1887, etc.).

W. Vischer, *The Witness of the OT to Christ* I (E.T. 1949).

F. W. Weber, *Jüdische Theologie* (1897).

J. Weiss, *History of Primitive Christianity* (E.T. 1937).

T. Zahn, *Introduction to the NT*, 3 volumes (E.T. 1909).

Idem, Skizzen aus dem Leben der alten Kirche (1908).

A. C. Zenos, *The Plastic Age of the Gospel* (1927).

VII. ANALYSIS OF THE EPISTLE OF JAMES

I. Salutation (1:1)

II. The Christian Faith (1:2–11)
   (a) In testing, in training, and in fruition (1:2–4)
   (b) In prayer for guidance (1:5–8)
   (c) As comforting the lowly poor and chastening the haughty rich (1:9–11)

III. The Gospel Promise (1:12–27)
   (a) For faithful endurance against temptations (1:12–21)
   (b) For doers of that gospel, not hearers only, with a special watch on the tongue (1:22–27)

IV. The Christian Life (2:1–26)
    (a) Social compassion amid social cleavage (2:1–13)
    (b) Christian faith expressed in Christian acts (2:14–26)
    Verse: Who would be a teacher? (3:1)

V. Some Christian Advice (3:2–18)
    (a) The power and treachery of the tongue as a menace of evil (3:2–12)
    (b) The contrast between the self-conceited controversies of the tongue and the fruitful peace of true wisdom (3:13–18)

VI. Love of the World and Love of God (4:1–10)

VII. Cautions (4:11–17)
    (a) Against speaking ill of another (4:11–12)
    (b) Against presuming on tomorrow's program (4:13–17)

VIII. Conclusion (5:1–18)
    (a) The judgment of the faithless rich (5:1–6)
    (b) Patience, a little: for the coming of the Lord draws near (5:7–11)
    (c) Swear no oaths (5:12)
    (d) Individual occasions for the services or exercises of the church or congregation (5:13–18)

Responsive Verse: The saving of human souls earns a great reward (5:19f.).

TEXT, EXPOSITION,
AND NOTES

CHAPTER 1

I. SALUTATION (1:1)

James, a bond slave of God and the Lord Jesus Christ, to the twelve tribes of the Dispersion, salutation.

1 Believing that the name in the opening signature is that of James the Lord's brother, let us on that basis consider the term *the twelve tribes of the Dispersion*. The Jewish Wisdom Literature, the Haggadah, and the Greek didactic parallels to which this Epistle shows affinities in style and method furnish no support for the theory[1] that the term is here used figuratively by an author of a later date than the Lord's brother to denote the whole multiracial Christian Church. That interpretation, without exact parallel in early Christian usage, is not possible for this Epistle, which reflects the very earliest stage, the most Jewish milieu, of the propagation of the gospel, in theology and eschatology, by a Jew, who, with complete goodwill toward men like Paul and their work among Gentiles, nevertheless, like Jesus, made the Christianization of his own people his present primary concern.

Even if an early or late Christian addressed his audience, Christians in general, as the twelve tribes of God, it seems paramount that in so doing he must not try to stand in both worlds of thought at once. If he has a new spiritual meaning for *the twelve tribes* he must not at once add *of the Dispersion,* for this at once anchors it again in the old historical application. The term *of the Dispersion,* here only in the NT in the absolute sense,[2] is

---

[1]See Ropes, pp. 125, 10ff., 15ff., and several others, e.g., Hort, Parry, Dibelius.

[2]The force of the article, omitted in 1 Pet. 1:1, shows that the term is still nontechnical and is used concretely, as Ropes says (p. 120), "of the Jews so dispersed"; what he means by "so" is obvious in the context; his continuation, "or even of the districts in which they were dispersed," is correct enough, but the result in this verse of James is practically the same. The

49

alive with the ancient, restricted, physical and national privileges of those Jews under the Covenant, and, we submit, could never have been used by James to symbolize the spiritual catholicity of Christianity. Neither may we interpret the term as limited to the non-Palestinian Jewish Christians;[3] in fact, the rabbis regarded the Palestinian Jews as representing all "the twelve tribes of Israel."[4] "The Twelve Tribes," as Ropes points out (p. 119), always "has a genitive of nearer definition" added, "unless it is clearly implied in the immediate context," usually "of Israel" (Exod. 24:4). Of the other citations, we emphasize especially "the tribes of Yahweh" (Ps. 122:4). In James's signature (1:1), the genitive, *a bond slave of God* . . . , has force also (psychologically) in the naming of the Lord's *people* here addressed: instead of a genitive, of the same or equivalent significance ("the Lord's" or "of Israel"), James substitutes as his supplement to the bare name "the twelve tribes," rare even in the LXX (e.g., Exod. 24:4; 28:21; 36:21; Josh. 4:5), this description, "of the Dispersion." This is quite excellent, in grammar, style, and apposite relevance to the "broadcast" he is about to begin; and, Ropes notwithstanding, we submit that it is equivalent to "the Jews."[5]

James calls himself the *slave* of God and Jesus in a spirit of loyalty and devoted service to both. Paul uses the term thus in the opening only in the Epistle to Titus. It is a thoroughly Hebrew (*'ebed*) rather than a Greek concept, used in loyalty and respect toward prophets and rabbis, e.g., Gamaliel, Johanan b. Zakkai,[6] and here toward God and our Lord Jesus Christ, as in the (non-Pauline) Epistle to the Hebrews. Hort even thought that the combination *God* and *Lord,* though grammatically possible, and despite Tit. 2:13 and 2 Pet. 1:1, violated scriptural analogy; but it seems scarcely reasonable to fault this Epistle for not elsewhere, except 2:1, naming Christ and at the same time to question the exceptionally reverent use of this title

---

phrase does indeed belong to the physical, the shadow, not to the spirituality of the new religion (see Ropes, p. 120); its meaning is mortal, terrestrial, ethnic, material, and geographical, and has no more spiritual, celestial, or eternal significance than the regular Jewish Diaspora. On the various, sometimes indistinguishable, related meanings of *the Dispersion,* see Ropes, pp. 121ff. After the small print Ropes's important note on ἐν τῇ διασπορᾷ (pp. 120ff.) refers to the Jews so dispersed, and so forth, with a concrete application which seems confined to the (literal) Jews, and here and on the next page he seems scarcely to remember his metaphorical and transferred application to Christians in general, nor does he seem to realize the bearing of the phrase *of the Dispersion* on his interpretation; we think this same objection applies to all he has on this point, right down to p. 127.
[3]With, e.g., Selwyn, Marty, Beyschlag. If James had intended so to limit its scope, he would probably have used some such phrase as ταῖς ἐκ τῶν δώδεκα φυλῶν ταῖς ἐν τῇ διασπορᾷ, or τοῖς ἀπὸ τῶν δώδεκα φυλῶν διασπαρεῖσιν (see Ropes, p. 124).
[4]See Acts 26:7; Justin Martyr *Dialogue with Trypho* 126.
[5]τοῖς Ἰουδαίοις.
[6]Schlatter; see H. St. J. Thackeray, *Grammar of the OT in Greek* I (1909), p. 8.

here and in 2:1. It need not be from a later hand any more than the tradition of the confession of Thomas: "My Lord and my God" (John 20:28).

Since proverbially no man can be the servant of two masters, it may be that James, in order to obviate any possible offense to the cherished monotheism of orthodox Jewry, is here emphasizing that service to Christ is also service to God, since they are both One (John 5:17; 9:4; 17:4); but we doubt whether such subtlety in the opening is truly in keeping with the character of this Epistle.

We hold that James, the Lord's brother, is here writing as a Jew—not "a Jewish Christian" (Ropes, p. 17), but *a Christian Jew*—to Jews, and that he was writing with full hope that the Jews as a whole would turn to Christ. In his Epistle he is to preach both aspects of the Christian religion, both faith and works, both of which he is impressing on the Jews as the carnal descendants and heirs of Abraham. Jas. 2:21 is not parallel to Gal. 3:7. Paul is concentrating on one aspect of Christian duty and that same aspect of God's Fatherhood, the spiritual aspect, of which Abraham's fatherhood of Jewry is only symbolic. In James we note also the traditional prominence given to God, without prejudice to Christ, in 1:1, 5–8, 12–15, 16–21, 26, 27, before James turns, in full faith, to Christ, in 2:1, and then reverts to God, in 2:19–25; 5:1–6 (esp. v. 5), and in the prophetic tone of the whole passage 5:7–8, 9–11, 14–15, and the example of Elijah in 5:16–18. James thoroughly understands that Jesus did not come to supplant but to supplement the Father, and did not come to supersede but to reinforce God's OT lessons to the Jews and to extend them to the Gentiles. To James, therefore, Christianity is not a new religion but the consummation of the old; and we shall never see OT and NT as an intrinsic unity unless we grasp this fundamental truth enshrined in our Epistle.

In our view, then, James is addressing his Epistle both to Christian and (hopefully) to non-Christian Jews, outside and within Palestine itself: see Paul's practice in Acts 17:1–4 (esp. v. 2, "as his manner was"); also Gamaliel's attitude (Acts 5:34–40). To Christian Jews Jesus is peculiarly the fulfilment of their eternal hope of ultimate restoration from the Dispersion (see 2 Esdras 13:40; Tobit 13:3–5, 15–18; and Rev. 21:10–21). On that note James opens his Epistle, the note of suffering but hopeful brotherhood.

Salutation[7] is the usual greeting with which, as the papyri show, Greek letters of all periods opened (see Acts 15:23; 23:26). In Hebrew (and ancient Syriac and modern Arabic) the regular greeting is "Peace!" In Latin it is "Health!" (*Salve* or *Salvete,* in letters *Salutem,* i.e., *salutem dicit*). In Greek it is "Joy be to you."[8]

---

[7]χαίρειν, depending on the regularly unexpressed λέγει, "bids you χαίρειν."
[8]χαίρειν or χαίρετε: in letters χαίρειν.

The significance of this greeting should not be altogether over-looked. Here, as in the two passages quoted by Ropes (p. 131), the word "joy" is taken up in the sequel, "All joy. . . ." James both writes and thinks in Greek better than any other NT author. His mind is no less, but usually more, in tune than theirs with the capacity for joy manifest in ancient Greek art and literature. One mark of this characteristic appears at once in his opening words, in his exhortation to us to see joy even in the trials of life. No NT author expresses more sympathy for the poor or more indignation at their sufferings than James does in every chapter except the third of his Epistle; and yet the joy he saw in their sufferings makes him stand out among the Christians who included in their Lord's Prayer the *ne nos inducas* ("Lead us not. . .") petition, so different from the spirit of these opening words of James.

Not only in his thought but in his mastery of language he is close to the Greeks, closer than any other NT author, except perhaps the unidentified author of the Epistle to the Hebrews. James's style, of course, does not rival that of the greatest classical Greek authors, but is not unworthy to be mentioned in the same breath as one of the most powerful of Aeschylus' utterances:

> *This is Agamemnon, my*
> *Lord husband, slain, the deed of this right hand*
> *Fulfilling justice; thus this matter stands.*[9]

(See especially Jas. 1:16–18; 2:1–26; 3:3–6, 17f.; 4:1–10; 5:1–6.)

II. THE CHRISTIAN FAITH (1:2–11)

a. In testing, in training, and in fruition (1:2–4)

> 2 *Deem it nothing but an occasion for joy, my brothers, whenever (on each occasion when) you encounter trying assaults of evil in their various forms.*
> 3 *You must realize that your approbation is accomplished by constancy in endurance.*
> 4 *But let that constancy perfect its work, so that you may be perfect, and complete in every part, lacking in nothing (but able to withstand any kind of assault of evil by which you may be tried).*

2 James impressively begins his message with *peirasmos*, the great common experience of the Redeemer and the redeemed. This present world is a battlefield where the powers of good and evil are embroiled in a war

---

[9]οὗτός ἐστιν ᾿Αγαμέμνων ἐμὸς/πόσις, νεκρὸς δέ, τῆσδε δεξιᾶς χερὸς/ἔργον, δικαίας τέκτονος. τάδ᾿ ὧδ᾿ ἔχει. (Aeschylus *Agamemnon* 1403–1405).

hastening hard to its predestined climax, the triumph of God. The Christian convert must be God's soldier to the end: "there is no discharge in that war." The two dominant ideas of the Epistle are the duty and the reward of endurance under *peirasmos*—certain and not distant victory. The inspiration of the words and the example of Jesus here is clear (see Luke 6:22f.).

Pleasure is not synonymous with joy, and Christian joy is a kind of *activity,* as in Aristotle's notion of happiness—a word that falls short of his thought in Greek as "joy" falls short of the Christian's in English. Christian joy is a man's pleasure in his (*and his brothers'*) progress toward Christian salvation; and it is not undiluted pleasure. Judaism also "baptized moral joy into religion."[10] The rabbis taught that the "chastisements of love" are precious,[11] bestowing on Israel the finest gifts from heaven,[12] like a father's chastisement of his son;[13] and R. Joshua B. Levi declared: "He who gladly accepts the sufferings of this world brings salvation to the world."[14] Pagan philosophy knew much of the same truth: "True joy is an exacting business," says the Stoic Seneca.[15] See Excursus A (pp. 88f.).

James is not, as is often held, here thinking of an alleged distinction between "internal" and "external" temptations. In the Christian life there is really no effective difference between the two: only the defects inherent in human nature make it possible for external or internal stimuli to goad a man into sin; thus to sexual lust straying thought is a temptation no less real, and not less potent, than a provocative temptress. In the Greek of this verse the picturesque adjective *various,* or "varied,"[16] is in an emphatic position; and it would not have been wasted here by a master of the language on a tepid armchair dichotomy to signify or emphasize such difference as may exist between "external" and "internal" temptations. There are no otiose adjectives in James's style; in 1:2 (against Ropes) "varied," as the order shows to the discerning, is as emphatic as the noun "endurance" in the next verse and the adjectives and participial phrase in v. 4, and the noun "wisdom" and the adverb "simply" in v. 5. If James had wanted to use *peirasmos* in a selective sense he would scarcely have given it the expansive and emphatic "varied" in hyperbaton without any indication that the sense of the noun was restricted. It is only in a clear context that *peirasmoi* has the narrower

---

[10]C. G. Montefiore and H. Loewe, in their *Rabbinic Anthology* (1938), devote a chapter to "Suffering." On the mistaken notion that "rejoicing in suffering is specifically Christian," see W. Nauck, "Freude im Leiden: Zum Problem einer urchristlichen Verfolgungstradition," *ZNW* 46 (1955), pp. 68–80.

[11]b. *San.* 101a.

[12]Exod. R. i.1.

[13]Minor Tractate, *Semachoth* 8.

[14]*Ta'an.* 8a.

[15]*Verum gaudium res severa est* (*Epist.* xxiii).

[16]ποικίλος.

meaning.[17] The Greek verb, *encounter,*[18] is apt for both kinds of temptation (Hort; against Mayor). Like the Latin *incido* it can have a deliberate meaning, as in a memorable passage in Xenophon, but it often indicates an unplanned and frequently, as here, an undesired incident. Much of the strength of temptation lies in our never knowing what it is going to do next.

3, 4 As in a scholastic Examination Course persevering study leads toward success, so we must realize that in Christianity approbation can follow only the effort of steadfast endurance under trial and temptation (subject, of course, to conditions of age and mental and physical health). Experience itself shows the probationary function of *peirasmos*: the wind of tribulation blows away the chaff of error, hypocrisy, and doubt, leaving that which survives the test, viz., *the genuine element of true character.*[19] Here we find striking similarities to the teaching of Judaism: both regard *peirasmos* as training and testing the seeker after righteousness in his battles with adversity (*Prüfungsleiden*) and with his own evil inclinations; of the latter Judaism has much to say. "As a goldsmith, who allows the silver in the fire and the gold in the crucible to be purified not longer than necessary, so God purifies the righteous each one according to his rank and his deeds."[20] The Jewish concept of the *yetser hā-rā'* or evil inclination is important in James's doctrine of *peirasmos,* not only in Jas. 1:13ff., where he specifically describes its activity, but also, we believe, in the preceding section (Jas. 1:2ff.); and it is never far below the surface of his thought. Judaism speaks much of internal testing, especially by the *yetser hā-rā'*, the willful animal impulses indispensable to the survival of the human species. On the other hand, Abrahams, pointing to the admittedly neutral meaning of both the Greek[21] and the Hebrew,[22] is inclined to doubt whether "temptation" bore this meaning in the first century. It is interesting, however, to note that it is James's use of *peirasmos* that seems to dispel his doubt, for he concedes

---

[17]E.g., Luke 8:13 has πειρασμοί where Mark 4:17 and Matt. 13:21 have θλῖψις and διωγμός (διὰ τὸν λόγον); but Luke does not give πειρασμός *simpliciter:* after πρὸς καιρὸν πιστεύουσι we have ἐν καιρῷ πειρασμοῦ and the verb ἀφίστανται, "desert": "who for a season believe, and in the season of attack of evil, desert," which readily suggests the translation "persecution": so, though not in form, does NEB, "in the time of testing they desert." The parable does not imply any real difference between the two classes of unfaithful men; in Jas. 1:2 as in 1 Cor. 10:13 there is nothing to narrow the scope of the term, and there is a whole background of thought to extend its meaning to the full.

[18]περιπίπτω. Cf. Xenophon *Anabasis* i.8.28: "when Artapates saw Cyrus fallen (πεπτωκότα), he leapt down from his horse and threw his arms around him" (lit. "fell around him," περιπεσεῖν αὐτῷ).

[19]On the meaning and spelling of δοκιμεῖον, see Moule, *Idiom Book,* pp. 96, 202; P. Chantraine, *La formation des noms* (1933), p. 53.

[20]b. *Pes.* 118a.

[21]πειράζειν.

[22]*nissāh.*

that "the use of 'temptation' in the first chapter of the Epistle of James may illustrate the double use of the term."[23]

In the usual text "endurance" is the result achieved; in our emended text, *in endurance,* it is the means and method by which we strive for (and, we hope, win) approbation.[24] In his note Ropes (pp. 135f.) well describes Christian constancy as "that permanent and underlying active trait of the soul from which endurance springs," and translates "steadfastness," "staying power," "not 'patience' " (KJV), citing Rom. 5:3f. and 2 Pet. 1:6. In Rom. 5:4 the present tense "works" signifies *progress,* not completion: cf. the teacher's motto, "Time teaches patience." So here it is not a question of more of our fruits which will give completeness of Christian character but of continued striving by God's grace to see that our endurance be unremittingly carried on till our death. In 1:4, therefore, "perfect" and "complete" and "lacking in nothing" are not perfunctory doublets, as Ropes suggests; they are of the essence of the doctrine.

Perfection, at first conceived in terms of OT cultic requirements (e.g., Exod. 12:5), later came to mean completeness in wholehearted dedication to Israel (Deut. 18:13), as in Noah and others (e.g., Gen. 6:9); here James continues the OT idea of perfection as a right relationship to God expressed in undivided obedience and unblemished life.[25] Balance pervades the Epistle of James: here—characteristically—James has sounded the prelude (1:3f.) to the theme to be developed in 1:16–21.

b. In prayer for guidance (1:5–8)

5 *But if any of you is lacking knowledge (of God's way and will), let him ask of God, who gives it to all as a simple (unconditional) gift and chides not (the petitioner for previous ignorance).*

6 *But let him ask in faith, with no halting between two opinions: for the man who halts between two opinions is like a sea of waves, the way it is blown and beaten under the winds.*

7 *Let not that (sort of) man imagine that he will get anything from the Lord.*

8 *A man who is of two minds is unsteady in all his ways.*

5   Whatever the doubtful meaning of Gen. 2:17 and 3:22 may be, it is clear that in the antecedents of the cult of Yahweh knowledge is often a jealously monopolized attribute of divinity: in later Hebrew religion, however, the bond of wisdom between God and his believers plays a part analogous to that of faith in Christianity. Sometimes "Wisdom means Law

---

[23]I. Abrahams, *Studies in Pharisaism and the Gospels* II (1924), p. 105.
[24]See Excursus B, pp. 90ff.
[25]See P. J. DuPlessis, *Teleios: The Idea of Perfection in the NT* (1959), pp. 98, 241.

(Torah)," says an old commentary on Ps. 99:4 (Midr. Ps. on 99:4). This Wisdom/Law was needed for defeating the wiles of the Evil Spirit in man;[26] but wisdom is a *gift,* from on high, which cannot be bought by man; its sole source is God: so OT Wisdom literature, Philo, and the rabbis. "Blessed be Thou, O Lord our God, King of the universe, who hast imparted of Thy wisdom to flesh and blood."[27]

In all Christian temptation wisdom is to be had "just for the asking," a gift here described by James with an adverb etymologically meaning "simply," a word often used in Greek in contrast to another Greek word connoting complex variety, in nature or art, from a patchwork quilt to an elaborate financial fraud.[28] For the mind of such a giver we confess that no single sufficient word occurs to us: "kind," "generous," "whole-hearted,"[29] are neither inapposite nor completely adequate.[30] KJV has "liberally"[31] for the Greek here,[32] and this suits the equivalent Greek noun[33] as "generosity." "Liberally" would be the best translation if we could confine it to its ethical signification (Hort, p. 9); as it is, "liberally" smacks too much of "profusely." "Graciously," says Hort (against Mayor), "is perhaps the best word for it," since it recalls the OT *ḥesed* (Gen. 24:49) and NT "kindness" (Rom. 2:4), i.e., benevolent goodness or grace of God. But even that has unfortunate overtones. We think that of the possible variants, "freely" has the fewest and least defects.

God gives his wisdom to men not only just for the asking but also without chiding a man for his previous sins, many of which the man may not even know he has committed. In this context the paramount function of wisdom is to keep a man from otherwise scarcely avoidable sin; hence we prefer our present explanation to other suggestions, such as that of Ropes (p. 140)—namely, James is thinking of human beings who are apt to keep casting up to a man any good turn they may have done him: see Tyndale, "God casteth no man in his teeth" (Moffatt, p. 12). Bunyan is right: referring to Jas. 1:15, he writes: "It appeareth that He (Christ) is free,

---

[26]E.g., b. *Baba Bathra* 16a; see S. Schechter, *Some Aspects of Rabbinic Theology* (1909), pp. 273ff.

[27]See Oesterley, p. 423.

[28]Cf. LS *s.v.* ἁπλῶς and ποικίλος.

[29]*TDNT* I, *s.v.* ἁπλοῦς (Bauernfeind), p. 386.

[30]Also unhelpful are Hermas *Mandates* ii.4 (cf. also 6) and the close parallel from the fourth-century Himerius *Ecloga* v. 19 (see Hort and Dibelius). More helpful is the reference in Matt. 6:22; Luke 11:34 to the "single" and "evil" eye, with the possible contrast between "generous" and "niggardly."

[31]Cf. Vulg. *affluenter*; ff *simpliciter*.

[32]ἁπλῶς.

[33]ἁπλότης.

because he giveth *without* twitting'' (i.e., ''rebuking'' or ''taunting'').[34] See Ps. 19:12, ''Who can be aware each time he offends? O cleanse thou me of my unconscious sins.'' Here in vv. 7–11 the psalmist praises the law of the Lord; he then very naturally proceeds to ask pardon for any offenses he may have committed against it, either unconsciously (v. 12) or ''presumptuously,'' that is at least, ''knowingly'' (v. 13a): only thus could he hope for remission in both classes of offense (v. 13b). In essence Ps. 19:12f. is a typical Hebrew prayer for wisdom in righteousness, and here in 1:5 James voices the characteristic Jewish faith in God as its source.

6 Here, in what Luther justly calls ''one of the best verses of this Epistle,''[35] James teaches that faith is the essential condition of prayer. The best light on this verse (and the kindred 5:15) is Heb. 11:6 (NEB): ''anyone who comes to God must believe that he exists and that he rewards those who search for him.''

In our present verse (1:6) ''faith'' does not, as in v. 3 above, denote ''constancy in the Christian religion''; it means ''confidence in prayer,'' as in Sir. 7:10: ''Be not of faint confidence in thy prayer.''[36] It means the petitioner's faith, his belief and trust, that God will heed his prayer, and grant it or only in his superior wisdom deny it: thus Jesus in Matt. 26:39 and in Mark and Luke. In this as usual the teaching of James is identical with that of Jesus; as Mitton says (p. 30): ''Here and in the Synoptic Gospels it means primarily the simple act of coming to Jesus with some need in complete confidence that He can and will deal with it. It was this attitude of faith that seemed to release powers in Jesus that made all things possible. Often when Jesus had healed an ailing man or woman, his explanation of the healing was: 'Thy faith hath saved thee'.'' We would venture to add that these links of faith reveal most clearly the relation of God and men as *partners* in human life.

The doubter has not such confidence that his prayer will be heeded: the picture in the middle voice of the verb[37] here is of a mind so filled with uncertainty and indecision that it cannot make any choice between the alternatives with which it is faced, i.e., whether or not to believe that God

---

[34]Hort, p. 6, shows that ''chide'' (ὀνειδίζω) is often used, e.g., by Aristotle, of reproachful giving: we think ὀνειδίζοντος would be quite pointless here unless it and ''gives'' (διδόντος) firmly continued the thought of ''wisdom'' (σοφία) and the sins to which ''wisdom'' is the sole antidote.

[35]*optimus unus locus huius epistolae.*

[36]See G. F. Moore, *Judaism in the First Centuries of the Christian Era* II (1927), p. 232, n. 2; also Montefiore and Loewe, *Rabbinic Anthology,* pp. 346ff., on the Jewish doctrine of prayer and the undivided heart, *kawwanah.*

[37]διακρίνομαι.

will be moved to grant the prayer being made: the man who is praying believes in God right enough, probably, but (as sometimes with child and father) is not at all confident that he will get what he wants.

The rendering "uncertainty and indecision" is supported by the versions and the Greek commentators on the NT, from Chrysostom and Hesychius, as well as the context of all the passages (see Hort, p. 10). The indisputable, though unprecedented NT meaning seems to have developed from the verb, meaning in the present, "I am making up my mind between two alternatives," as in the classical use, closely akin, too, to the idea of self-debate contained in the middle.[38] Hence, apparently, I am "undecided" in judgment between two alternatives. In our opinion, though argument is superfluous when the meaning is not disputed, this is more likely than Hort's association (p. 10) of the NT sense with "dispute." This is corroborated by v. 7, which shows, says Ropes (p. 141), that "the kind of waverer whom James has in mind fully *expects* to receive some benefit from God." *Halting between two opinions,* with its root idea of division, obviously has the same meaning as in v. 8, undecided between two choices, like Burian's ass (see Hermas *Mandates* ix.2, 4, 6).

The interpretation of the marine analogy in this verse is typically simple. The doubter here inclines (but no more) toward one alternative (say, to believe in prayer) and then inclines (but no more) toward the opposite alternative, and never is able to settle upon either: he is thus in constant agitation without making any progress to any result. In this he resembles the Lake of Galilee, *a sea of waves*. The noun[39] is a strong word, no "ripple": it can mean "wave," but on consideration we think that here it means an expanse of storm or at least swelling sea,[40] with emphasis, as Ropes observes (p. 141), "rather on size and extension than on separateness and succession (*kyma*), hence often used in a collective sense." The doubter is like "a sea of waves," now wind-driven toward the southeast, and now toward the northwest, with nothing that could sensibly be called progress. Though we know there could be a storm on the Lake, we are here assuming no more than normal winds and their effects on the waters. For the Mediterranean see, for example, Acts 27:4, 7, 9 and (v. 14) "a tempestuous wind": so much for Hort's improbable hypothesis (p. 11) of "a slight rufflement" of a waveless Mediterranean. The first verb,[41] rare, describes any movement of the wind, perhaps implying here, as Hort thinks, "gentler motions of the

[38]Cf. Euripides *Medea* 609, cited by Mayor, p. 39.
[39]κλύδων.
[40]As in, e.g., Sophocles *Oedipus Tyrannus* 1527.
[41]ἀνεμίζω.

air." The second verb[42] means "to fan," "fan" itself being used with fiercer applications than we find in a lady's drawing room: sometimes it is also used of bellows, and James here (besides others in other texts) may be using it in the other sense of bellows, perhaps another local Palestinian allusion to the winnowing of wheat. Hort's whole motive is to deny the meaning "storm" in James's simile, and so he argues that a fan could not raise a storm. But it is not true that we are confined to the amount of blast proper to an actual fan. A metaphorical fan can be as big and forceful as the proportion of the metaphor suggests, as we can say that in the Great Fire of London or Chicago the flames were fanned by a high wind.[43] We cannot possibly exclude, but neither do we here insist upon requiring, the extreme set up by Hort, as "the *prima facie* notion of billows lashed by a storm." All that is necessary is a real, vigorous wind, not any slight rufflement: it *can* come in a tempest, as in that which wrecked Odysseus' ship—"the surge loosed the sides from the keel."[44] But we think what James has in mind is the more normal, but quite vigorous action of the winds exemplified in Thucydides ii.84, in the naval battle off Naupactus.

The point of comparison in James here is strictly *not* "the ordinary instability of the heaving sea," as Ropes thought (p. 142), but the unsettled behavior of the waves (as to their direction, to and fro, like the doubter's mind) under the perpetually varying winds that keep driving them now in one direction and perhaps next day in another, like the man hesitating before a choice to be made—and perhaps never made after all. The sentence, says Ropes (p. 142), is made less forcible through the excessive elaboration of the figure. The elaboration is *not* excessive; it is typical of the author's skill: since the action in this scene proceeds from the winds, they naturally figure prominently in the script, which only needs to be understood.

We suggest that this figure, no fantasy of the closet, corroborates the ascription of this Epistle to the Lord's brother, James of Galilee.[45]

7 See Excursus B (pp. 92ff.).

8 This adjective "of divided mind"[46] occurs only here and at 4:8,

---

[42]ῥιπίζω, n. ῥιπίς.

[43]The metaphorical uses of ῥιπίζω cited by LS imply *vigorous* action; and there is nothing mild about ἀναρριπίζω in Philo *On the Giants* 51 (cf. *Unchangeableness of God* 175), cited by Ropes, p. 142 *ad init.*, but apparently ignored by Hort: "an *indescribable storm* that is *fanned up* in the soul by the *extreme violence* of life."

[44]*Odyssey* xii.421.

[45]For concurring views see, among others, Rendall, pp. 37f.; E. F. F. Bishop, *Apostles of Palestine* (1958), p. 184; D. Y. Hadidian, "Palestinian Pictures in the Epistle of James," *ExT* 63 (1951–52), p. 228.

[46]δίψυχος.

and never in the LXX or in Greek literature before James; but it as well as its cognate derivatives soon became current in postapostolic writings, especially in Hermas, sometimes linked with "prayer" and "simplicity" (40 times), Clement of Rome, Epistle of Barnabas, Didache, and the Apostolic Constitutions.[47] We are aware of scholars who have judged that the Epistle of James has neither structure nor pedigree, but if James was the author of this Epistle it is not surprising but rather inevitable that the occurrence (and perhaps invention) of this word here set Clement (c.A.D. 96) and the others to using it profusely: Lightfoot, Westcott, and Zahn, among others, believed that Clement knew and used the Epistle of James. The hypothesis that James here is quoting from a lost book like *Eldad and Modad* appears unnecessary.

Literally meaning *of two minds,* the word is rightly explained by Ropes (p. 143) as "with soul divided between faith and the world," "a fence-straddler" (Jordan). Here and in its recurrence at 4:8 the point is *doubt,* not duplicity: in James the word describes a mind distracted by lusts and temptations. This idea is epitomized by Bunyan's "Mr. Facing-Both-Ways," and, in real life, by Augustine's prayer: "O Lord, grant me purity, but not yet."[48] But doubt and indecision, as Kierkegaard clearly saw, can degenerate into despair; hence his observation:

> Is not despair simply double-mindedness? For what is despairing other than to have two wills? For whether the weakling despairs over not being able to wrench himself away from the bad, or whether the brazen one despairs over not being able to tear himself completely away from the good: they are both double-minded, they both have two wills.[49]

The idea of a man divided in doubt or hesitation is common enough in Greek; thus Homer says Achilles' heart within his breast "was divided in counsel" whether to ... or ....[50] The OT notion of the double heart, literally in Hebrew "with heart and heart," obviously lies at the root of James's locution (see Ps. 12:2; 1 Chr. 12:23; Sir. 2:12–14). Closely akin and illuminating is the rabbinic doctrine of man's spirit as originally pure and so to be returned to God, and of the two *yetsers,* good and bad, though essentially one, seated in the heart; for example, prayer must not be offered with a divided heart, part for God, part for the world.[51] More recently,

---

[47]See Mayor and Ropes for references. The word was used by A. H. Clough for the title of his poem, *Dipsychos.*
[48]*Confessions* vii.17.
[49]S. Kierkegaard, *Purity of Heart Is To Will One Thing* (E.T. 1938), p. 61.
[50]*Iliad* i.188f.; xvi.435. LS, *s.v.* δίχα, cite Homer six times in much the same sense.
[51]*Tanḥuma* on Deut. 6:5; see Schechter, *op. cit.,* p. 255.

60

evidence from Qumran[52] has shown a similar type of dualism. This evidence suggests that the topic of the single/double heart was in the air in (and before and after) the time of James.[53] The importance of the topic in the minds of James and other apostles is confirmed by the emphasis on single-mindedness, the opposite of double-mindedness: e.g., Jas. 1:5; 4:7ff.—in the former of these two passages the adverbial form of the Greek word ''simple'' (unconditional)[54] recalls a similar association with prayer, as in 1:8 (see 1 Cor. 14:20; Hermas *Mandates* ii.1; ix.1; xii.1).

c. As comforting the lowly poor and chastening the haughty rich (1:9–11)

9 *(In the equality of Christian brotherhood) let the brother of humble degree exult in his being made high,*

10 *and the rich (brother) in his being made low: for he (in his being-only-rich) shall pass away like the flower among the grass.*

11 *For the sun arises, with the scorching wind, and parches the grass, and the flower among it falls off, and the beauty of its appearance perishes: so he who is (only) rich shall wither in his ways.*

9 The wording in the Greek is significant. We must read *brother* with *the rich* (v. 10) as well as with the lowly (*of humble degree*). The other view, that *the rich* refers to the non-Christian man in general, has little to commend it.[55] The reference would then become ironic and eschatological. Such an interpretation is adequately rebutted by Ropes (p. 146) on three grounds: (1) the unnatural refusal to supply ''brother''; (2) the excessive irony required by the supply of ''let him exult''; and (3) the loose connection with the context and especially with the initial and continuing idea of *peirasmoi*. ''Let the lowly brother rejoice in his being exalted.'' The verb *exult* is used in the OT of any ''proud and exulting joy'' (Ps. 5:11; 32:11; Jer. 9:23; Sir. 39:8) and frequently in the NT, especially by Paul, more than thirty times, in Christians (2 Cor. 7:14); in sufferings and infirmities (Rom. 5:3; 2 Cor. 12:9); and even by way of a personal apologia (2 Cor. 11:12).

[52]See W. I. Wolverton, ''The Double-Minded Man in the Light of Essene Psychology,'' *ATR* 38 (1956), pp. 166–175; O. J. F. Seitz, ''Relationship of the Shepherd of Hermas to the Epistle of James,'' *JBL* 63 (1944), pp. 131–140; ''Antecedents and Signification of the Term ΔΙΨΥΧΟΣ,'' *JBL* 66 (1947), pp. 211–19; also ''Afterthoughts on the Term 'Dipsychos,' '' *NTS* 4 (1957–58), pp. 330ff.; ''Two Spirits in Man: An Essay in Biblical Exegesis,'' *NTS* 6 (1959–60), pp. 82ff.

[53]Compare similar neologisms διχόνους and δίγλωσσος in Philo *On the Sacrifices of Abel and Cain*, 32; Sir. 5:9 (and see Ropes, p. 143).

[54]ἁπλῶς (adverb from ἁπλοῦς).

[55]Demanding that we should supply some verb like καυχάσθω, or less naturally καυχᾶται (Alford), αἰσχυνέσθω (Oecumenius), or ταπεινοῦσθαι (Grotius).

(See Ropes, p. 145.) Here the verb renews the exhortation to joy of 1:2, its prominent position clearly stressing the opposition to "doublemindedness" (1:8); see Mayor, p. 42. The moral quality of the exulting joy depends on its occasion. In 4:16 it is bad; cf. Rom. 2:17, 23 (God and Torah); 3:27; 4:2; 1 Cor. 1:29; 4:7 (self-righteousness); 2 Cor. 11:18; Gal. 6:13 (the flesh); and 1 Cor. 5:6 (sin). Here the exulting is good, as often in similar directive contexts, or, for instance, exulting in "hope of the glory of God" (Rom. 5:2), in God himself (Rom. 5:11), and in Christ Jesus (esp. Phil. 3:3; also Rom. 15:17; 1 Cor. 1:31).

James's thought must not be spiritualized. By "lowly" he had in mind not the Christian grace of humility but simply outward social status, e.g., that of a slave or beggar (Luke 1:52; Rom. 12:16), "poverty in relation to 'glorying' and contempt, a state despised by the mass of mankind" (Hort). The Greek word,[56] like Latin *humilis*, means "low"—not a virtue, in mind or status, in classical thought, but rather like our "poor-spirited." In the LXX the word may mean literally "poor" (1 Sam. 18:23), but sometimes with a special religious connotation when contrasted with the "rich" (Ps. 10:2, and esp. Pss. of Solomon 2:35). Later James also uses "lowly" in an inward spiritual way (4:6), recalling that the two ideas were sometimes so associated in Jewish literature (Sir. 10:30f.). Among Christians, humility is the virtue of voluntary acceptance or confession of a low or subordinate status in esteem or function; cf. Phil. 2:1–13, the *locus classicus* on Christian, and Christ's, humility. Even under Christianity, the metaphor implicit in the word "humility" is not very pleasing in an equalitarian age. In Jas. 1:9 the meaning is literal, referring to a man's mean social station in life. "Highness," "exaltation," refers to the present spiritual status which, by virtue of his relation to Christ, the Christian now enjoys.

10 Abasement, here virtually reflexive, like "humble yourselves" (4:10, in a similar context), is self-abasement: it refers to the adoption of that new mind of humility which James also in 4:10, 13–16, enjoins upon some (obviously of the richer) of the brothers. Mayor rightly takes this to refer to "the intrinsic effect of Christianity in changing our view of life." "For the rich man (in his being-only-rich) shall pass away, will vanish into the past." This, as Hort points out, is not an explanation of the previous clause, but "one reason why the rich brother should glory in it, or more strictly why he should not be startled at the command to glory in it." Like the aorists and the future in the next verse, *shall pass away* is gnomic, and speaks not of the rich convert but of the rich man in general, "*qua* rich" (Mayor), "the typical rich man" (Ropes), strangely typified for Arnold Meyer also in Asher (Gen. 49:20), "the worldly rich man." He and his riches are as fleeting as "the

[56]ταπείνωσις.

flower of the field" (Jas. 5:1ff.). Like Peter (1:24), James quotes Isa. 40:6f. with its theme of "all flesh is grass"; and both in turn may be reproducing a catechetical source. For the sake of continuity in translation we have written here *the flower among the grass*: for similar translation Greek of the Hebrew "flower of the field" cf. Ps. 103:15 (LXX). The Greek word for *grass*[57] is cognate with our "garden, yard," and the Latin *hortus*, and may mean either a place such as a feeding ground, or fodder, usually grass or hay. Flowers like the anemone, cyclamen, and lily (Matt. 6:28, 30) are profuse in Palestine. Hort (p. 15) writes: "By 'the flower of the field' the prophet doubtless meant the blaze of gorgeous blossoms which accompanies the first shooting of the grass in spring, alike in the Holy Land and on the Babylonian plain." This is another of those vivid "Palestinian Pictures in the Epistle of James";[58] so H. B. Tristram also writes: "The downs of Bethlehem in February are one spangled carpet of brilliant flowers. . . . In May all traces of verdure are gone."[59] The image then is both familiar and forceful, recalling the special and distinctive climate of Palestine. In the Mediterranean region the spring is brilliant but very brief.

11 Mention of the implications for the rich leads to a poetic elaboration of the figure of "the flower." The rare use of the Greek aorist here (also 1 Pet. 1:24; Matt. 13:44, 46, 48), which has been called "narrative" or "gnomic," may well represent the Hebrew perfect to "emphasize the suddenness and completeness of the withering."[60] The theory that finds an obscure tribal reference to Jacob in Gen. 32:31 (Arnold Meyer) is as bizarre as that which equates "the rising of the sun" with Christ and "the day of the Lord" (Laurentius). NEB translates "scorching *heat*" (so KJV, RSV) and the *Living Bible* "scorching *summer sun*": in the Bible the word (*kausōn*) can mean "heat" (Matt. 20:12; Luke 12:55) or "wind" (Jer. 18:17; Ezek. 27:26, and others). We prefer to translate *scorching wind*, for the admittedly inconclusive reason of its more particular vividness of the country life. No one who has ever lived in Palestine can forget the sirocco (*sharqiya*)— the blasting, scorching southeast wind which blows there in the spring; once begun, it blows incessantly night and day.[61] Vivid is E. F. F. Bishop's comment: "The temperature hardly seems to vary. Flowers and herbage wilt and fade, lasting as long as 'morning glory'. Anemones and cyclamen,

---

[57]χόρτος.
[58]Hadidian, *art. cit.*, pp. 227f.
[59]*Natural History of the Bible* (1868), p. 455.
[60]Moule, *Idiom Book*, p. 12.
[61]See G. A. Smith, *Historical Geography of the Holy Land* ([25]1931), pp. 67ff.; *Encyclopaedia Biblica*, *s.v.* "Wind" (Cheyne), cols. 5304f.; Hadidian, *art. cit.*, pp. 227f.; Savas C. Agourides, "The Origin of the Epistle of James," *Greek Orthodox Theological Review*, Vol. 9, No. 1 (1963), p. 73.

carpeting the hillsides of Galilee in spring, have a loveliness that belongs only to the past, when the hot wind comes. Drooping flowers make fuel. The fields of lupins are here today and gone tomorrow."[62] Although our rendering "sirocco" points more clearly to a Palestinian milieu, the other envisages similar conditions. It is difficult to resist the conclusion that James had often seen the flowers blooming on the Galilean hills wilt and perish in the intense scorching wind. The flower of the grass that fades has a forceful reminder of the transience of earthly wealth.

Hort gives two renderings for the Greek word *prosōpon* (here translated *appearance*): (i) "face," as in Hebrew; that is, outward appearance or "fashion" (Lat. *facies*); or (ii) as in late Jewish Greek, especially in the old Hebrew idiom "to accept the face," that is, "receive with favor": on "personage" as the possessor of dignity or honor, see Sir. 29:27; 32:15; Wisd. 6:7; 2 Macc. 14:24. On this latter basis he thinks "pride" does best here. But such a semantic extension seems to us unlikely. The texts cited in Ropes (Gen. 2:6; 2 Sam. 14:20; Job 41:13) support the easier *appearance* (or "show"), that is, the appearance presented. Again Hort gives two renderings for the word we translate *beauty* (*euprepeia*): (i) "beauty," "grace," or "comeliness"; or (ii) "dignity" and "splendor"; "majesty" as in Ps. 93:1; 104:1 (Vulg. *decor*). We prefer the former ("goodly appearance," Ropes) for this NT *hapax legomenon*. Of Hort's citations, besides Ps. 93:1, Ropes gives Wisd. 7:29; but in this KJV has "more beautiful" and RV (attributed to Westcott), "fairer (than the sun)." In any case Hort's "the glory of its pride" seems to allegorize the similitude too far. We do not think of the "pride" of flowers, but of their short-lived beauty. And the point is mainly evanescence, *perishes*: hence *grass* is often included in such OT comparisons. Even when we speak of the glory of flowers or of the sunrise or sunset, it is not the glory of pomp and pride as in plutocrats.

The fate of the unbelieving *rich* (generic singular) is climactically described, the eschatological thrust anticipating the fuller treatment later on (Jas. 5:1ff.). The picture of the rich "withering" continues the simile of the fading flower: the verb, found only in the NT, is picturesque and may be used of the dying out of a fire,[63] "many kinds of gradual enfeeblement," and (rarely) plants like roses (Wisd. 2:8), as well as ears of corn (Job 15:30; 24:24). The figure itself is found in Philo,[64] in connection with wealth; in 2 Baruch 82:7, of the Gentiles; frequently in papyrus epitaphs, and also in the Talmud. Thus Rab says: "The children of man are like the grasses of the field, some blossom and some fade."[65]

[62]*Op. cit.*, p. 184.
[63]Aristotle *De Vita et Morte* 5.
[64]*Special Laws* i.311.
[65]b. *Erubin* 54a; Sir. 14:11–19.

Ropes is right in adding Prov. 2:7; 4:27 to the instances given by Hort (Ps. 68:24; Isa. 8:11; Hab. 3:6; Sir. 1:5) of this use of *ways* (*poreiai*) in the sense of "going" as a mere trope for "doings," which Hort quite needlessly questions as "too weak here." It is as forcible as the other words for 'way' so "abundantly" thus used in the LXX. The suggestion that James here means journeys of merchants on business (Mayor, Hort, Herder, following Jas. 4:13f.) is too subtle. Hort's own notion that the word is here used to suggest the unquiet restlessness of the worldly rich is also unlikely. To anyone approaching James as an artist the reason for the word is clear: he had used another trite Greek word for 'way' in v. 8, not two dozen words from the beginning of the elaborately studied sentence of v. 11. Besides being less trite, besides avoiding repetition, besides the alliteration[66] (and Mayor has shown the attraction alliteration has for James), the longer word[67] adds strength to the central limb of the rhythm before the smashing close of the final verb (*shall wither*),[68] itself noticed for its effect by Mayor.

"Which passes away, the rich man or his riches?" asks Hort. He answers that the point is in the separation of a man from his wealth at death, and he quotes to this purpose Ps. 49:16f.; Luke 12:20, and Horace *Odes* ii.14.21ff. The tradition to which such similes as this belong goes back to the days when the Hebrews, having little faith in a real personal immortality (compare the state of the dead in Ps. 88 with the Homeric Hades), looked for the reward of the righteous and the wicked, in themselves or their prosperity, in *this* world (see Ps. 58:10f.; 34:1–22; 37:38). Wealth without righteousness shares the lot of the wicked; indeed in the ancient world it was often the wicked that prospered—for a time (Ps. 73:12, 18f.). Hort rightly takes "he will pass away" as a reference not to the rich brother, but to the rich man in general, as, we may suggest, Belshazzar came to an abrupt end. Hort continues, however: "But a difficulty remains. St. James would hardly say that the rich man is more liable to death than the poor, and the shortness of life common to both is in itself no reason why the rich should glory in being brought to poverty." But James does not say that the rich brother is impoverished, either here or in 4:7, "Submit yourselves to God," or 4:8, "Cleanse your hands, purify your hearts," or in 4:13–16, on the pride of money-makers, where 4:14 could scarcely be closer to our present 1:10f. Hort's objection is not well taken. The common fact of mortality has a quite special lesson for the rich (among other magnates of this world), for they have a special temptation to forget it, as Pindar is never tired of telling his patrons: "If any man who has riches excels others in beauty of form and has

[66]πλούσιος and πορείαις.
[67]πορείαις (dative).
[68]μαρανθήσεται, future indicative passive of μαραίνω.

proved his strength by victory in the Games, let him remember that he puts his raiment on mortal limbs and in the end of all is clad with earth'';[69] "If any man fosters his wealth with honesty, abounding in possessions and winning good fame, let him not seek to be a god.''[70]

Yet Hort perceives the truth. James indeed, as Hort says, has in view "not death absolutely but death as separating riches from their possessor and showing them to have no essential connection with him." The pride of wealth "substituted another God for Jehovah and denied the brotherhood of man." Speaking of his friend, a poor Christian, a wealthy unbeliever remarked: "When I die, I shall leave my riches. When he dies he will go to his.''[71] In effect this is what James is saying: Remember you are mortal, and wealth *per se* does nothing for your soul: so be glad that by humbling yourself in Christ and the brotherhood you are likely to win the treasure of life everlasting. The old Hebrew thought of the premature end of the wicked and rich appears in James's statement of his principle, which in fact is equally valid if the rich man lives in wealth to the age of a hundred; besides, James is convinced that the end is at hand (see 5:3, 8).

III. THE GOSPEL PROMISE (1:12–27)

a. For faithful endurance against temptations (12–21)

12 *Happy is the man who with constancy endures trying assaults of evil; for when (upon trial) he has been approved, he will receive the crown of life, which God has promised to those who love him.*

13 *Let no one under trying assault of evil say, "My trial by assault of evil comes from God." For God is invincible to assault of evils, and himself subjects no one to assault of evil.*

14 *But each man is tried by assault of evil by his own lust, as he feels the pull of its distraction and the enticement of its bait.*

15 *Then his lust having conceived gives birth to sin: and when sin is full grown it brings forth death.*

16 *Make no mistake, my beloved brothers (I'm not arguing, I'm telling you):*

17 *Every good gift, yes, every perfect gift, is from above, coming down from the Father of lights of heaven, whose nature (unlike those lights) suffers neither the variation of orbit nor any shadow.*

18 *He of his own wish begot us by the Word of truth, for us to be a kind of firstfruits of his creation.*

[69]*Nem.* xi.13–16.
[70]*Ol.* v.23f.
[71]See J. Blanchard, *Not Hearers Only* I (1971), p. 68. Cf. K. Menninger, *Whatever Became of Sin?*, on "the sin of affluence" (pp. 149ff.).

19 *Wherefore, my beloved brothers, let every man be swift to hear, slow to speak, slow to wrath:*

20 *for a man's wrath (or "anger") does not express in action the righteousness of God.*

21 *Wherefore strip off all filthiness and prodigality of vice, and with meekness accept the implanted Word (implanted by those who have preached the gospel to you), which is able to save your souls.*

12   Following Hort, in order to avoid the admittedly slight element of ambiguity, we prefer the translation *happy* (*beatus*) to "blessed" (*benedictus*) in this context. A. Meyer (pp. 270ff.) and B. S. Easton (p. 26) find supposed tribal references to Jacob and Issachar. The idea is familiar in Judaism: "Happy is the man who can withstand the test, for there is none whom God does not prove."[72] The thought is quite typical of James. Happy is the man who here and now, from day to day, withstands *peirasmos*: he is progressing *toward* salvation (as in 1:3), and if (as 1:4 requires) he endures to the end, then at last, winning final approval, he will receive the final reward, the crown of life.

Peirasmos here must still be taken in its most comprehensive sense. Ropes (p. 150) is right when he says that *has been approved* is another way of saying *endures,* not a further condition of receiving the crown. "The word will, in almost every case, imply that the proof is victoriously demonstrated, the proved is also approved, just as in English we speak of 'tried men'."[73] The word therefore contains not only the notion of trial, but also trial and approval (2 Cor. 10:18; 13:7; 2 Tim. 2:15). This notion of genuineness is well brought out if we contrast the antonym,[74] which means "rejected" or "reprobate" (as of silver in Jer. 6:30).

The crown, head-wreath, chaplet, circlet was the victor's prize in the Greek games; it might be given to a man the public wished to honor; it was worn in religious and secular feasts. There is no need to catalog its secular and religious uses (see Ropes, pp. 150ff.). But whereas Paul finds occasion (1 Cor. 9:24, 25) to remind us that in the races only one competitor received the prize, in Christianity, as in scholastic examinations, there is no reason why all candidates should not pass the test. The Christian is not competing against his fellows as do the athletes; yet the image was felt to be, and was, relevant. The clue to our understanding its appropriateness is in Heb. 12:1. There we have the crowd of spectator-witnesses, the past heroes of the faith, the stripping off of encumbrances, as it were of clothes (see Jas. 1:21), for

---

[72]Exod. R. xxxi.3; Sifre Deut. 32, p. 57; Dan. 12:12; Sir. 14:1; 4 Macc. 7:21f.; 10:15.
[73]MM, *s.v.* δόκιμος; R. C. Trench, *Synonyms of the NT* ([12]1894), No. lxxiv.
[74]ἀδόκιμος.

the race: it is the race of *endurance*; and the model of endurance, and the founder and perfecter of the faith which by endurance we must maintain, is Jesus. Whereas the athletes have human competitors, the Christian's adversaries are the powers of darkness, trying to drive him out of the course and prevent his ever finishing it. The metaphor of the fight (and some fights did come into the Games) would have been a closer parallel; so R. Simeon b. Lakish said: "It can be compared to two prize-fighters, one of whom was stronger than the other. The stronger prevailed over the weaker and then placed a garland over his own head."[75] Yet, notwithstanding his opening verses, James, unlike Paul, does not elaborate the metaphor of athletic competitions. The crown is the reward of the Christian's effort, which against the powers of evil is no less agonistic than the athlete's against his fellow competitors: the crown as his reward is eternal life.

Some later manuscripts—apparently contrary to Jewish custom[76]—specifically mention "the Lord" or "God" as giver of the promise to "those who love him." This promise does not appear in so many words in the OT, and it means that here and in 1 Cor. 9:25; 1 Pet. 5:4; 2 Tim. 4:8, and especially Rev. 2:10, we have an otherwise unrecorded saying of Jesus;[77] confirmation is also found in its "strong liturgical flavor" (von Soden). Dibelius shows (p. 87) that the words "those who love him," common enough in the LXX and later Jewish and Christian tradition, are traced back by the rabbis to Judg. 5:31. Man's duty of love to God is as old as any in Hebrew religion, and from Ezekiel onward the prophets take up the theme with renewed emphasis, in which they are followed by Jesus and, after his example, by James and Paul.

13–21 Let us try to summarize the sequence of thought (in short, the logic) of Jas. 1:13ff.: James is no backwater eccentric; he is in the midstream of apostolic doctrine.

The Christian is God's man, not the world's; and so, as his loyal child, he is bound by God's law. "James has no philosophical answer to the problem of evil," notes John Coutts. "He cannot explain why people are pushed almost beyond endurance—but he offers a practical answer: faith in a God of pure goodness."[78] There is a reward for the faithful who resist the assaults of evil; these assaults spring from lust, which is alien to God. Endurance under such assaults obviously comes from sincerity of faith, not from the amorality of 1:13. The theological duplicity of 1:13 is an amoral philosophy; for, if God is not constantly good, there is no such thing as

---

[75]Exod. R. xxi.11.
[76]SB III, p. 751; Windisch, p. 8.
[77]A. Resch, *Agrapha* (1906), p. 253.
[78]*The Soldier's Armoury* (Jan.–June 1976), p. 108.

"good." The opposite implications of the truth are clear in 1:19-21. God's attribute is unmixed good. He has given us Christians the "word of truth" with a view to our becoming a sort of "firstfruits." Therefore, *in accordance with that gift and purpose,* we must live as in v. 19 (say, in a word, "peaceably"); for as Christian children of God we must by our conduct manifest God's implanted gift (of "truth," involving "righteousness," v. 21), and that is not achieved by "wrath" (and its concomitants, as in 4:1-4).

13 Oesterley suggests that the warning against charging God with responsibility for temptation is intended to correct a misunderstanding of the *ne nos inducas* clause of the Lord's Prayer by which certainly some later Christians and possibly even some of the first generation were perplexed.[79] The idea, however, is as old as Homer. "Our nature in itself doth abhor the deformity of sin, and for that cause [men] study by all means how to find the first original of it elsewhere" (R. Hooker). B. S. Easton suggests (p. 27) that this "may or may not be a polemic against the common Jewish doctrine that God implants in every man two impulses, one good and one evil" (see Jas. 1:2). Again, without setting the Epistle of James in a Gnostic context, as Schammberger, Pfleiderer, and others attempt to do, it is not impossible to assume that James might have been aware of some kind of nascent Gnosticism which even at an early date cast doubts on divine integrity.

Moffatt (p. 19) conjectures that the phrase "the Father of the heavenly lights," 1:17, contains an implicit denial of the power over human destinies which the prevalent astrology ascribed to the stars. Shakespeare's *Julius Caesar* (I.ii.134) offers a possible parallel:

> *The fault, dear Brutus, is not in our stars*
> *But in ourselves, that we are underlings.*

James has no sympathy with sentimental fatalism. The use of "tempt" in the OT and NT, as when the Israelites tempt God in the desert, or when God tempts Abraham, is certainly apt to cause perplexity in some readers (see R. A. Knox, p. 94). But God's "tempting," unlike the devil's, is a test in which he does not desire the candidate to fail but to succeed. Nevertheless, if this innocent interpretation is the true meaning of "temptation" by God in the Lord's Prayer,[80] it is palpably not the meaning of the word in James, who

---

[79]See F. H. Chase, *The Lord's Prayer in the Early Church* (1891), pp. 60ff.

[80]Probably the best paraphrase, if not direct translation, of the petition in the Lord's Prayer is "Grant that we may not fail in the test" (cf. C. C. Torrey, *The Four Gospels* [1933], p. 292), with which may be compared our Lord's admonition to the disciples in Gethsemane: "Keep awake, and pray not to fail in the test" (Mark 14:38a). The Jewish service for morning prayer contains the similar petition: "Do not bring us into the power of temptation; let not the evil inclination (*yetser*) have sway over us," See C. F. D. Moule, "An Unsolved Problem in the Temptation-Clause in the Lord's Prayer," *Reformed Theological Review* 33 (1974), pp. 65-75.

uses it in its most sinister sense and, even so, emphatically tells us to rejoice in it, and no less emphatically insists that it never comes from God.[81]

That "assault of evils" here refers to *moral* evil, i.e., sin, and not, for example, leprosy, nor even God's sorrow at men's sin or his own Son's crucifixion, surely cannot be seriously doubted. As for the construction "invincible to assault of evils,"[82] *grammatici certant* on the classification of this genitive case: the meaning is not obscure. Adjectives formed like this regularly negative the idea of the cognate verb.[83]

The second half of this sentence expressly denies that God ever instigates a man to sin, but both halves are co-equal elements in a single truth.[84] If God were not invincible to evil he could not escape becoming at least sometimes the ally of sin; as it is, the invincible good is *ipso facto* incapable either of leading others or itself being led into sin (see Jas. 1:17; 3:10–12, on the argument from natural consistency). Moffatt (p. 18) effectively quotes Marcus Aurelius: "The Reason (Logos) which rules the universe has no cause in itself for doing wrong." Exactly so Mayor (p. 50) summarizes James: "God is incapable of tempting others to evil, because He is Himself absolutely insusceptible to evil." Tempting others to evil would require a delight in evil, of which he is himself incapable.

14 "Desire" in the NT is not always evil (Luke 22:15); so of human desire, in Col. 3:5 the adjective "evil" is necessarily added. "Animal desire is not in itself evil," wrote John Baillie; "it only becomes evil when, in man, it seeks the aid of spirituality—of freedom and reason and the judgment of value—in order to convert its relativity into an absolute and its finitude into infinity."[85] The fifteenth-century poem *The Cuckoo and the Nightingale* furnishes an excellent illustration of the neutral use of the

---

[81]Cf. 1 Cor. 10:13, where indeed Paul may be deliberately supplying an interpretation of the clause "Lead us not into temptation."

[82]ἀπείραστος κακῶν.

[83]E.g., as ἄγευστος, "without taste," negatives that of γεύομαι, "to taste"; ἀστέγαστος, "uncovered," that of στεγάζω, "to cover"; and ἄπαυστος, "never ceasing from," that of παύω, "to make to cease." With verbs like παύω and θεραπεύω, forms like ἄπαυστος and ἀθεράπευτος usually signify an impossibility—"incapable of being stopped," and "incurable," in these two verbs cited. So here, as Mayor and Ropes agree, ἀπείραστος has this negative gerundive meaning, "incapable of being tempted." Ropes (*ad loc.*) rightly says: "In favour of the meaning 'untemptable' (E.V.) is the sharp verbal contrast then afforded to πειράζει οὐδένα." Origin (on Exod. 15:25), the Vulgate, Luther, R. A. Knox, and others have taken ἀπείραστος as active, "incapable of tempting"; but even if possible this would be unlikely here, both as a very rare use of such a form (see Mayor), and as giving a vain tautology to the two clauses, and—above all—as denuding αὐτός of all its force. Unacceptable also is Hort's attempt (p. 23) to equate ἀπείραστος with the almost proverbial ἀπείρατος (Plut. *Moral.* 119f.), meaning "without experience in evils."

[84]See Mayor, p. 50, with his reference to Jelf's *Greek Grammar*, § 797.

[85]*Invitation to Pilgrimage* (1944), p. 56. Cf. Menninger, *op. cit.*, pp. 138ff.

English *lust*:[86] "Worship, ease, and all hertes lust."[87] In Jas. 1:14 "desire," and 4:2 "you desire," however, the context clearly imports sin.

The themes of 1:9–21 are renewed in the second section of the Epistle, in 4:1–12; our most important need is to relate 4:5 (and 6) to 1:14. On the relevant points we agree with the NEB translation of 4:5, "Or do you suppose that Scripture has no meaning when it says that the spirit which God implanted in man turns towards envious desires?" In 1:14 "his own" (lust) emphasizes the antithesis, "not God's instigation but a man's own 'desire'," which often, as Hort says (p. 24), "substitutes some private and individual end for the will of God." Thus, as Gal. 5:16f. indicates, a carnal "desire" is very apt to be sinful; but as we remembered above, on Jas. 1:2, only an ascetic extremist would think that desire for a good dinner must necessarily be evil. In Jas. 1:15 the personification of "desire" is only literary (against Schammberger, Hauck).

In such cases the influence toward evil comes, when it does come, from the appetite of man's body (part of "the world of iniquity," 3:6), in which since the Fall some evil is inherent. There is no reference to Satan as the tempter (contrast 1 Enoch 49:4ff.; Clem. Hom. 3:55), because this would have been "only substituting one excuse for another" (Hort). The language recalls the function of the *yetser*.[88] James's metaphors of the "pull of its distraction and the enticement of its bait" are probably based on his fishing experience in Galilee,[89] like that of displenishment, in the Council's letter, from his farmhouse observations in Galilee; but he was assuredly not the first to use a fishing metaphor. The rabbis wrote: "As man throws out a net whereby he catches the fish of the sea, so the sins of man become the means of entangling and catching the sinner."[90] "Hooked" is also the way we describe a drug addict. The present tenses of the participles, as Hort insists (pp. 25f.), have only the inchoate sense shown in our translation, a sense common in the Greek present tense; we have already noted it in 1:3 and 12 ("works" and "endures"): each man experiences assault of evil by his own lust, as he feels himself being pulled astray by it and enticed by it as by a bait.

The choice of participles and especially the combination of *as he feels the pull of its distraction* with *the enticement of its bait*[91] has caused the

---

[86]Here used to render ἐπιθυμία.
[87]Similarly in the papyri; see MM, p. 239.
[88]See Moore, *Judaism* I (1927), pp. 481f.
[89]Bishop, *op. cit.*, pp. 184f.; Hadidian, *art. cit.*, p. 227.
[90]Midr. Prov. 5; see also Qumran Hymn Scroll 3:26; 5:8; Philo *Every Good Man Is Free* 159; Antipho; Xenophon; Demosthenes; contrast Hos. 2:14.
[91]ἐξέλκω with δελεάζω.

commentators difficulty. Though the *simple* Greek word for "draw,"[92] as Hort (p. 25) says, *is* used metaphorically—for example, of a love charm[93] or seduction from the truth,[94] actually with the Greek "entice by bait"[95]—the compound[96] is not used metaphorically like this in Classical Greek. Its association with "entice by bait" suggests the drawing of a hooked fish out of the water by a line;[97] but as Hort says (p. 25), that does not fit Jas. 1:14. It could be conjectured that the Epistle of James is here inventing a special use of the compound to mean "draw astray."[98] We are sure that the true reading, not in any manuscript, is "attracted,"[99] a proper Classical Greek verb, with that meaning—as in the proverb, "And do not be attracted ([almost] tempted)[100] by this—that they are offering you a strong naval alliance."[101] "Attraction" (or better, *distraction*) forms a better pair with *enticement* than "being led astray," recalling in some ways perhaps the enticement of the harlot (Prov. 7:16ff.). In any case we think the emendation is less bold than it is to ascribe to the expert classic who wrote the Greek of the Epistle of James a dubious and quite unnecessary neologism, unparalleled in this metaphorical sense in *any* extant Greek.

The theological implications of this verse are another matter. So far, we think, there is enough basis for it in the OT and Judaism, and there is no need to resort to Qumran. We think James's view of the flesh as inherently but not entirely evil agrees with that of Paul: "it is better to marry than to burn" (1 Cor. 7:9); "tempts" here introduces a sentence about lust which the mind in the case to be contemplated happens to have a duty to disobey. Only the apparent attempts by some theologians to dissociate lust and the body from Satan made some of our remarks necessary.

15 James obviously had the scene before his mind's eye as he wrote of the birth of sin and death in v. 15, just as in vv. 16–17 he had sunsets and sun's shadows in his mind's eye. Inevitably we are reminded of Thomas à Kempis' analysis of temptation,[101a] which is almost certainly inspired by these verses.

---

[92]ἕλκω.
[93]Pindar *Nem.* iv.6.
[94]Ael. *Hist. An.* 6.31.
[95]δελεάζω—so Plutarch *Moralia* 1093D.
[96]ἐξέλκω.
[97]Herodotus ii.70, of the crocodile.
[98]A meaning not unusual in παρα- compounds; Hort (*ibid.*) cites ἐξάγω, ἐκκλίνω, and a few others.
[99]ἐφελκόμενος.
[100]μηδὲ τούτῳ ἐφέλκεσθε.
[101]Quoted in Homer *Od.* xvi.294 (middle) and Thucydides i.42.
[101a]"At first it is a mere thought confronting the mind; then imagination paints it in stronger colours; only after that do we take pleasure in it, and the will makes a false move, and we give our assent" (*The Imitation of Christ*, tr. Ronald A. Knox and Michael Oakley [1959], p. 32).

Here the theology and the psychology may well be illustrated in a little dramatic fiction.

Consider these three stages. "Then his lust . . ."—the meaning is temporal (then) not logical (therefore), there being no hint, however, when this submission takes place, only that this is the next step in sin's deadly fruition. *If* he yields to it. . . .

(1) STAGE ONE: *I see something in a shop. I say to myself: "I should love to have that—but I can't afford it."*

That is the first stage: I am feeling the (still inchoate) pull and lure of the bait, but no more harm has been done or suffered as yet.

(2) STAGE TWO: *"I know! I will steal it!" That is, lust, impregnated by the devil, "conceives" the notion and "gives birth" to the act of theft.*

Too much should not be read into the twin image of conception and birth. The grammar behind "having conceived gives birth" recalls the Hebrew construction rendered "she conceived and bore" (Gen. 4:1, etc.), the participle and finite verb in this instance bringing "thought and act together as a single stage between the temptations on the one hand and death on the other" (Hort). "Lust" produces "sin," and James expresses this single idea by the metaphorical parallel of motherhood, signified (quite properly) by the two chief steps—the first and the last—of that single process: we do not find (against Hort) two separate points in "conceives and bears."

(3) STAGE THREE: *That sin, unless (however late, like the penitent thief) I properly repent before my physical death, will, "being fully grown," cause my damnation and my spiritual "death" at the Day of Judgment.*

This agrees with Ropes and without inconsistency supplements him. The "consummation" and the *death* are in the "next world," not in our earthly existence.[102]

Hort points out that the verb "to be fully grown"[103] connotes "completeness of parts and functions . . . accompanying full growth as opposed to a rudimentary or otherwise incomplete state"; as an example he contrasts the winged insect with chrysalis and grub.[104] To preserve the analogy of chrysalis and grub and winged insect we could say "fully developed and grown." But James is obviously picturing the growth of sin from birth onward in the analogy of a human infant growing to full manhood, in the human context of conception, birth, and growth to maturity. "Sin, when full grown, when it becomes a fixed habit . . . brings forth death." The immediate cause of death is sin, and sin, when full-grown, is in its very

---

[102]See A. C. Zenos, *The Plastic Age of the Gospel* (1927), p. 135.
[103]ἀποτελέω.
[104]Hort cites Plato *Timaeus* 73d, and others.

nature self-destructive, containing seeds of death in its womb and nurturing its unborn child until the time of delivery.[105]

16–17 All human good comes from the perfect Father of the universe. The analysis and interpretation of James's high-toned expression of this truth has, perhaps inevitably, raised some doubts and disputes among the commentators.

Of the three notable ways of taking the opening words of v. 17 we prefer that of KJV and RV and (among others) Ropes: *Every good gift . . . is from above, coming down*: i.e. taking *from above* as the predicate, with *coming down* as an explanatory expansion.

To couple *is* with *coming down* as expressing "comes down" (Syriac version) is here less likely in style; and so is T. Erskine's "Every giving is good and every gift is perfect from above" or "from its first source" (see Hort), which, besides giving *from above* a meaning it cannot here bear, is a statement that all God's gifts are good, *not* that all good gifts come from God, which seems to us the sense required both in the verse here quoted and in the present context.

James, we are sure, had in mind here some older Greek verses.[106] Nothing in the language or substance of the Epistle of James suggests that James was less able and willing to use a pagan hexameter than Paul (Acts 17:28, from an extant hexameter: see commentators).

The meaning of the rest of v. 17 is clear enough; the difficulties are textual (see Excursus D, pp. 96f.). The word for *variation*,[107] used only here in the NT and once, or twice, in the LXX,[108] is used in Greek for the setting of the teeth in a saw, or for stones set alternately, for a sequence of beacons,[109] or seasons.[110] *Variation* (RV) is preferable to "variableness" (KJV) as denoting some regularity or system in change.[111] There is no need to assume a technical sense, e.g., parallax; the prime reference is to the light of the sun and its change from hour to hour and from day to night, and we consider this quite proper to the Greek of the Epistle of James as signifying the variation of an object in constant orbit. The genitive is a genitive of

---

[105]Though sometimes of abnormal birth (Hort), ἀποκυέω, which occurs in the NT only here and in v. 17 (but of God), has the same meaning as τίκτω, of a mother delivering her child: see MM, *s.v.*

[106]πᾶσα δόσις (τ') ἀγαθὴ καὶ πᾶν δώρημα τέλειον/ἐκ Διός ἐστιν ἄνωθεν ἐπ' ἀνθρώπους καταβαῖνον/ἡμερίους. . . .

[107]παραλλαγή.

[108]2 K. 9:20, and (Aquila) Job 4:13.

[109]Aeschylus *Agam.* 490.

[110]Epictetus *Diss.* i.14.4.

[111]See Hort's excellent note (p. 30), esp. on the Emperor Severus in the north of Scotland (Dion Cassius lxxvi.13).

definition, "a variation consisting in turning,"[112] like "the city of Athens" or "the gift of (i.e., which is) sleep."

No recondite meaning is ascribed to *shadow*[113] (here only in the NT; not in LXX or Philo); it can mean:

i. The shadow cast by an object, as in an eclipse (Plutarch ii. 891);
ii. The act of overshadowing;
iii. A reflected image.

God's benevolence is like a light which cannot be extinguished, eclipsed, or "shadowed out" in any way at all. The light of the sun may be blocked, for example, by some material object, so as to cast a shadow: indeed, for a time in an eclipse, the direct light of the sun (or moon) may be shut off from the observer. Nothing like that can block God's light, interrupt the flow of his goodness, or put us "in shadow," so that we are out of the reach of his "radiance." It is not necessary to confine "shadow" to eclipses or any other specific sort of shadow. God's light or radiance lets nothing stop it. Horatius Bonar expresses a similar thought in his fine hymn:

> *Light of the world! for ever, ever shining,*
>> *There is no change in Thee;*
> *True Light of Life, all joy and health enshrining,*
>> *Thou canst not fade nor flee.*

We now follow with Hort's conjecture of an emphatic "he,"[114] to be read not at the end of v. 17 but at the beginning of v. 18.[115]

18 *Of his own wish*[116] is rather emphatic as the beginning here in this context. We have accepted Hort's suggestion that in the Greek text "shadow"[117] was incorporated with a following *he*,[118] which is actually found in one minor manuscript. Hort, we believe, did not wish to add *he* to 1:18: we think he only assumed it as a false reading in 1:18 which by another error produced the reading in 1:17. Personally we think the emphatic *he* is right, and rhetorically better, as taking up "the Father of the Lights." Consider the resulting translation we have given: *He of his own wish.* . . . He (God) is the author of our Christian being and purpose, a being which is endowed with truth, and a purpose which is to be holy as firstfruits. In contrast to man's "desire," which begets spiritual death (1:13ff.), God's

---

[112]παραλλαγὴ τροπῆς.
[113]ἀποσκίασμα.
[114]αὐτός, on the supposition that the reading ἀποσκιάσματος at the end of v. 17 is a corruption of ἀποσκίασμα αὐτός (αὐτός being then the first word of v. 18).
[115]See Excursus D, pp. 96f., and exposition of next verse.
[116]βουληθείς.
[117]ἀποσκίασμα.
[118]αὐτός.

deliberate, purposive will is gracious, choosing to initiate and to beget new spiritual life.

The conjecture then of the emphatic *he* further emphasizes the omnipotence as well as the benevolence of the great Father; emphasis on that benevolence is already inherent in *of his own wish,* i.e., *deliberato consilio, sponte sua.*[119] This "emphatic" use of *he* is common in Greek and a commonplace in Greek grammars.[120]

In Jewish tradition God is sexless; divine birth-giving is neither "a remarkable blunder"[121] nor a polemic against "Gnostic feminine emanations."[122] The idea of begetting can be figuratively applied to God as easily as the concepts "Father" (Ps. 68:5; 103:13; Matt. 6:9), "Mother" (Isa. 66:13; cf. "breasts of Son and Father," Odes Sol. 8:16; 19:3), or even "birth-pangs" (Deut. 32:8).[123] The figure was also familiar to the rabbis: "I made thee (Israel) a new creation as a woman conceives and brings forth."[124]

The view of several scholars (e.g., Hort, Spitta, Arnold Meyer, Cadoux) that this refers to the creation of man deserves consideration. In 1:18 as in the previous verse the perfection of God's gifts and the constancy of his nature could embrace all men in his benevolence. If God is said to have begotten all mankind by the word of truth, the metaphor "begot" and the gift of knowing the truth would aptly give man priority over the brute creation, in his capacity and appetite for truth. On this hypothesis James would be saying, in effect: "Therefore, having this potential for truth bestowed on you in the creation of mankind, *use* it: be swift to hear, slow to speak, and open your hearts and minds, not to strife and other vile passions, but to the innate Word of God-given reason."

Against this view, however, there are serious objections. On this hypothesis, James would not be arguing, as in 3:13–4:10, that Christians should behave like Christians, but simply that they should not behave like

---

[119]See J. C. Wolff, *Curae Philologicae et Criticae* (1735), p. 20; *TDNT* I, *s.v.* βούλομαι (G. Schrenk), pp. 632ff.; also "gladly" in 2 Cor. 11:19, which, however, is sarcastic.

[120]See Moule, *Idiom Book,* p. 121, II, ii, and our note on 2:6, 7. Moule discusses this αὐτός. It is not truly "unemphatic": it has a sort of deictic force which is *not* "quite unemphatic," *pace* Moule on οὗτος in John 18:30, any more than *hic,* which Moule gives as equivalent. So in Luke 5:1 (see Moule) and 4:30, αὐτός has the force (emphasis) of antithesis: we mean the pointed contrast between Jesus and the others, 4:29, the "crowd" of 5:1: exactly the same emphasis often leads to use of a personal name, as in Luke 4:35—Jesus contrasted with the demoniac, 4:33, 34. αὐτός may also carry this force by epanalepsis, as we think in Jas. 1:18.

[121]W. L. Knox, "The Epistle of St. James," *JTS* 46 (1945), p. 14.

[122]C. M. Edsmann, "Schöpferwille und Geburt," *ZNW* 38 (1939), pp. 28ff.; Schammberger, p. 59; H. Greeven, supplement volume to Dibelius, comm. ([8]1956), p. 13, n. 99.

[123]See S. R. Driver, *Deuteronomy.* ICC ([3]1902, 1952), p. 363; L. E. Elliott-Binns, "James i.18: Creation or Redemption?" *NTS* 3 (1956–57), p. 150.

[124]*Tanḥuma* on Exod. 4:12.

beasts; and, other things being equal, we feel bound to hold that here, as usual, James is preaching not just humanity, but Christianity. Thus Ropes (p. 166): "The objection which seems decisive" against the view of Spitta and especially Hort "is that the figure of begetting was not used for creation."[125] In fact, human knowledge of good and evil, which is tantamount to the gift of truth, came through another channel (Gen. 3:22), "whereas it came early into use with reference to the Christians, who deemed themselves 'sons of God.' The idea of divine begetting and of the entrance into Christian life as a new birth has its roots in Greek not in Jewish thought." This dictum of Ropes (pp. 166ff.), who quotes Clement of Alexandria[126] in illustration, may give us pause when we recall John 1:13; 3:3ff.; nevertheless we have already observed that no NT writer is more Greek than James.

The idea of the new birth is actually found in Judaism and flourished in Palestine via Hellenism.[127] It is true that the rabbinic notion of the new creation does not include in the new spirit or heart of the proselyte the NT concept of moral renewal in our Christian rebirth. Elliott-Binns,[127a] among others, declares that "James knows nothing of any 'new' creation" in Christian theology: that was "later"; but it is known in Eph. 2:10 and the Fourth Gospel, which (3:3, 7, like James 1:17) has the word for "from above": this remarkable coincidence suggests that in both these sources we have evidence of yet another *verbum Christi*.

The "firstfruits" of body or field were sacred and were often offered to God: the Greek particle, *kind of* or "as it were,"[128] as often indicates a figurative use of the term. The figure is used of Israel in Jer. 2:3 but it is not so common in Jewish as in Greek thought. Liddell and Scott[129] say that "firstfruits" was used not merely of that which was first in order but of that which was first in honor.[130]

The biblical use of the noun *creation* (1 Tim. 4:4; Rev. 5:13; 8:9) follows from the Jewish use of the verb[131] and its derivatives in this sense, a sense in which "creation" is not found in secular Greek.

19   The moral logic of James's thought becomes even clearer in v.

---

[125]See Introduction, p. 27.

[126]καὶ παρὰ τοῖς βαρβάροις φιλοσόφοις τὸ κατηχῆσαί τε καὶ φωτίσαι ἀναγεννῆσαι λέγεται (*Strom.* v.2.653).

[127]See, e.g., E. Sjöberg, "Rebirth and New Creation in Palestine Judaism," *Studia Theologica* 4, fasc. 1–2 (1951–52), pp. 44ff.

[127a]"James i.18: Creation or Redemption?" *NTS* 3 (1956–57), pp. 148–161.

[128]τινα.

[129]*s.v.* ἀπαρχή.

[130]See Paul S. Minear, *Images of the Church in the NT* (1961), 53: *The New Creation*, pp. 111ff., esp. on the NT doctrine of *aparchē*.

[131]κτίζω.

19 with the introductory *wherefore,*[132] *my beloved brothers....* He has already spoken of the new birth, and he now proposes to show that this experience should evince itself in conduct.

Besides insistence on the "Word" James adds a warning against hasty speech. The Christian must obey the moral demands of the gospel and exhibit a receptive spirit. *Swift to hear* recalls "Be swift to hear and let thy life be sincere; and with patience give answer."[133] The hearing to which James refers is to the "Word" of v. 18 preached or catechized. *Slow to speak* may refer to the hasty tongue and the perils of overmuch speaking—a stock theme of the ancient moralist. "Be not hasty in thy tongue, and in thy deeds slack and remiss."[134] In the second part of the Epistle (chs. 3, 4) James mentions one particularly vicious sin of the tongue, viz., malicious slander (4:11), which the rabbis called "the third tongue" (*lishan telitay*), for it slays three persons—the speaker, the spoken to, and the spoken of[135]—and because of which the Shechinah departs.[136] *Slow* here and following means humility and patience; *every man* means teachers. He then gives a warning against "what men ordinarily know as anger, against whomsoever directed. Its opposite is good temper and self-restraint" (Ropes, p. 169). It was believed that the 'angry' man had not mastered his *yetser*.[137] To lose one's temper was to lose the Shechinah (Jas. 2:1).[138]

20 A. H. McNeile thinks that this verse is probably a quotation, that an iambic line lies behind *for a man's wrath*, etc., and that *the righteousness of God* was substituted for another word: "A man's anger does not promote virtue."[139] But this has neither the force nor the meaning to chime with James's thought and power. What we wrote (on vv. 7, 8) has (we hope) both.[140]

Wrath is wrong. As Ropes says (p. 170), this is a warning against the wrong but common Jewish doctrine that anger "is sometimes valuable as an

---

[132]The emendation ὅθεν for ὥστε is attractive, but we doubt if it is much, if at all, stronger than ὥστε; ἴστε is certainly wrong. ὥστε quite effectively carries on the thought of the righteousness of God (v. 13) and the Word of the truth (v. 18) to the thought of cleansing and the implanted Word (v. 21 and the rest of the chapter), and is quite plausibly consistent with the corruption ἴστε: the case for ὅθεν seems (to us at least) rather too speculative.

[133]Sir. 5:11; cf. also the Talmud's four kinds of disciples, b. *Ned.* 22b; M. *Aboth* v.18; *TDNT* I, *s.v.* ἀκούω (G. Kittel), pp. 216ff.

[134]Sir. 4:29; A. Cohen, *Everyman's Talmud* (1932), p. 100. Cf. Menninger, *op. cit.*, p. 143.

[135]b. *'Arakin* 15b; Cohen, p. 99.

[136]Deut. R., *Kî Tētsē* vi.5.

[137]b. *Baba Bathra* 16a; Hermas *Mand.* v.2a, 3–4.

[138]For an alleged reference to Simeon, see A. Meyer, pp. 282ff.; Gen. 49:5ff.; Test. Levi 6f.

[139]I.e., χρηστὸν (for δικαιοσύνην θεοῦ): A. H. McNeile, *NT Teaching in the Light of St. Paul's* (1923), p. 88, n. 1.

[140]ὀργὴ γὰρ ἀνδρὸς θεῶν δίκην οὐκ ἐκτελεῖ: see pp. 93f.

engine of righteousness.''[141] While man may imitate certain divine qualities, according to the Jews, certain ones, notably anger, are forbidden: ''Thrice was Moses angry, and thrice he failed to produce the mind of God.''[142] The verb's present tense obviously has the same inchoate meaning; hence the simple verb is emended in some minor manuscripts to the compound used in 1:3, which rather emphasized the result. Here it means something like ''does not forward the righteousness of God,'' i.e., in the usual sense of ''work,'' ''do,'' rather than in the other rarer sense of ''produce.''[143] The objection to wrath is not simply that it is bad tactics and futile. Even if a pedagog's wrath—contrast God's patience (1:5)—*may* produce righteousness in his pupil (Zahn), Christians are not told to eschew wrath because it has no good effect on the persons wronged. The reason is not necessarily the possible effect on the target of my wrath: you might be more grieved, and even damaged, by cold, calculated, and justified censures than by any heated chastisement from my tongue. In Christianity, sin is forbidden primarily because of its effect on the sinner.

It is tempting to see here a reference to ''the justice of God'' (NEB), the penal judgment of God upon sinners; this verse would then become an injunction to Christians when wronged not to revenge themselves. Thus R. A. Knox (p. 95) believes that James is thinking of ''resentment against our persecutors,'' after the tradition of Rom. 12:19: ''Vengeance executed by man is not the proper vehicle of the Divine punishments.'' God's vengeance on sinners is one of the oldest ideas for both the Greeks[144] and the Hebrews.[145] In Rom. 3:5, God in his righteousness is said ''to inflict his anger on us'' (Moffatt). Human self-help by revenge is forbidden in (e.g.) Rom. 12:19 (in the context of vv. 17–21). This notion is not in itself inapposite in the Epistle of James. The eschatological urgency of the NT springs from the conception of God as Judge (e.g., Acts 17:30, 31), and throughout James, from 1:2 to 5:20, this is the dominant idea of God; see particularly: ''and there stands the Judge, at the door'' (5:9, NEB).

In our opinion, the foregoing interpretation is too narrow: we prefer *righteousness,* both for that reason and as more in keeping with the Epistle's habitual rotary (rondo) structure. With his characteristic cohesion of

---

[141]For Hort (*ad loc.*) ἀνήρ instead of ἄνθρωπος for ''man'' meant ''the petty passion of the individual,'' eliminating the possible distinction between divine and human anger: against which, however, see, e.g., Sophocles *Ajax* 7—a point that led Hauck, *ad loc.,* to see here a Hebraism, ''menschlicher (not männlicher) Zorn.''

[142]b. *Pes.* 66b; I. Abrahams, *op. cit.,* II, p. 161.

[143]ἐργάζεται: the compound is κατεργάζεται (see above and 1:3, 4).

[144]E.g., Sophocles *Ajax* 1390.

[145]E.g., Ps. 58:10, 11, where there is just award for good men and evil: see Acts 28:4.

thought, James continues this theme of righteousness in 3:13–18 (not in 4:11, 12, which is only about censoriousness, not "anger," 1:19, 20): in 1:19, 20 he exhorts to meekness and peace, and in 1:21 to purity.

It is notoriously impossible to find one word (just(ice)/right(eous)ness) for the Hebrew *tsedeq* and the Greek *dikē* and their cognates. It is used here in the conventional Jewish, nontechnical, un-Pauline sense of "righteous action" (Easton, p. 31, against Hofmann and others); compare similar OT phrases (e.g., Gen. 18:19; Ps. 15:2), but contrast the parallel of Jas. 2:9. In Hebrew the word is much richer than the classical notion of "justice"; it is a *modus vivendi* or conduct required by Christian faith and obedience to God, as, for example, in accordance with 1:25–27. It depicts the Christian life under the scrutiny and standards of God. A man's animosity toward his fellows does not create that kind of life. God's righteousness here refers not to the righteousness that is part of his character (subjective genitive) but to the way of life, in deed and thought, that he requires in us. Such righteousness will become ours, if we genuinely accept what is called, in the next verse, "the implanted word."

21 The convert to Christ must cleanse himself not merely of defilement arising from words (Mayor), nor merely of malice manifested in speech (Hort), but of all sin contemplated in 1:12–15, which is well called "the abounding evil . . . which we find in our hearts" (Ropes). We cannot find any merit in Ropes's theory that the word for *prodigality*[146] "calls attention to the fact that wickedness is really an excrescence on character, not a normal part of it." Ropes rightly rejects "malice" (RV mg., Mayor, Hort, Moffatt) and *malitia* (Vulg.; Beza, instead of *pravitas*) and rightly points out that *meekness* is in contrast with "wrath"; but he fails to see that the exhortation to meekness in 1:21b harks back to 1:19, 20, while the conversion from sin enjoined in 1:21a catches up the earlier verses, 12ff. Translators have had difficulty with this phrase:[147] so Bauer, *s.v.*, "all the evil prevailing around you"; Beza, "excrement"; Spitta, "all the finery of sin"; R. A. Knox, following Hofmann, *residuum*; NEB "reckless dissipation"; and KJV "superfluity of naughtiness"—the last quaintly implying that perhaps a certain amount of malice was indeed proper for a Christian (Mayor). We cannot find a better word here than *prodigality*, though some may prefer "enormity of vice."

"When James, like Peter, hastens to urge the moral and spiritual qualities of Christians," Moffatt cogently remarks (p. 24), "he passes from

---

[146]περισσεία.
[147]περισσεία κακίας.

the idea of the regenerating Word to the conception of the Word as seed which has to be cared for, if it is to thrive; indeed he develops the metaphor more definitely than Peter. Give the divine seed a clean soil." But how are we to accept the seed of the Word, especially since, as James declares, it is already *implanted* (*emphytos*)? Hort maintains (p. 37) that here *emphytos* signifies "innate," not implanted; but even he cannot deny that this adjective denotes a postnatal acquisition in Herodotus ix.94. Though *emphytos* can mean "congenital," like the instinct for self-preservation, or wickedness (Wisd. 12:10), Hort admits it can also mean something added later to our nature, i.e., for Euenios a divine gift of prophecy long after birth (Herodotus ix.94). Hort, however, prefers to call it "a secondary ingrowth" or "second nature" rather than *implanted*. But since in Herodotus, and here in James, the postnatal ingrowth was started by "a Divine gift" (Hort's phrase), we may very well say "sown" or "planted" (but not "engrafted," KJV), in the regularly used metaphorical sense. We think it has the same meaning here, and that *implanted,* though not a perfect translation, does very well. (See Excursus E, pp. 98ff.) Like Wisdom, Torah was said to be implanted in God "from the very beginning," and then rooted in every Jew from the earliest years.[148] There may be a reference to the Parable of the Sower (Beza; Alford; against Ropes, hesitantly, p. 173). By nature the seed must be implanted, and since the gospel has been preached, this has already been done. But the soil of the heart must be hospitable, if the seed of the Word is to grow. And so we must give up impure living, and fully accept the "Word of truth," showing (by acceptance and obedience) *meekness,* that self-subduing gentleness which is among the fruits of the Spirit (v. 19).

The end of the logic is the reward: *Accept the implanted Word*: for that *is able to save your souls*. The Jewish Torah was held to be redemptive, the medicine of life and a "spice" against the *yetser*.[149] "Torah is the only way that leadeth to life."[150] Like the Torah, the *implanted Word* was redemptive, uniquely so since this was the "Torah of the Messiah." James may not mention Christ by name, but Christ's Saviorhood, if not explicitly elaborated here or elsewhere, is everywhere implied. The reference to salvation is to be interpreted in the light of the rapidly approaching Day of Judgment (see Acts 17:30). It is charged with the eschatological urgency of the NT, including (conspicuously) the Epistle of James. No soul can be called saved, or lost, until the Final Judgment; hence James's gospel of faith continuing at work in hope of that final approbation, 1:3. It is faith expressed

[148]Num. R. xiv.4; Oesterley, p. 433.
[149]b. *Qid*. 30b; b. *Baba Bathra* 16a.
[150]Wayyiqra Rabba 29; see Oesterley, p. 432.

81

in action (*magna efficacia,* Bengel) that puts the power of the divine Word into human life, to the saving of the soul at the Last Judgment.[151]

b. For doers of that gospel, not hearers only, with a special watch on the tongue (1:22–27)

22 *But be doers of the Word and not merely hearers of it, deluding yourselves.*

23 *For*[152] *if anyone is a hearer of the Word and not a doer of it, he is like a man observing the face of his mortal, physical birth (created being) in a mirror.*

24 *For he observes himself, and is gone, and immediately forgets what he was like.*

25 *But he who has bent over to look into the perfect law of liberty, and has stayed by it, since he has not been a hearer who forgets but a doer who acts, he shall be blessed in his doing.*

26 *If anyone among you thinks he is a model of piety, and is one who does not bridle his tongue but deludes his own heart, this man's piety is vain.*

27 *The way to win an account with God the Father for piety pure and undefiled is this, to visit the fatherless and widows in their affliction, and to keep oneself unspotted from the world.*

22 As we have already noted in some other verbs, *be* has a continuative sense: "Keep on striving to be doers of the Word." The Hebraic *doers* (Vulg. *factores*), comparable to "doer of the law,"[153] is almost adjectival, like "law-abiding," "law-breakers" (Hort). *The Word* is the gospel as taught by Jesus, then practiced and proclaimed by his followers (Matt. 7:21, 24ff.). In Hebrew "hear" often implies hearing the Bible read; but probably it is now to be understood to embrace any oral religious instruction, in the synagogue, as was usual, or elsewhere.[154] To attend such instruction as *merely hearers*[155] was not enough, as any teacher knows: the lesson must enter into the hearer's heart and mind. The implanted Word can only flourish in the soil of true obedience: to think otherwise is to delude oneself (see Moffatt, p. 26).

23 In 1:23ff. there are two contrasts: (i) between a hasty, forgetful glance and an attentive, sustained study; (ii) between the picture, glimpsed in a mirror of a mortal, physical face, and the picture, contained in the divine law, of the ideal pattern of each immortal soul for the time being inhabiting the mortal flesh, and, while still in that flesh, striving to approach that

---

[151]For power in operation, see Ps. 29; Rom. 1:16 ἐνέργεια with δύνασθε (Phil. 3:21); and ἐνεργουμένη with ἰσχύει (Jas. 5:16).

[152]ὅτι in James (and NT) is often almost like γάρ.

[153]See Rom. 2:13; Acts 17:28; Sir. 19:20; 1 Macc. 2:67; Jas. 1:23, 25; 4:11.

[154]Cf. *TDNT* I, *s.v.* ἀκούω (G. Kittel), p. 218.

[155]So B ff.

immortal ideal. We have a man who "notices" or "observes" his face in a mirror; but the degree of attention given to it is clear from the sequel, including the instantaneous perfect: at once he is gone, and immediately he forgets what his face was like.

To make both points clear, both the haste contrasted with the studiousness and the *physical* as contrasted with the *spiritual,* we add "mortal" (birth), taking no great liberty with the Greek language or Hebrew religion; so Ropes shows (p. 176): ". . . the created world (including man) as distinguished from God, and with a suggestion of its character as seen and temporal." That is valid, though we do not equate *genesis* with *rerum natura* here, but with the man's individual birth, *genitura; genesis* does have that meaning in Greek (e.g., Matt. 1:18; Luke 1:14), but it sometimes means coming into being, birth, creation. So we translate *created being.*

Here, as is clear from the next verse, in the Greek "perceive"[156] is used in the lowest value of the word "perceive," and what the man perceives is not anything like "his face as a constituent of the cosmos and cosmic law" but, quite simply, "the face he was born with" (so R. A. Knox). Thus in Jas. 3:6 NEB translates the Greek *genesis* by "existence." As the word may mean the creation of the universe so it can regularly mean the birth of an individual man. We feel that a thing so personal as our face is more naturally and immediately associated with the notion of our personal incarnation, *ab initio,* than with the notion of the *kosmos,* undeniable though this latter association is. We cannot believe that James, of all men, would import an abstruse cosmic element into the homely clue intended to help us understand a vital truth. So we translate: "the face of his (mortal, physical) birth."

24   The two aorists, *observes, forgets,*[157] are gnomic—of something that naturally, normally, or repeatedly happens (Ropes). The gnomic aorist occurs only in the indicative: hence "noticing" (*not* "looking at," against Ropes, p. 175) in 1:23, present participle with the same force as the gnomic aorist in 1:25. The perfect, *and is gone,* denoting the immediacy of the sequel, is equally dramatic: "He is off!"[158] He "catches sight" of

---

[156]κατανοέω.

[157]κατενόησεν, ἐπελάθετο.

[158]The force of the perfect ἀπελήλυθεν does not necessarily express a lasting state but an *immediate sequel,* e.g., a swift result, as in Plato *Protag.* 328B, cited by Ropes: "As soon as one has completed my course of instruction, then, if he wishes, he (forthwith) *pays* the fee I charge (ἀποδέδωκεν, perfect); if not, he goes to a temple, swears an oath, and *pays* (lit. puts down: κατέθηκεν, gnomic aorist) just so much as my instruction is worth." An even clearer parallel than this passage is Demosthenes *Against Timocrates* 139: "Among the Locrians the proposer of a new law must propose it with his neck in a noose. If the law is approved, well and good; if not, they pull up the noose, and it's all up with him (τέθνηκεν ἐπισπασθέντος τοῦ βρόχου)."

himself, and (at once) *is gone,* and forthwith *forgets what he was like* (in the mirror). Modern man, constantly using shaving mirrors, may be surprised at this statement; but even a good artist may hesitate to do a self-portrait from memory. And James is speaking of a man of the normal sort that do not care much about remembering their face: he does not say *all* men are equally forgetful in this matter.

25 The discrepancy found by R. A. Knox (p. 96) in 1:25 disappears if we remember that the *look* in the first case is literal, in the second not merely a literal "look" but a mental and spiritual study. There is no ground for demanding that both men should be presented as looking in the same literal sense at the same thing, say a polished "silver bowl" (Knox). The words *bent over*[159] imply a deliberate intention to look (against Hort), sometimes frivolously or cursorily, but here, in this context, with serious attention.[160] Mayor quotes with approval Westcott's view that "the idea conveyed is that of looking intently with eager desire and effort at that which is partially concealed";[161] *look* implies no such deliberation (see Eph. 3:10). James is thinking of the Word/Law presenting in words (through sermons or catechesis) a picture of the righteousness prescribed by God for us to live by and fulfil with his grace. The one, hearing the Word/Law, listens only perfunctorily, with no more effect than a fleeting glance at his face in a mirror; the other, hearing the Word/Law, gives it sustained attention, not only then but throughout life—just as if he were poring over God's design for living and trying to fulfil it in thought, word, and deed. The contrast between a casual look into a mirror and a study, in another sense of *look,* given to the law and an effort to live by that law, is quite effective for James's purpose here. On the blessedness of doing God's will, see John 13:14.

For the *law of liberty,* see the Introduction, pp. 33ff.

26-27 The two closing verses of this chapter clinch the immediately preceding section, v. 26 dealing with vv. 19–21 on the tongue and v. 27 with vv. 22–25 on doers of the Word. Ropes (p. 181) is correct when he says that the advance is from "the more general precept of reality, 'not hearing but doing', to the more specific, 'not mere worship but doing good'." For the latter phrase we prefer and substitute: "not a vain and corrupt illusion of worship." "Vain" and "illusion" come from James; "corrupt" is the opposite of his ideal.

The Greek words in v. 26 correspond closely in sense to our words

[159]παρακύψας.
[160]John 20:5, 11–14; 1 Pet. 1:12; Sir. 14:20–23; Epictetus i.1.16.
[161]"Hort's Posthumous Commentary on St. James," *Expositor,* ser. 7, 9 (1910), pp. 562f.; also comm., p. 69.

"pious"[162] and "piety"[163] denoting the scrupulous observance of religious exercises—in action or words—sincerely or hypocritically performed in the guise of devout religion; see our Lord's criticisms in Matt. 6:2-6, "Be careful not to make a show of your religion before men" (v. 1, NEB).

In Greek the adjective *thrēskos* is exceedingly rare and describes "one who stands in awe of the gods, and is tremulously scrupulous in what regards them" (Hort); the noun *thrēskeia* occurs once in Herodotus, never in Attic, and in the LXX only in the Apocrypha. Ropes correctly says (p. 181) that both "have the same considerable range of meaning as the English word 'worship' with reference to the inner and the external aspects of religious worship." So in John 4:22, Jesus says to the woman at the well: "You Samaritans worship without knowing what you worship, while we worship what we know" (NEB): here the first "worship" (on Gerizim) and to a less extent the second (at Jerusalem) are defective, in comparison with "worship" in the next two verses ("in spirit and truth"). Since the self-proclaimed "worshipper" thinks his "worship" is the full and true religion, KJV can withstand criticism.

We observe the continuing close-knit unity of thought of these two verses with this whole chapter and Epistle—here we have "doublemindedness" as in 1:6 and later in 4:8, called "instability" or "anarchy" in 1:8 and 3:16; purity, as always in Christian homiletics, as later in 4:8; and lust, wrath, strife, and all other aspects of *the world*. It is all linked up with 1:13ff., and indeed, with 1:4. "Pure and undefiled . . . unspotted from the world" is just a variant of putting off all filthiness.

Verse 27 is not, and is not intended to be, a comprehensive definition of Christianity: it is an assertion of one element positively but not exclusively indispensable in that religion. Devout godliness does not consist merely of regular and punctilious praise of God and scrupulous obedience to his rules relating to specifically religious observance: the spirit of the religion and service of God must live also in our lives, as, for example, Lev. 19:18 testifies. Nothing could be more alien to the spirit of the good servant of God (or of man, as immortalized in P. G. Wodehouse's character Jeeves) than "working to rule." Nor is this intended to be a denial of the value of true worship: he is simply insisting, with the prophets, that "our participation in it is only acceptable to God when it is accompanied by love to our neighbour" (Cranfield, p. 8). Like Jesus, James sees worship not in terms of external law but as an expression of inner active goodness. On the notion that piety is the

---

[162]θρησκός.
[163]θρησκεία.

true form of purity, see, for example, Isa. 1:16, 17: "Wash yourselves and be clean. Put away the evil of your deeds, away out of my sight" (NEB). The rabbis held that "upon three things the world is based: upon the Torah, upon the Temple Service, and upon the doing of loving deeds,"[164] the last two of which are said to control the evil *yetser*.[165] Jesus declared: "Let what is in the cup be given in charity, and all is clean" (Luke 11:41 NEB; also Matt. 23:14, 26).[166]

First, *to win an account with God*[167] genuine religion must always be practical. Observance of outward ritual is no substitute for interior righteousness, nor attendance at church services for performance of Christian service, even though attending what we call "divine service" should mean that we *do* something for God. Kierkegaard poked fun at the "religiousness" that calls itself Christianity which is "just as genuine as tea made with a bit of paper which once had been used to wrap a few dried tea-leaves from which tea had already been made three times." The Fatherhood of God implies the brotherhood of man, specifically in this case the fatherless and widows, both of whom figure prominently in the social concern of the early Church (Acts 6:1ff.; 9:39; 1 Tim. 5:3ff.). Later William Booth said: "We will wash it (our money) in the tears of the widows and orphans and lay it on the altar of humanity."[167a] The rabbis also taught that those who looked after orphans will enter "into the gates of the Lord,"[168] and for ample OT precedent see, for example, Exod. 22:22; Deut. 14:28, 29; 16:11; 26:12; 27:19; Ps. 68:5; 146:9. The "affliction" to which James refers may be sickness or old age, in the case of widows; the orphan and widow through bereavement were usually poor and needed money and other practical help.

Here, as elsewhere, Paul is James's best interpreter. In James, as in Paul, Christianity is word (*logos*) plus deed (*poiēsis*). "Worship" or "service" (*thrēskeia*) is what I *do* to please God: and if I do not do it outside the church and similar observances, I am not doing it *at all*. In Rom. 12:1 Paul uses another word for it (*latreia*), and there, as in James, it means *deed*

---

[164] *Aboth de-Rabbi Nathan* version I, iv.11a.

[165] b. *'Ab. Zar.* 5b.

[166] See W. L. Knox, *art. cit.*, p. 11; *idem, Some Hellenistic Elements in Primitive Christianity* (1944), p. 76; Montefiore and Loewe, *Rabbinic Anthology*, pp. 286ff.

[167] So rendered to suggest the picture suggested in this use of παρά ("with"), as when one thinks of an account with (or at) a bank. The conventional "in the judgment of God," or "in the sight of God," also has merit. But we think an artist in words like James would welcome a translation retorting to these mercenary hypocrites with a mercenary word (*win an account*) transfigured by its sincerely religious use: the hypocrites only want to have an account of worldly credit.

[167a] Richard Collier, *The General Next to God* (1965), p. 217.

[168] See Midr. Pss. on Ps. 118:19; Exod. R. xxx.8; I. Abrahams, *op. cit.*, I (1917), p. 81, "Widows' Houses."

(*poiēsis*) of the *word* (*logos*), that is, of the *logos* which, as James says, is implanted in the Christian by God: hence Paul very accurately and deliberately calls that deed (*poiēsis*) "your reasonable service" (KJV) or "the worship offered by mind and heart" (NEB), not just a "churchy" *thysia* ("sacrifice") but a living *thysia*, a *thysia* made by a way of thinking and living. Exactly similar is James's doctrine of *poiēsis* of the *logos*; and its foundation (1:17) is the same as Paul's foundation in the last verse of Rom. 11. It is not a definition of religion, but a characterization of Christian conduct as the *poiēsis* of the Christian *logos*. Worship must be related to life, in the sense of being contemporary and relevant but also essentially practical. By its very nature, however, Christian worship is redeemed from that barren moralism of which George Tyrrell spoke, "the kind of doing good which is chiefly going about." Worship and *latreia* and *thrēskeia* can be properly done in the narrower scope of the narrower sense of these words; but unless it is a real part of the full scope (as in Heb. 9:1, 6) of these words in their all-embracing sense, it is nothing.

Second, *to win an account with God,* genuine religion must always be pure: *unspotted from the world.* Christian "faith" means trusting God, trusting oneself to God. We cannot choose him with part of our minds, for part of our life, and give part to the world, the flesh, and the devil (1:8). "Firstfruits" are holy (1:18); therefore the Christian must not live like the unconverted or the renegade converts of 1 Cor. 6:8–10, a passage which, like Jas. 1:16, has the same warning: "Make no mistake about this fact." It is abundantly plain that the first Christians did not all live up to their faith. That is why Paul and James and others are *constantly* preaching the duty of conduct in keeping with faith. But Christian conduct, says Paul, must be pure, unmixed, unalloyed, unadulterated[169] (1 Cor. 5:8), rather like James's words here, *pure, undefiled,* and *unspotted.* Such purity is ethical, never ascetic nor ritual. *Unspotted,* for example, is a good illustration of "the way in which the NT gives new religious and moral content to originally cultic concepts."[170]

The best comment on the concept of *the world* is found in Jas. 4:4; so, in our opinion, even though James has not used the word until 1:27, it is not really "sudden." The Qumran Scrolls, though not parallel, show that the Qumran covenanters took a sinister view of the world as a domain of evil in the present age, as do James, John, and Paul. In 1:27 James finds it convenient to use the word *kosmos* to epitomize the evils he has been

---

[169]εἰλικρινής.
[170]*TDNT* I, *s.v.* ἄσπιλος (A. Oepke), p. 502.

describing in other words (vv. 14, 15, 20, 21, 26). "Flesh" also occurs in the NT in this sinister sense: see Jas. 4:4.

EXCURSUS A
JAMES 1:2: "ALL JOY"

The phrase "all joy" (πᾶσαν χαρὰν) is discussed in a long note by J. H. Ropes, p. 129. The point at issue is the precise grammatical significance and sense of "all" (πᾶσαν). It is our purpose here to investigate its meaning.

"That *peirasmos* was all joy": here "all" agrees grammatically with *peirasmos*. "That *peirasmos* was pure joy": the effect is scarcely different, but now we have the adjective agreeing with the noun (χαρὰν) in the predicate. In such sentences Greek practice retains the word *all*, πᾶς, but makes it agree with the noun in the predicate (e.g., "joy"). Nothing could be simpler. Ropes (p. 130, about line 28) quotes Plato *Philebus* 27E, to the effect that pleasure is not *all* a good thing, nor pain *all* a bad thing, i.e., pleasure has some evil in it, and pain some good. The Greek makes *all* agree with the predicate ἀγαθόν, not with the subject ἡδονή, and with κακόν, not with λύπη.[1] Ropes (p. 129, last line in large print) quotes Euripides *Medea* 453: "Being punished with exile (only, and not death), count it (that fact) all gain" (pure gain, nothing but gain). Similarly James, using the same order, and the same verb (but he has it in the aorist, and plural), ἡγήσασθε,[2] says: "When you encounter trials, count it (the fact that you are encountering one) all joy" (pure joy, nothing but joy—i.e., an occasion for such). Since English often best translates this

---

[1] For κακόν used as a noun, "a bad thing," cf. Susarion's old comic jibe, κακὸν γυναῖκες, "Women are an evil." In Aristophanes *Acharn.* 908f., Dikaiopolis says: "Here comes Nikarchos to start an information." The Boeotian replies (in dialect), μικκός γα μᾶκος οὗτος (i.e., μικρός γε μῆκος οὗτος), "He's little in size, this fellow." Dikaiopolis ends the line: ἀλλ' ἅπαν κακόν, "But he is *all* an evil" (every inch a pest). Logic might expect ἅπας κακόν, "He, all of him is a pest": but the attraction to the neuter κακόν is irresistible. Speech is not the child of logic, but of ill logic.

[2] Our translation seeks to bring out the proper *nuance* of the tense of the verb, and the previous quotation shows that there is nothing odd, or even nonclassical prose, about ἡγήσασθε. To illustrate: μανθάνω may mean, "I understand": but it may also mean, I am learning, am studying, am toying with the subject. So ἐσθίω *may* mean, I am busy eating; γράφω *may* mean, I am busy writing. If we want to give someone an order (or request) connected with any of these verbs, and we want to make it perfectly plain that we do not wish him just to get on with learning, or eating, or writing, but to learn, eat, or write something completely, we shall use the Greek *aorist* imperative—μάθε, φάγε, γράψον. So, if we want him to form a decided opinion (not διακρινόμενοι [1:6]—note the present), to "conclude," as common in bygone American, we use the aorist imperative, ἡγήσασθε (as the classical orators—or νομίσατε of which they were actually much fonder). This is why James used—and why we translate— ἡγήσασθε: "Conclude (or deem) it nothing but joy."

predicative use of πᾶς by the adverb "wholly," e.g., "Pleasure is not wholly good" (or "entirely," or the like), many Greek grammars and editors call this the "adverbial" πᾶς. Other adjectives, too, are so used, and so described, e.g., "He watches quietly," where Greek says ἥσυχος, "He watches quiet."[3]

It is unnecessary to examine all the points raised by Ropes's note (pp. 129f.). Some we would like to question, e.g.: We do not know what "an intensifying adjective" is, and whereas he says, "not to denote strict completeness of extension," his translations in *1* "every," *2* "whole," "entire," *3* "full," "complete," "utter," *4* "unmixed," "wholly," all denote completeness of extension in one mode or another. The paradox with which James begins is that the experience of *peirasmos* is completely, wholly, a ground for rejoicing and nothing but rejoicing. When Ropes, in *4*, p. 130, writes, "through its position in the sentence," he shows defective grammatical insight: "through its function" would be right enough. He misses the significance of the predicative function which gives his *4* its distinctive character.[4] And we note that "utter" is ambiguous. "This is utter folly" *may* mean, "This is unsurpassable folly: it embodies all the foolishness that ever any man could fall into: there is no foolishness that is not to be seen in it." But it *may* (and, we think, usually does) mean rather less: "This is sheer folly: it may not be as foolish as some fools can be, but yet it is entirely foolish: there is no mixture or tinge of wisdom in it: it is nothing but folly." Ropes actually says (p. 129, middle, large print) that our πᾶσαν means either "full" (i.e., our first meaning of "utter" above) "or (less natural) 'nothing but', 'unmixed' (*merus,* German *lauter*)"—which is our second interpretation of *utter,* five to eight lines above. In truth, the meaning he calls less natural is the only one possible for our present πᾶσαν χαράν. James does not say there is no greater joy than that of *peirasmos*: he does say that *peirasmos* is an occasion for unmixed joy, i.e., joy and nothing detracting from that joy.

---

[3]Sophocles *Philoctetes* 385f.: πόλις γάρ ἐστι πᾶσα τῶν ἡγουμένων στρατός τε σύμπος. Jebb tr., "For an army, like a city, hangs wholly on its leaders" (lit. "is all of its leaders," i.e., belongs, all of it, to their sphere of influence). Now we quote Jebb on *Philoctetes* 622: ἢ κεῖνος, ἡ πᾶσα βλάβη . . . , "Hath he, that utter pest, sworn to bring me by persuasion to the Achaeans?": ". . . when a man is called a βλάβη, instead of saying ὁ πᾶς βλάβη ὤν, 'he is altogether a bane', we can say ἡ πᾶσα βλάβη, 'the bane which is altogether such'. The tendency is the same that appears, e.g., in λέγει . . . εἶναι ταύτην (instead of τοῦτο) ὀρθότητα ὀνόματος [Plato *Cratylus* 443E; Sophocles *Oedipus Coloneus* 88 note]." Cf. *Philoctetes* 927: ὦ πῦρ σὺ καὶ πᾶν δεῖμα. πᾶν δεῖμα: utter monster. As ἡ πᾶσα βλάβη (622), said of a man, is equivalent to ὁ πᾶς βλάβη (ὤν), so here πᾶν δεῖμα is equivalent to πᾶς δεῖμα ὤν (being, all of you, a monster).

[4]At the foot of p. 130 he speaks to no purpose about "heightening the effect of the noun." The meaning of good is the same in "The good man learns Greek" and in "Too few men are good": the distinction "which our analysis reveals" (p. 131, *ad init.*) is that between attributive and predicative (the latter is here the so-called "adverbial" use): that is what grammatically divides his *4* from all his other 3 groups. And he puts παντὶ σθένει, "with all (say, my) strength," in *3*: it should go with 2—"my whole strength," "the whole time," "a whole city." Only his *4* is relevant to James's πᾶσαν χαρὰν, but in *2* and *3* it is necessary to remember not to confuse *a*, "with all my strength" (i.e., with all the strength we do in fact possess) and *b*, "with all zeal" (i.e., with all the zeal that can possibly be manifested in any performance, i.e., nothing short of the ideal).

EXCURSUS B
JAMES 1:3: A SUGGESTED EMENDATION

We propose to follow a suggestion by G. Zunz (in a personal note) and emend one Greek word in this text, reading the dative ὑπομονῇ for the usual accusative ὑπομονήν, translating thus: "You must realize that your approbation is accomplished by constancy in endurance."

It is hardly necessary to point out that this translation differs significantly from the conventional KJV: "Knowing this, that the trying of your faith worketh patience." To justify our emendation we need to show that it makes better sense of this verse and indeed of the entire context, and this is what we will now try to do.

The key to this verse is the word δοκίμιον (or δοκίμειον, as Peter Katz insisted we should spell it), which we translate "approbation" and the KJV "trying." In effect, as Ropes says (p. 134), δοκίμειον means, first, something that tests a person or thing; then, the application or (as here) the undergoing of a test. In 1 Pet. 1:7, however, according to traditional exegesis, δοκίμειον is said to have a different meaning from Jas. 1:3. It is the neuter of δόκιμος, an adjective used as a noun (as an adjective often is in Greek, e.g., τὸ ἡδύ, or τὸ ἀγαθόν), and means not merely "tested"—for what is "tested" may be rejected upon "test"—but *tested and approved*. The difference is important: to illustrate simply, when a gastronomist speaks of "tested recipes," he means they have been tested and proved good. We are forced, therefore, as things stand, to accept the view that the same word, δοκίμειον, means two different things: (i) in James "testing to find out if you pass or fail"; (ii) in Peter "approval," "approbation," i.e., passing the test. It has always seemed odd to us that the same word should mean two different things in two writers whose thought and language otherwise coincide so remarkably at so many significant points. Yet, unless so translated in the text as it stands, δοκίμειον would make no sense, and the argument would be wrecked. This is really an exegetical dilemma, and one that has led us to reexamine the current text of James. We have found that the dilemma can be eased by a simple textual correction, viz., the omission of the last letter of ὑπομονήν (*endurance*), reading, instead of the accusative, the dative ὑπομονῇ or perhaps the nominative ὑπομονή. The former, in our opinion, is clearly right. It is true that the nominative (with κατεργάζεται of course as middle deponent) gives the same sense, and the order does occur a few times in the Epistle; but our feeling is very strongly for the dative, with κατεργάζεται of course as passive: "is accomplished by endurance." This would straighten out what is a very crooked argument in the current text. With ὑπομονῇ, too, we get the same meaning for δοκίμειον in both James and Peter (as well as Paul, cf. Rom. 5:4 [not 3]), each referring to the successful outcome of the test, or *approbation,* not mere probation (for probation may end in rejection). In 1 Pet. 1:7, τὸ δοκίμειον means that which has been tested and approved ("faith which has stood the test," NEB) and in James now, too, we believe the word connotes not merely testing but approval. Ropes says (p. 135): "In other usage also the word makes a natural advance from 'test' to that of 'purification' (as with metals) or of 'training' (as Herodian ii.10.6: δοκίμειον δὲ στρατιωτῶν

90

κάματος ἀλλ' οὐ τρυφή)." Cf. Plutarch *Mor.*, p. 230, already cited. We may put it thus: δοκίμειον sometimes means merely "testing," sometimes "approval," sometimes "the means or method of bringing a person or thing up to standard," i.e., to a state worthy of approval (as σωτηρία and *salus* sometimes mean "salvation," sometimes "means or methods of salvation"). In Jas. 1:3 δοκίμειον simply means (we believe) "approval." Herodian means: "Toil, not luxurious living, is the means or method of bringing soldiers up to standard." The meaning of δοκίμειον also passes to "the thing subjected to test," as cited in LS, *s.v.*, or "the thing approved after being tested," as in 1 Pet. 1:7 NEB quoted above. But, obviously, approval does not work endurance: endurance works approval. The text of Jas. 1:3 must be emended as we suggest, with ὑπομονῇ for ὑπομονήν: "approval is accomplished through endurance." One further point—and we find this very persuasive: our emendation restores the strength of the unity of structure in 1:2–21, by giving 1:3 the same sense, in outline, as 1:12. Thus: 1:3, "the approbation of your faith (i.e., its being approved as 'satisfactory' by the Divine Examiner) is accomplished (or 'achieved') by 'endurance' "; 1:12, ". . . being approved (passed as 'satisfactory'), he shall receive. . . ." And 1:21 sounds the same note of result and reward, "save your souls." So "endure" (ὑπομένει) /"trial" (πειρασμόν) /"approved" (δόκιμος) in 1:12 now correctly echo the three key words in 1:2 and 1:3, and now we see how "blessed" (μακάριος) of 1:12 echoes "pure joy" of 1:2, for now we see that the reasons are not different (probation and approbation) but the same (approbation) in both places. In our Introduction we have shown that we cannot overrate the significance of what we have called the "circular" or "rondo" form in James, and in this I believe we find further corroboration of our emendation. For some time, we must confess, we have been uneasy at the 'jerk' which the conventional text of 1:3 forces upon 1:12. So emended it now fits in with the rondo form and links up beautifully and characteristically with the rest.

Ropes says (p. 135) that the evidence of the Mss. raises a bare suspicion that τῆς πίστεως was added by conformation to 1 Pet. 1:7, and that to omit τῆς πίστεως does not alter the general sense. "The Greek text underlying ff and m [which omit τῆς πίστεως] was of the same type as that of the older Greek uncials, and resembled B [the best ms.] more closely than does any extant Greek Ms. (not excluding even ℵ)" (Ropes, p. 84). The question of the omission is not entirely negligible, and the deletion does slightly affect the sense of the argument for the better—in our present opinion. It brings 1:3 into line with 1:12, giving a reference to "approval" *simpliciter* in both: and it may be thought that it makes the introduction of σοφία in 1:5 much—or a little—easier. If we include τῆς πίστεως, even with our emendation, then (after the mention of "the approval of your faith") "lacking nothing" at least suggests "lacking nothing in faith," which makes the relation of σοφία to the previous verse a little difficult. The difficulty disappears if we take πίστις in its comprehensive sense ("faith working in life"); but Ropes, and others who confine *peirasmoi* here to "tribulations from without," take πίστις in its narrower, credal sense, "faith in Providence and in a good God . . . that fundamental attitude of the man's soul by virtue of which he belongs to the people of God" (pp. 133, 135)— though so much faith, be it noted, might well be Jewish, Greek, or Roman, and not

Christian. In 1 Pet. 1:7, τῆς πίστεως follows naturally from διὰ πίστεως in 1 Pet. 1:5, where πίστις has the special meaning it has in any such statement, or, e.g., in Jas. 1:6 or 5:15; 2 Pet. 1:5. In Jas. 1:3–5, it may be thought that the argument runs better without τῆς πίστεως: "Deem it nothing but an occasion for joy when you encounter trying assaults of evil in their various kinds. You must realize that your approbation is accomplished by constancy in endurance. But let that constancy perfect its work, so that you may be perfect and complete in every part, lacking in nothing. But if any of you lacks wisdom . . . let him ask. . . . But let him ask in *faith*, with no halting between two opinions. . . ."

EXCURSUS C
JAMES 1:7: AN EXPLANATION

More accurately, the discussion here covers vv. 5–8 and the problem of punctuation. μὴ γὰρ οἰέσθω ὁ ἄνθρωπος ἐκεῖνος ὅτι λήμψεταί τι παρὰ τοῦ κυρίου · ἀνὴρ δίψυχος ἀκατάστατος ἐν πάσαις ταῖς ὁδοῖς αὐτοῦ. (7) "Let not that (sort of) man imagine that he will get anything from the Lord: (8) a man who is of two minds is unsteady in all his ways." The Greek, depending on the way we punctuate, is capable of three interpretations. We may:

(i) Omit a stop and form a general statement with ἀνὴρ δίψυχος as the subject (RV mg.), thus—"that a man who is of two minds, unsteady in all his ways, will get anything from the Lord"; or

(ii) Insert a comma, making v. 7 a complete statement and v. 8 in apposition (RV): "let not that (sort of) man imagine that he will get anything from the Lord"; or

(iii) Insert a colon and, like the KJV, form two separate statements: "Let not that (sort of) man imagine that he will get anything from the Lord: a man who is of two minds is unsteady in all his ways" (cf. Vulg. *non ergo aestimet homo ille quod accipiat aliquid a Domino. vir duplex animo inconstans est in omnibus viis suis*).

Arguing that "that man" (ὁ ἄνθρωπος ἐκεῖνος) refers to "the man that lacks wisdom" (τις ὑμῶν λείπεται σοφίας, v. 5) rather than to "the man of two minds," as is usually thought, Hort opts for the first interpretation, offering a highly individual approach to this difficult verse. His view, in our opinion, has no foundation in fact or Greek. Hort says that ἄνθρωπος in James carries no trace of reproach. It is, however, obvious that in "O vain man" the phrase as a whole is disparaging; in fact, in the vocative, addressed in the ordinary way to an individual, the word is usually disrespectful, or at least clearly without respect. In 1:7 "that man" is, in the context, disparaging, and so is "let him not imagine," as Ropes points out (*ad loc.*).

Here, as sometimes elsewhere, οἴεσθαι means not simply "thinking" but "vain thinking," as when any father says to his son: "Don't think you can bamboozle *me*!" i.e., "Don't *imagine* you can do that." So in James: "Let not that (sort of) man imagine that he...." But we base no argument on the inherent quality of the expression "that man" *per se*: let it take its meaning and quality from the context. Surely, only a man blinded by his own preconceptions would say that there is "nowhere... a trace of reproach" in 2:20, ὦ ἄνθρωπε κενέ, or that there is "emphatic opposition to other beings" in 2:20 or 2:24; and ἡμᾶς in 1:19 means not "mankind" but "Christians" (*pace* Hort). In 1:19 πᾶς ἄνθρωπος is just a weightier πᾶς, as in John 2:10.

On the point of the two words for *man*, which Ropes too cursorily dismisses (p. 143), we may note that James uses ἄνθρωπος in 1:7 and 19; 2:20 and 24; 3:8 and 9; and 5:17—always with generic implications, i.e., with implicit thought of the character, rights, duties, or (usually) limitations, of human nature: in 3:9 the context asserts the dignity of the species; elsewhere the limitations are in point, especially in the contemptuous 2:20; 1:7 is at least chastening.

This sense and tone of ἄνθρωπος appear already in Homer: cf. *Od.* iii.48, "All men have need of gods." Without them the word is not much used in the singular, at least not with respect. Pilate's use of it in John 18:29 and 19:5 is not disparaging (for he is sympathetic), but it is *de haut en bas*; Paul's use of it, of himself, in Acts 21:39 and 22:25, is deliberately modest in expression; in 22:26 it obviously has the tone of the governing class. The individualizing word is ἀνήρ, as, for instance, the first word of the *Odyssey*; and often, as there, the man is singled out as really being "somebody"; but that need not be so, as when this word is used in telling that some ships perished, "men and all." So in Jas. 1:8 ἀνὴρ δίψυχος is quite in keeping with the normal individualizing use of ἀνήρ. This use is familiar in sententious maxims and the like in Greek Tragedy and the later Comedy, where besides being an individual ἀνήρ is a type, but not necessarily of humanity as a whole, e.g., a bore: ἀνὴρ γὰρ ὅστις ἥδεται λέγων ἀεί, "For a man who delights in talking all the time (gets himself disliked without knowing it)." It may be a type of virtue: ἀνὴρ δὲ χρηστὸς χρηστὸν οὐ μισεῖ ποτε, "But a good man never hates a good man (but knave cleaves to knave in pleasures)." Sometimes the scope is quite general: οὐκ ἀνδρὸς ὅρκοι πίστις ἀλλ' ὅρκων ἀνήρ. "Oaths are not a guarantee of a man, but a man (is guarantee) of his oaths," or κατθανὼν δὲ πᾶς ἀνὴρ γῆ καὶ σκία, "But when a man has died, every man is but earth (clay?) and a shadow."

Adopting, as I think we must, the third and KJV treatment of 1:7f. (see iii above), we find ἀνήρ in James in 1:23 and 2:2 as an individual, but representing a typical experience and a type of man, respectively, and we find it in maxims or generalizations about a type in 1:8 and 20, both censured, and in 1:12 and 3:2, both commended. It may be noted that, accepting KJV, we find ἄνθρωπος in 1:7 and 19, both times in admonition, and followed in each case in the next verse, 1:8 and 20, by ἀνήρ in a chastening maxim. We believe also that the maxim in 1:20 is in the same tradition of style and thought, illustrated in the extant ἔξω γὰρ ὀργῆς πᾶς ἀνὴρ σοφώτερος, "For every man is wiser without (lit. outside) anger." Indeed, and the original for James's maxim there almost suggests itself, if we may offer it: ὀργὴ γὰρ

93

ἀνδρὸς θεῶν δίκην οὐκ ἐκτελεῖ. "For the wrath of man does not accomplish the justice of the gods." That James was influenced as much by the style of the pagan Greek maxim as by that of the biblical proverb is suggested by his use of the word ἀνήρ in 1:20; for *prima facie* it is as clear a case for using ἄνθρωπος in contrast to θεός as Rom. 3:4 μὴ γένοιτο·γινέσθω δὲ ὁ θεός ἀληθής, πᾶς δὲ ἄνθρωπος ψεύστης. Of Greek preachers in their diatribes, Ropes (p. 14) writes: "Not originality but impressiveness was what they aimed at. The argument is from what the readers already know and ought to feel. . . . The writers of diatribes were fond of quotations from poets and sages, but these were used not for proof of the doctrine but incidentally, and often for ornament of the discourse. So is it usually with James." (These last words do less than justice to James.) James obviously owes much to the diatribe, be it said without prejudice to his originality. We are certain that James's mastery of style in Greek (for he is a master of his kind) includes as much familiarity as Paul's with the poetry from which Paul actually makes two quotations in his Epistles, not to forget Jas. 1:17. So we have a (quite conjectural) notion here that James is quoting (not exactly) some line from a Greek play (Comedy). This is just the sort of maxim they indulged in.

The description of the doubter in 1:6–8 follows a pattern common in James and easily illustrated from Paul in Rom. 2:7–10, a sort of A B A rondo form: To A (well-doing), eternal life; to B (contentious), wrath; but glory to A (that worketh good). So here in James, *A,* the doubter is like the tossing sea; *B,* for he cannot win an answer to his prayer; *A,* he is like a rudderless vessel (if we may give the effect in another form).

In the above we have followed KJV. The NEB follows the second (ii) and RV interpretation (see above), which, literally translated, would show this construction: "Let not that (sort of) man imagine that he will get anything from the Lord, being of two minds, unsteady in all his ways." The confusion among the commentators seems to have been planted, or at least watered, by Hort, who claims that ὁ ἄνθρωπος ἐκεῖνος means the man of v. 5, who "lacks wisdom." He says that even if ὁ ἄνθρωπος were a "cumbrous reproachful description" of the doubter in v. 6, it would have no force, thus closely preceding an explicit rebuke. This is the only place where James has ἐκεῖνος in any of its case-forms: we find it not cumbrous but forceful, as in Matt. 12:45; 26:24 (cited by Hort), and as also we find ὦ ἄνθρωπε κενέ (2:20), no less closely preceding another explicit rebuke. Jas. 1:7 is (we think) no less solemn in subject than Matt. 12:45; we are not sure that it is even very *different* in subject. Of course Matt. 26:24 is very much more solemn.

Hort says of the six places with ἄνθρωπος in James, besides that in 1:7 under discussion, that the word is used by him "nowhere with a trace of reproach" (of which statement no more need be said), and "apparently always in emphatic opposition to other beings," among others, "to the devils" in 2:20 "and probably in 2:24." Does any reasonable man see any such "emphatic opposition" in the use of ἄνθρωπος in these verses? In all Hort's pleading against either inherent or contextual suggestion of disparagement in ἄνθρωπος (1:7), he is incited by his wish to refer "that man" to the man of v. 5. He explains the insertion of ἄνθρωπος as in opposition to "the Lord"—which few can find convincing. There is no need to make heavy weather of ἐκεῖνος, which Hort says ''is the obvious way of setting aside the last person and pointing back to the person mentioned before him.'' The matter is not as simple as that: the paramount rule of grammar, here and everywhere, is the rule of sense. Kühner-Gerth, § 467.11, gives opposite cases, including Dem. viii.72, which has both ἐκεῖνο and τοῦτο, and ἐκεῖνο means the nearer (the latter) of two equally emphasized alternatives. When οὗτος and ἐκεῖνος *both* occur in a sentence, after mention of two (say) persons, ἐκεῖνος refers to the remoter, i.e., the first. But *by itself* ἐκεῖνος ''generally refers to what has gone *immediately before*'' (LS, *s.v.*). Thus it is often used as almost equal to αὐτόν or αὐτοῦ or αὐτῷ, etc., e.g., Σωκράτει συνεῖναι καὶ μετ᾽ ἐκείνου διατρίβειν, and οὐχ ὡς ἀδελφὸν αὐτῆς, ἀλλ᾽ ὡς ἄνδρα ἐκείνης (= same person: ''not as her brother but as her husband''). ''The phrase,'' as Ropes rightly observes (*ad loc.*), ''is highly effective with reference to the person just described elaborately, and on the other hand it is impossible to see why the warning that follows, which is of universal application, should be addressed with such special emphasis only to 'the man that lacketh wisdom'.'' ὁ ἄνθρωπος ἐκεῖνος is not a simple *ille*. The only rational course is to relate this designation, unique, as we mentioned, in James, to the vividly depicted doubter just mentioned in v. 6, not to the εἴ τις of v. 5, who is no more visually realized than the *si quis* of banns of marriage or ordination.

Hort's proposal, amounting to, ''let not the man who lacks wisdom and is to pray for it think that a two-minded man, unsteady in all his ways, will get anything from the Lord,'' cannot stand against the simple, forcible, downright intelligible version of KJV, or even against that of RV and NEB. Hort's view has no merits, and few, if any, followers. As Mayor rightly says, Hort's feeble version lacks the energy characteristic of James, appealing less directly to the person addressed—by not making him the subject of both οἰέσθω (let him imagine, v. 7) and λήμψεται (he will receive, v. 7)—and weakening the force and rhythm of the following clause (ἀνὴρ . . . αὐτοῦ, 1:8). Against the KJV, Mayor with approval quotes Alford, who says: ''It is hardly possible that the writer could have introduced a hitherto unknown, or at any rate a very unusual, word in this casual way''; but we see nothing casual about it. Jas. 1:6–8, like 1:19, 20, is a piece of careful art; it is not casual to introduce a striking word, δίψυχος, in a short, striking maxim which revives and balances the studied simile of v. 6 with its picture of the tossing sea driven now this way and that, by the proverbially inconstant winds.[1]

---

[1]At this point we note (from a personal communication through the kindness of Professor C. F. D. Moule) the opinion of Ernst Bammel. He writes: ''Both Mayor and Ropes state that B puts a stop before ἀνήρ and both follow this interpretation of the Vatican Codex, although in a different way. Indeed, there is a stop before ἀνήρ in B (as in A) and perhaps even a small spatium. But there is a stop between v. 9 and 10 too, and only if the spatium can be taken into consideration, is it possible to separate v. 7 and 8 more (KJV) or less (RV) completely. But I do not think that the punctuation of B is right. It is the seconder's attempt to disentangle the difficult structure of the sentence. The same tendency is even more emphasized in those variants which omit δίψυχος and place γάρ instead (88; 1837); cp. the Vulgate reading: 'inconstans *est.*' ℵ and C show neither a lacuna nor a stop—but they seldom do. Dibelius, *Der Brief des Jakobus*, p. 80, considers v. 7 and 8 one entity. Unfortunately I could not check p74; but the papyrus is late (6th or 7th cent.).''

In support of his view Mayor offers parallels from 3:2, 6, 8 ("though here the apposition is irregular"), and 4:12. In his note on 3:8 he says it is "more probable that there is a sudden change of construction, ἀκατάστατον κακόν being the predicate of an independent sentence with ἡ γλῶσσα understood as subject." Jas. 3:6, we are convinced, is irrelevant; we are sure the Peshitta reading is right. 3:2 and 4:12 are easy and single appositions with immediately antecedent connections in the sentence: they show nothing like the alleged apposition in 1:8 to the remote ὁ ἄνθρωπος ἐκεῖνος (as Mayor supposed) or (as Ropes has it) "the unexpressed subject (WH mg., RV)." The approximate (not exact) resemblances to 3:2 and 4:12a, at a pause in the flow of the reasoning as in 1:8, are in 1:4, 21, 22; 2:9; 3:6; 5:16; and these show (*pace* Bammel) no "difficult structure of the sentence" to provoke a scribe's vain "attempt to disentangle" it.

The moral maxim and gnomic style of 5:16b, on the effectual prayer of the δίκαιος, are exactly parallel to 1:8, on the opposite kind of prayer by the opposite sort of man. For, as we have seen (see comment on 1:8), already in the Dead Sea Scrolls is evidence that the Jews had early developed a philosophy of the δίψυχος as the opposite of the righteous. It also seems plausible that James knew the word δίψυχος from the vocabulary of this topic, possibly from an apocryphon, which Lightfoot conjectured to be the Book of Eldad and Modad (mentioned by Hermas in *Vis.* ii.3), or from some early commentary on Num. 11:26–29 (see following comment).

Both A and B punctuate before ἀνήρ. Ropes, following Mayor, claims that this evidence supports their theory of apposition. Punctuation in these mss. has little or no evidential value: but any value it has supports the separation adopted by KJV. The whole style of the Epistle of James is against Mayor, Ropes, and evidently the position of Bammel. To begin a new sentence with δίψυχος is forcible, and like James, much more so than any dim, disjointed apposition. Of all the proposals, the only one worthy of James is that in the KJV, which has the support of A and B, two excellent manuscripts.

EXCURSUS D
JAMES 1:17: DISCUSSION OF THE TEXT

The chief variants of v. 17b are these:
1. Bℵ* ἡ τροπῆς ἀποσκιάσματος.
2. 𝔭²³ 614 ἢ τροπὴ ἀποσκιάσματος; ff *vel modicum obumbrationis*; Boh. "nor a form of a shadow which passed."
3. A, TR ἢ τροπῆς ἀποσκίασμα; Vulg. *vicissitudinis obumbratio*; Jer. adv. Jov.

conversionis obumbraculum; Aug. *momenti obumbratio*. Cf. D. R. Goodwin in *JBL* 5 (1886), pp. 126f.

4. 876 1518 ἢ τροπὴ ἢ τροπῆς ἀποσκίασμα.

5. Sah. ἀποσκίασμα ἢ παραλλαγὴ ἢ τροπή.

Παραλλαγή as in the NT is in all our *testimonia*; and (3) is in all our printed editions. KJV "shadow of turning."

RV "shadow that is cast by turning."

These both seem tantamount to "turning shadow," i.e., cast by the sun in its daily course. Cf. Ropes, p. 165: "ἀποσκιάζω—to cast a shadow: ἀποσκίασμα therefore is either 'shadow cast' or 'the act of casting a shadow'." "The word for shadow on a dial is ἀποσκιασμός," he continues, "and even that word requires a context to define it in that meaning." But, we may remark, a sundial may be included with other things partially resembling a sundial, as in saying that the sundial and the trees in your garden all give a turning shadow; this point, however, may not arise in our exposition.

Ropes in his commentary, p. 163, favored the reading of Bℵ* P. Oxy. 1229, ἡ τροπῆς ἀποσκιάσματος. This, he says, "makes excellent sense, if only η is taken as the article on which τροπῆς depends, the meaning being that given above," viz., "with whom is none of the variation that belongs to ('consists in', 'is observed in') the turning of the shadow." "The general sense," he adds, "is the same as with the usual reading."

We offer a different suggestion. We think ἤ has been displaced in transmission and should follow, not precede, the word for 'turning': "from the Father of lights, whose nature suffers neither the variation of orbit nor any shadowing out (as in eclipse)"; we take ἔνι (i.e., ἔνεστι) to mean inherent nature rather than inherent possibility; cf. 1 John 1:5, "God is (ever) light, and in him is no darkness at all." See Ropes, p. 161, for more on the contrast between the sun and the divine immutability. Though τροπή, which in the NT occurs only here, can mean "solstice," we assume no technical meaning in this passage, only "turning" or "orbit": so Ps. 19:6, where "circuit" (Vulg. *occursus*) translates the Hebrew noun from *qûph*. On later Jewish superstitions connected with the four "turnings of the sun" (*Tekufot*), see J. Trachtenberg, *Jewish Magic and Superstition*, p. 257. In God there is no "turning" (τροπή) from light of day to darkness of night.

We have read ἀποσκίασμα, not the genitive; and we also think Hort's conjecture was right, viz., that it was followed by αὐτός in earlier mss. (see also Ropes, p. 163, line 9). We further think that αὐτός is right, and should be restored to the text, as the first word of 1:18, properly and emphatically taking up the "Father of lights" of 1:17. So we read: παρ' ᾧ οὐκ ἔνι παραλλαγὴ τροπῆς ἢ ἀποσκίασμα · αὐτὸς βουληθείς, "from the Father of lights, whose nature suffers neither the variation of orbit nor any (occluding) shadow. He of his own wish. . . ." This fits the ms. confusion, and makes the quoted "parallels" really parallel: Isa. 60:30; Wisd. 7:29; Sir. 17:31 (see Ropes, p. 161).

EXCURSUS E
JAMES 1:21: "THE IMPLANTED WORD"

This apparently simple phrase "the implanted word" is deceptively so and constitutes a notorious *crux*, which has caused at least one commentator[1] to devote 120 pages in Latin to its interpretation. The difficulty springs from the essential meaning of the word ἔμφυτος itself—only here in the NT and Wisd. 12:10 in LXX—and also from the way in which it is used in this particular context. If, as we have suggested, the word is to be translated "implanted," it is still not clear how we can accept something already "implanted." Broadly speaking three explanations of ἔμφυτος have been offered:

1. "engrafted" (KJV);
2. "innate" or "inborn" (RV mg); cf. *genitum* ff; and
3. "implanted" (RV; RSV).

Incidentally, the usual Latin rendering *insitus*, which may mean either "implanted" or "innate," is of little help.

    1. The first KJV rendering, "engrafted," which goes back to Tyndale's "that is grafted in you" (1526) and other early English versions (but not Wyclif), finds little support among the commentators.[2] The word employed for "engrafted" is ἐμφυτευτός, although ἔμφυτος is also used sometimes in the papyri (see M.M. *s.v.* ἔμφυτος). This first imterpretation therefore can be safely rejected.

    2. There is less unanimity about the other two interpretations. "Innate" or "inborn" was strongly favored by Hort[3] who, following up his views of 1:18, sees a reference not to the reception of the gospel, but rather to "the original capacity involved in the creation in God's image which makes it possible for man to apprehend a revelation at all."[4] So understood—*eigentlich ein stoischer Schulausdruck*[5]—the phrase may be taken as proof of Stoic influence,[6] and almost equivalent to the λόγος σπερματικός,[7] although Windisch himself[8] is inclined to dismiss such a possibility. Certainly there is a wide difference between the metaphysical Logos of the Stoic and the practical exhortation of James: "Be doers of the Word. . . ." No Stoic could ever say this about his Logos. Even more serious, however, if this interpretation were adopted, is the difficulty inherent in the idea of accepting a Word which is already

---

[1]Heisen, *Novae Hypotheses*, who himself (p. 671) thought ἔμφυτος was used in contrast to διδακτός, ἐπίκτητος, etc.

[2]Typical is the comment of Ropes (p. 172): "The rendering 'engrafted' (AV) . . . is unsuitable because it directly expresses the idea of "foreign," "applied from without," "not a natural growth," a meaning for which a derivative of ἐμφυτεύειν, "engraft," would be required.

[3]*Op. cit.*, p. 37.

[4]*Op. cit.*, p. 39. He further asserts (*op. cit.*, p. 37) that it is impossible to take τὸν ἔμφυτον λόγον as the outward message of the gospel. He could never have used in that sense a word which everyone who knew Greek would of necessity understand in the opposite sense.

[5]Windisch.

[6]Dibelius, Marty.

[7]See C. H. Dodd, *The Parables of the Kingdom*, p. 14. Also W. L. Knox, *art. cit.* (*JTS* 46 [1945]), pp. 14f.

[8]*Op. cit.*, p. 11.

"inborn," a meaning which, notwithstanding Hort's appeals to Lk. 21:19 and I Thess. 4:4, James Moffatt[9] rightly declares "impossible here."

In effect, Hort is saying every Grecian would here understand logos as *ratio*, not *narratio*. He is saying that logos here means a God-given enlightening power, "the original capacity involved in the Creation of man in the image of his Maker, which makes it possible for man to apprehend a revelation from God at all." But Hort's attempt to reconcile δέξασθε with this notion obviously fails. The gap between the faculty of apprehension, it is not "always sounding," to be "received" or "rejected": if anything, it is listening, not sounding. If we do not listen with our faculty of listening intelligently, what we do not accept, δέξασθε, is not the faculty, but the sounding message which we disregard—not the *ratio*, but the *narratio* and *hortatio*. Apart from all we have already said we simply cannot believe that James is here saying, "Accept your inborn power of comprehension," or anything like that! We take logos in 1:18, 21, 22, in the same sense; and in the last of these verses logos obviously includes the "message." Besides, the distinction Hort fixes between logos, *ratio*, and logos, message, must never be pressed too far. The Christian must hear the Word and also comprehend its immediate and consequential meaning. James 1:22–25 shows what he meant by δέξασθε τὸν λόγον. The λόγος Θεοῦ, implied in Tit. 1:3, is the word expressing the *ratio Dei*. The Word/Gospel/Law is not just a sequence of noises of words; it includes all the meaning and power, the reason and life, that the NT constantly identifies with Word/Gospel/Law—as in this passage James identifies the Law with Liberty. We might add, a reminder that the Word/Gospel/Law is not planted in our hearts to do some active magic in a passive, inactive mind. We do not become part of the logos: the logos may become part of us, but we remain morally responsible creatures, even in the Court of Mercy.[10]

---

[9]*MNTC*, p. 25. Hort tries to get over the difficulty of accepting an "inborn" word by citing Lk. 21:19 and I Thess 4:4. He might also have appealed to the Latin *genitum* of ff.

[10]Let us also urge, in reply to Hort, that some truths are fundamental to the interpretation of James. He writes the nearest to Classical Greek in the NT, except perhaps Hebrews. He is an expert in argument and exposition, dogmatic and parenetic, and an expert artist in language, i.e., in the art of rhetoric as beautiful and effective speech. He never fails in relevance, unity, and coherence. Any interpretation that presumes otherwise is *ipso facto* suspect, e.g., E. C. Blackman's (*The Epistle of James* [1957], p. 63), at which point he suggests: "It may be saner to pay less respect to James's competence with Greek, and to allow that he misunderstood the meaning of *emphutos*, innate, and tried to make it mean, viz. engrafted, as in AV." Sic! For this reason, especially when we observe his pervading habit of epanalepsis (e.g., ὑπομονή/ ἡ δὲ ὑπομονή *ad init.*—not always so obvious) and what we label as his "rotary" or "rondo" form, we hesitate to take λόγος in 1:18, 21, 22 in any but one and the same signification, unless cause can be shown to the contrary. At least nearly all commentators agree that James is a Christian-Jew addressing Christians (even if none but Christian-Jews); so we have rejected Hort's interpretation of 1:18 as expounding a doctrine of the creation of men at large (for there were no Jews till Abraham), for such an argument is not *properly* Christian. The λόγος, as we have seen, can only be taken to mean the gospel. If this is correct, what can the ἔμφυτος λόγος in James's chain of argument mean but the λόγος of the gospel, implanted by such as the Apostles ("the doctrine implanted by your teachers" [Thayer-Grimm]), which their hearers must let root and flourish in their lives? In this connection, Ropes (p. 173) points out that:

> The ἔμφυτος λόγος itself is called in v. 25 νόμος τέλειος and in vv. 22f. is described as something to be done. It seems to mean the sum of present knowledge of God's

3. On the balance of evidence the third interpretation, "implanted," is to be preferred. The main and decisive reason, of course, is semantic. Careful consideration of ἔμφυτος and its Greek cognates has led us to the conclusion that this is the correct meaning. The proper Greek word for "innate," i.e., implanted at birth, is σύμφυτος, which occurs often enough in that sense, i.e., set into a man at birth as part of his congenital nature. But ἔμφυτος means only "implanted," without any inherent indication of the time of life at which the implanting occurs; it may be set into a man after birth to be another part of his nature. Since σύμφυτος is, as we say, "timed" with birth, ἔμφυτος, which is "untimed," is the word for an "implanting" not at birth but later in life. "Implant" in this sense is used metaphorically to mean "set into a man to be, or to grow to be, a new part of his nature (including his mind)." Thus ἐμφύω in Od. 22.348, where the gods "implanted" lays (songs) in a minstrel, may—but we think does not—refer to the time of birth, but in Hdt. 9.94 (cited by Mayor) a certain man receives *in manhood* a gift of prophecy "implanted" in him by the gods (μετὰ ταῦτα ἔμφυτον μαντικὴν εἶχεν). It is not *enough* for Mayor to call it "a secondary growth," "a second nature." Nor is it *enough* for Hort to say that "he had a Divine gift of prophecy, not as a receiver of prophecies, but as the possessor of a power within himself," or to go on to say that "such passages as these are useless for showing that the word can mean implanted." Just as the gods had set the wolves on those who blinded him, their promise δώσειν Εὐηνίῳ δόσιν suggests that they "implanted" in him, as a new gift, the power of prophecy—he had it set into him as an additional part of his nature, i.e., of his thereby enhanced natural powers. "Implanted" seems the best English word to express what happened. Mayor's reference to σύμφυτος in Rom. 6:5 has no relevance to our understanding of ἔμφυτος. But since ἔμφυτος is "untimed" in its reference, it is quite often and quite easily used of an "implanting," the setting of something in a man as part of his nature, at birth no less than at any other time of his life; the context makes the meaning clear; e.g., Wisd. 12:10 ἔμφυτος ἡ κακία αὐτῶν; Philo (*Quod Deus* 22; *De Fuge* 22; *De Fort.* 5; *De Praem.* 1); Josephus (*Ant.* XVI. viii.1; *B.J.* VII.iv.2); Ps. Phoc. 128. Clem. Alex. *Protrept.* X (77 pp.) speaks of ἔμφυτον πίστιν as a natural gift in man; but to say, like Mayor, that the word *starts* by meaning *innate*, from birth only, leads to trouble.

---

will. It is inwrought into a man's nature and speaks from within, but this does not exclude that it should also exist for man's use in written or traditional form, whether in the law of Moses or in the precepts of Jesus.

Strictly, of course, the λόγος ἔμφυτος implanted by the preachers of the gospel is the λόγος Θεοῦ (cf. Tit. 1:3), the word of the *ratio Dei,* God's will and work from everlasting to everlasting, described under the name of σοφία in 1 Cor. 2:4–16. We do err if we think that James did not know about baptism, crucifixion or resurrection; he succinctly expresses all that in 1:18. But since it is the message of the gospel, we may very well just think of it in James as the gospel truth.

CHAPTER 2

IV. THE CHRISTIAN LIFE (2:1–26)

a. Social compassion amid social cleavage (2:1–13)

1 *Do not try to combine faith in the Lord Jesus Christ, our Glory, with worship of men's social status.*

2 *For if there comes into your assembly a man with a gold ring and fine clothes, and there comes also a poor man in dirty clothes,*

3 *and you pay observance to the one wearing the fine clothes, and say: "Sit here in this good seat," while you say to the poor man: "Stand there," or "Sit here under my footstool,"*

4 *have you not lost your bond of unity (i.e., Christian brotherhood) and become judges to decree pernicious distinctions?*

5 *Listen, my beloved brothers: has not God selected the world's poor men to be rich in faith and heirs of the kingdom which he has promised to them that love him?*

6 *But you have had only contempt for the poor. Do not the rich use their power to oppress you? Is it not actually they who drag you to court?*

7 *Do they not actually sin impiously with their tongues against the noble name by which you are called?*

8 *If indeed you fulfil the sovereign law, according to the Scriptures, "Thou shalt love thy neighbor as thyself," you do well.*

9 *But if you are swayed by men's social status, you commit sin, and are convicted by the law as transgressors.*

10 *For whoever observes the entire Torah but contravenes a single commandment becomes guilty of all.*

11 *For he who said, "Thou shalt not commit adultery," said also: "Do not kill." If you do not commit adultery but do kill, you become a transgressor of the law.*

12 *So speak and so act as those who will be judged in accordance with the law of liberty.*

13 *For to him that has not shown pity, judgment (of God on Christians after death) is without pity; but where pity is (if it has been done by the Christian in his life), it triumphs over (legalistic) judgment (after death).*

The connection of this warning against social discrimination with the previous ch. 1 seems fairly obvious. Truckling to the rich and apathy or worse toward the poor are two sides of the same base coin rejected by the touchstone of 1:27 and of 2:8.

2:1–13 returns to and expands the theme of 1:9, on "respect of persons," the proper relations of rich and poor in Christian society and the Christian congregation. Respect of persons (2:1) and despising the poor (2:6) constitute a denial of Christian brotherhood—the essential theme, we believe, of 1:9, 10, as it is of 1:25; 2:12f. and 2:8, and (by implication) in the rule of 1:27. It is also a breach of the rule of wholehearted consistency in 1:6–8, as 2:4 indicates.

The gist of the diatribe against snobbery seems to be this: Faith must live in true brotherly love. Do not try to combine faith in Christ with worship of social status. That is a breach of the law of love, a breach which damns you under OT Law, and would throw you on Christ's mercy: but he that does no mercy has no right to expect mercy even that way—unless he repents and does his best to reform. So English lawyers still have an old, and still valid, saying, "He that comes to equity must do equity."

1 The Greek present tense has many possible meanings; one of them is to signify that something is happening now and continuing: "It is raining[1]—and there is no saying when it will stop." The dominant note in this use is incompleteness. Incompleteness is very apt to suggest effort in action: "I am defending the accused," that is, "I am trying to get him off"; or, "I am trying to drive off (my enemies)." Very often it is only the context that shows that this is the sort of meaning intended. It is *ex hypothesi* impossible to serve God and Mammon, or to be faithful to Christ and servile to the rich: hence here the command,[2] rather than question (Hort, Chaine), must mean: "Do not *try* to combine faith in Christ with (let us here say) worship of wealth." To translate otherwise, e.g., "Do not combine," would leave men to imagine it would be possible.[3]

Interpretations of this text have followed four main lines: we shall consider these and then propose our own.

---

[1] ὕει.

[2] μὴ . . . ἔχετε.

[3] On the Inchoative or Inceptive Present, see R. Kühner, *Greek Grammar* II, p. 140 (*sub fin.*); e.g., Xenophon *Comm.* ii.1, 14: ὅπλα κτῶνται, οἷς ἀμύνονται τοὺς ἀδικοῦντας, *quibus repellere conantur*, i.e., "with which they try to 'repel'. . . ."

i.   Some older scholars (e.g., Erasmus, Calvin) take what we have translated "glory"[4] to mean mere (and usually false) "opinion," and as dependent on "social status": i.e., "not with observance of class distinctions, which are only matters of worthless opinion": so Erasmus, *cum partium studio quo ex sua quisque opinione quemlibet aestimat.* This is thoroughly unbiblical and finds few modern advocates.

ii.   Others, e.g., Luther, Hooker, Ropes,[5] with biblical parallels in Hebrew, Aramaic, and Greek, see here a Semitic qualitative genitive: "Our glorious Lord Jesus Christ." This interpretation is arbitrary: such a genitive with a proper name is at least doubtful, while such parallels as 1 Cor. 2:8; Eph. 1:17; Ps. 29:3; Acts 7:2 are hardly relevant (see Mayor, Ropes).

iii.   The Syriac Peshitta[6] tried unsuccessfully to connect "glory" (construed as objective genitive) with "faith": "faith in the glory of our Lord Jesus Christ." But this has found few supporters (Grotius, Zahn, Schlatter); and there is no good parallel for this construction or the order, especially in the transposition of "glory."

iv.   The duplex construction of "Lord" (a) with the Name, "the Lord Jesus Christ," and (b) with "glory," "the Lord of glory" (EVV, RSV, Knowling, Windisch), imposes an intolerable strain on the order of the two nouns.

v.   We propose our own solution in two parts: (a) The reference to "glory" must go closely with the Name of Christ (*ipse Christus*), possibly as a title in apposition. Bengel suggested: "Our Lord Jesus Christ, the glory"; similarly NEB: "who reigns in glory."[7] But Mayor, like many others, with whom we concur, rejects Bengel's view as entirely lacking in evidence to support it. Indeed no translation or grammatical account satisfies us, and we reject the idea that "glory" is an afterthought (R. A. Knox) or a gloss (Spitta, Meyer), even if absent in two minuscules (Marty). Textual evidence[8] and alleged parallels to "the Lord of Glory"[9] are both palpably weak: why, too, should a Christian editor be content with such a superficial change? That "Jesus Christ" was originally a marginal gloss, possibly with "our" added, is equally untenable: no Jewish reader would break up the phrase; further, "Jesus Christ" ought to have come first or last. As the text stands, the Greek is hardly the kind one would expect from a writer like James, a circumstance underlined by the various and, in our opinion, unsatisfactory proposed renderings.

[4]δόξης.
[5]Also J. Brinktrine, "Zu Jac. 2, 1," *Biblica* 35 (1954), pp. 40ff.
[6]With 69 173 206 1518.
[7]See A. M. Ramsey, *The Glory of God and the Transfiguration of Christ* (1949), p. 149.
[8]13 Sah.
[9]1 Enoch 22:14, and many others; Ps. 29:3; 24:7–10; 1 Cor. 2:8; Eph. 1:17; see Jas. 5:14.

(b) We therefore propose transference of "our" to the end of the sentence, making Christ "our glory." He is "our hope," as in 1 Tim. 1:1, and in the *Nunc Dimittis* "the glory of . . . Israel." This suggestion, made originally by P. B. R. Forbes, is viewed favorably also by F. F. Bruce.[10]

Even if James did not write this, it would have expressed the latent argument more clearly, plainly, forcibly, in downright intelligible Greek—that Jesus Christ is the true Glory, viz., the Shechinah, and that a Christian is (or should be) the last person to be impressed by the sham glory of social status. So Hort (p. 48): "James rebukes the contemptuous usage of poor men, even such as the Incarnate Glory of God Himself became."[11] Certainly this brings out the contrast between the "great privilege of Christian faith and this petty discrimination" (Ropes), holding the faith, i.e., an objective genitive in the sense of "Christian profession"[12] and showing partiality. The essence of this profession, as the almost unique opening emphatic "my brothers" (see 5:19) shows, is brotherhood. Those who have the Lord Jesus Christ as their Glory cannot have "discrimination" in their brotherhood.

"Discrimination," i.e., the familiar KJV "respect of persons," represents an odd, non-LXX Greek compound,[13] going back perhaps to an Akkadian coinage,[14] and "among the earliest definitely Christian words." Originally of an Oriental ruler's favor in "lifting the face"[15] of the prostrate suppliant, this word, rather like the English "favorite," "favoritism," gradually came to mean "to accept the person (Lat. *acceptor personae*) instead of the cause," and eventually, "to show partiality." Perhaps here there is a subtle contrast between "receiving the person" in the bad sense, and "receiving the face of the Shechinah."[16] Also translated "partiality," "snobbishness," "flunkeyism," this compound means all that, but much more, viz., "the failure to oppose injustice for fear of the powerful."[17]

---

[10]Bruce wrote, in a letter to Forbes: "In support of the transference of 'our' to the end of the sentence—an attractive emendation—can be adduced the fact that in some MSS and VSS (614 *al;* syr. copt. h. (plur.) boh.) 'glory' appears before 'Lord'."

[11]See E. J. Goodspeed, *Problems of NT Translation* (1945), pp. 142ff.

[12]ἔχετε τὴν πίστιν. Though theoretically the genitive may be either subjective or objective, it is clearly objective here. Nowhere else, as Windisch points out, *ad loc.*, is Jesus Christ said to possess faith; see Acts 3:16; Mark 11:22. Hort took the passage rather differently, "Have faith from God. Trust on, as men should do to whom God is a reality," combining both subjective and objective senses, viz., "the faith which he makes possible and bestows." But it is best to take it in the simple, straightforward sense of professed belief. Cf. for the classical use of ἔχω with an inner quality, esp. faith: Mark 4:40; 11:22; Matt. 21:21; Luke 17:6; also Jas. 1:14, 18; 3:14.

[13]προσωπολημψία—cognates προσωπολημπτέω, προσωπολήμπτης; see MM, *s.v.*

[14]E. Dhorme, *Revue Biblique* 30 (1921), pp. 379f.

[15]Heb. *nāśā' pānîm*. See BDB, *s.v. nāśā'*; Job 13:8, 10; Prov. 18:5; 24:23.

[16]Heb. *meqabbēl pānîm*. See J. Abelson, *The Immanence of God in Rabbinical Literature* (1912), pp. 98ff., 101, n. 1.

[17]Cranfield, *The Epistle of James*, p. 9; see Lev. 19:5; Luke 20:21; Acts 10:34; Rom. 2:11; Gal.

2 The term *assembly*[18] or "synagogue," here only in the NT applied with a Christian connotation, confirms the early date of the Epistle of James, which, however, also uses the commoner Greek word for "church"[19] in 5:14. This picture is drawn from life.[20] It is neither necessary nor possible to decide whether "assembly" here means the building (Mark 1:21; Luke 4:16; Acts 18:19; 19:18) or the congregation present (and evidently, in part still arriving); the third common use, for the whole body of membership, is not likely here. Till the final rift between Judaism and Christianity both Christian and non-Christian Jews used, at least often, the same word for their sacred meeting-place, and possibly, in the time of James, here and generally they both met in the same place for worship, as, for example, the Christians James and Paul used the Temple (Acts 21:26; 22:19).[21] Though practically synonymous (cf. Prov. 5:14, where both are used together), apparently the word we translate "assembly" (*synagōgē*) had a more local, less purely religious connotation than the other word *ekklēsia*.[22] For the eschatological sense of the compound *episynagōgē* cf. 2 Thess. 2:1; every "gathering" was a foretaste of the final "mustering" at the Parousia.[23]

The Gospel writers, Matthew and Mark, speak of "their" (i.e., Jewish) synagogues, Luke, except once, of "the synagogues"; but it is possible that for a time early Jewish Christians in general, and not only James in this Epistle, used both *synagōgē* and *ekklēsia* for their place of worship. The usher who greets the rich visitor may have been the regular Jewish *ḥazzan*, the only paid synagogue official, whose custodial duties ranged from cleaning the premises to safeguarding the Torah in the Ark and blowing the silver trumpet to signal the Sabbath.[24] According to Rost,[25] this passage in James reflects "the liturgical given conditions of an older type [of synagogue] found in Galilee." (This accords with our hypothesis of the date and authorship of the Epistle.) He interprets "here"[26] as nearer to the entrance and the center of worship, and "there"[27] as remoter, as would be

---

2:6; Eph. 6:3; Col. 3:25; *Did*. 4:3; *Epistola Apostolorum* 24, 27, in M. R. James, ed., *The Apocryphal NT* (1926), pp. 493ff.
[18]συναγωγή.
[19]ἐκκλησία.
[20]For other views see R. B. Ward, "Partiality in the Assembly: James 2:2–4," *HTR* 62 (1969), p. 87.
[21]See J. Weiss, *Earliest Christianity* (E.T. 1959), p. 668.
[22]See *TDNT* III, *s.v.* (K. L. Schmidt), p. 528. Cf. the interesting use of ἐπισυναγωγή in Heb. 10:25.
[23]T. Zahn, *Introduction to the NT* I (E.T. 1909), pp. 94ff.; Dibelius.
[24]*JE* XI (1908), *s.v.* "Synagogue" (W. Bacher), pp. 640ff.
[25]See H. Greeven, revised supplement volume to Dibelius, commentary.
[26]ὧδε.
[27]ἐκεῖ.

apt for a Christian place of worship, modelled on the conventional Jewish synagogue: but we do not feel justified in so confining the scope of "here" and "there" in this passage; and the rebuke is plainly addressed to the entire Jewish Christian Church under the leadership of James with special reference to congregations betraying Christ, their ideal. Like a gazelle, the Shechinah skipped from synagogue to synagogue[28] and dwelt where two sat to study the Torah,[29] presumably in complete brotherhood (Jas. 2:1).

The scene is superbly described—on the one hand, the dignity of the rich man's grand clothing and beringed fingers (the Greek word,[30] not found elsewhere,[31] neither a plagiarism nor accident,[32] is a vivid and masterly coinage, another striking neologism) and the obsequious welcome he receives, and, on the other hand, the dirty rags of the poor man's beggary, and the mean place to which he is contemptuously relegated.[33] The ring, even if not official but merely ornamental, like the Prodigal Son's, had considerable social significance: attractive but pure conjecture are the suggestions that this refers to a Roman knight (Streeter), non-Christian politician (Reicke), or the like. Babylonians and Jews both wore rings.[34]

3 *Pay observance to*—this verb[35] is used for "look with attention, or interest (rarely, with envy), or respect or favor"; it is common in the LXX, usually of God looking on man, and occurs in the NT only in Luke 1:48, in the Magnificat (look with favor), 9:38 (look with the favor of healing), and here, expressing the preferential favor with which the rich man is regarded and accommodated.

"Please" (RSV and others) or "in a good place"[36] (KJV and others), like the "chief seats" of Matt. 23:6[37]—we can do little more than guess the right meaning here; but on grounds of style, a potent factor in the composition of the Epistle of James, we prefer the latter translation. It seems to us to be deliberately intended to give a sharper point to the contrast between the two attitudes here displayed toward the rich and the poor respectively, i.e., between the high and comfortable seat for the one, and, for the other, none at all (or an ignominious squat on or near the floor, under someone's stall). If the Greek here means "please," it only carries on the

---

[28]Num. R. xi.2.
[29]*Pirqe Aboth* iii.3.
[30]χρυσοδακτύλιος.
[31]Cf. Epictetus i.22.18; Lucian *Tim.* 20.
[32]Rendall, p. 55.
[33]On fine clothes and the allurements of the *yetser,* see Schechter, *Rabbinic Theology,* p. 249n.
[34]Herodotus i.196; *JE* X, *s.v.* "Rings" (A. Wolf), pp. 428–430; G. F. Kunz, *Rings* (1917), pp. 14ff., 252, 366; cf. the bejewelled ladies in P. G. Wodehouse, *passim.*
[35]ἐπιβλέψητε.
[36]καλῶς.
[37]See *Meg.* iv.21; Bacher, *JE art. cit.,* pp. 639ff.; SB I, pp. 314ff.

courtesy of the welcoming official; the other translation adds force to the antithesis, calling attention to the lack of both comfort and dignity for the poor man, standing or little better off at somebody's feet.

Hypopodium, "footstool," does not occur in classical Latin, but *podium* is common enough, as in Pliny's Epistles, meaning the balcony of a building, and regularly a balcony fronting upon the arena, where the emperor and other eminent persons sat. The classical Greek for *hypopodium* is *thranos* or *thrēnos*; but the former regularly means a bench, and in Homer the latter means at one time a footstool and at another a seven-foot bench for the helmsman or rowers.[38] The Latin *podium,* obviously borrowed from the Greek, in which the simple *podion* is cited only once, must have a meaning like the Greek word *hypopodion,* "footstool" (James's word here), and most probably indicates something such as Meistermann[39] and Orfali[40] found in a synagogue, at least as old as the second or third century, at Tell Hum, which has a stone bench running along the walls, with a lower tier for the feet of those sitting on the bench.[41] The construction in the Greek[42] indicates motion toward, "Sit down onto (i.e., upon) my footstool." R. B. Ward says of the biblical phrase "God's footstool" that it "connotes, at least, the place of the humble or, at the most, the place of enemies in judgment."[43] To come under or to lick the shoe for the Jew meant slavish subjection and even conquest.[44] Seating assigned, says Ward, "proves they are strangers."[45] Perhaps not: even in our present Christian churches how many let a ragged tramp, however regularly attending, get into one of "the best seats"? Moreover, in this passage there is no reason at all why they should not both be conceived as strangers to that church.[46]

This passage exemplifies the enduring value of the Epistle of James as a caution to us against any complacent illusion of progress. In church, even where we have abolished seat rents, we may still be tempted to covet "a good place," or to think uncharitably of a visitor who has innocently usurped our favorite corner pew;[46a] and out of church, let us ask ourselves: "If I

[38]LS, *s.v.*
[39]See *Capharnaüm et Bethsaïde* (1921), p. 163.
[40]*Capharnaüm et ses Ruines* (1922), p. 67.
[41]Cf. the galleries of Scottish Presbyterian churches.
[42]ὑπὸ τὸ ποδιόν μου.
[43]*Art. cit.,* p. 92. He cites a ms. variant ὑποπόδιον τῶν ποδῶν μου in the LXX of Isa. 66:1; see also Lam. 2:1.
[44]Esther R. 8; S. A. Cook, *The Religion of Ancient Palestine in the Light of Archaeology.* Schweich Lectures (1925), p. 20.
[45]*Art. cit.,* p. 93.
[46]For the interesting, if unlikely, suggestion that "stand without" means "exclusion from society," see T. H. Gaster, *The Scriptures of the Dead Sea Sect* (1957), p. 25.
[46a]For a striking modern example, see the early, unfortunate experiences of William Booth and the Salvation Army in Richard Collier, *The General Next to God* (1965), pp. 31, 32.

am completely honest with myself, can I claim to be entirely free from the snobbery of money?''

4 See Mitton (p. 84): "They are confessing a complete obedience to Jesus Christ, and yet in their conduct are defying and affronting Him."

Their duty to Christ forbids such snobbery: their conduct in fact fosters it. These men have made themselves judges, "sinful judges giving effect to sinful discriminations." The Greek verb[47] indicates their "facing both ways" in their rulings, nominally to Christ and actually to worldly snobbery. F. Mussner adopts an "internalizing interpretation" of "distinctions among yourselves" (*in eurem Innern*), saying "the author of James" ignores the point of religion, and considers only the reaction of the community; but Ward,[48] quoting 2:5, rightly finds no split in its members' attitude to the poor man of the episode narrated. Content and usage[49] suggest a juridical tone for both the verb and noun.[50] Their "facing both ways" makes each one of them like a divided jury or a divided court, and the distinctions they make between rich and poor are (by contrast) reminders of the valid distinctions a righteous judge has to make. Ward[51] quotes from rabbinic texts on the equal duty owed by a judge to a poorly dressed and to a rich party in the judicial proceedings before him, e.g.: "How do we know that, if two come to court, one clothed in rags and the other in fine raiment worth a hundred manehs, they should say to him, 'Either dress like him, or dress him like you'?"[52] These texts illustrate tradition descending from the OT (Lev. 19:15–18; Exod. 23:1–3; Deut. 1:16, 17; 16:18–20) and at least from early Tannaitic times. Like Jas. 2:2–3 these texts use apparel as an index of the contrast between rich and poor; in the rabbis it is also seen, as in James, in the distinction made as to seating: e.g., "R. Judah said, I heard that if they please to seat the two, they may sit. What is forbidden? One shall not stand and the other sit."[53]

Pernicious distinctions—this[54] is an ordinary objective genitive, as to which see Moule:[55] "judges who make evil discriminations," i.e., according to a man's poverty or wealth. Such judges are said to cause the Shechinah to depart.[56]

5 Not every rich man is doomed to be damned (e.g., Joseph of

---

[47]διεκρίθητε ἐν ἑαυτοῖς.
[48]*Art. cit.*, p. 89.
[49]See MM, AG, *s.v.*
[50]διακρίνω, διάκρισις.
[51]*Art. cit.*, pp. 89f.
[52]b. *Sheb.* 31a.
[53]Sifra *Qedoshim, Pereq* iv.4.
[54]κριταὶ διαλογισμῶν πονηρῶν.
[55]*Idiom Book*, p. 40.
[56]b. *Ber.* 6a; Exod. R. xxx.24; Schechter, *Rabbinic Theology*, pp. 229ff.

Arimathaea, Mark 15:43–47), and not every poor man is sure to be saved; but for the purposes of this chapter there is a deep difference between the rich, in general, and the poor, in general, and there is, in general, an equation of the poor and the world's despised (see "Rich and Poor," pp. 29f.), 1:9ff. shows how the behavior of 2:1–4 defies the ideal of Christianity. *Listen,* [57] in the oral style of the diatribe, is found in the LXX, the Synoptics, and the book of Revelation (2:7, etc.), but, not altogether unexpectedly, only here in a written Epistle, and, again not unexpectedly, in an Epistle with marked oral characteristics. Here the aorist[58] seems to be a sharp: "Take this in," as contrasted with a present as in v. 1, "Do not try to combine. . . ."[59]

The world tends to "choose" those who are rich in (say) money; God, those who are (*not* "those who are to be") *rich in faith,* i.e., "abounding in" (Mayor), "in virtue of" (Hort), or "in the realm of" faith (Ropes)—the last, with its contrast between judgment by God's standards and the world's,[60] is to be preferred.[61] James does not spiritualize or idealize poverty.[62] Poverty does not guarantee either faith or final salvation; but whereas the rich often have, and feel they have, a "heaven upon earth," the poor, in general, are much more likely and eager to believe in a celestial heaven to come, to compensate for the present purgatory, as it often has been, on earth. The ancient Anatolian Greek shepherds, who put up a stone, "To the Nymphs," at their remote well, remind us that the ancients, pagan or Jewish, especially of the humble peasant type, had much faith in the divine, and in divine justice, a faith which our high modern economic prosperity seems to be far on the way to destroy. (Not many of our fountains, wells, faucets, or water-taps are inscribed with a tribute to God.[63]) But it is not just a matter of indigence or affluence. The "poor in spirit" (Matt. 5:3), who are to have a place in the kingdom of heaven, do not include those of the poor who are without faith, and do include those of the rich who have not succumbed to their wealth.

The mention of inheritance in Jas. 2:5, not so expressed in Matt. 5:3 or Luke 6:20, probably represents the more accurate form of this testimony

[57]ἀκούσατε.

[58]ἀκούσατε.

[59]ἔχετε.

[60]Lit. "in the sight of the world," τῷ κόσμῳ, probably *dativus commodi* (cf. Acts 7:20; 2 Cor. 10:4).

[61]See Aristeas 15, "rich in spirit"; also the rabbinic "rich in goodwill," "rich in law," *Tanhuma* xxxiv.3.

[62]See Moule, *Idiom Book,* p. 46; contrast Matt. 5:3.

[63]W. M. Calder, "Inscriptions of Southern Galatia," *American Journal of Archaeology* 36 (1932), p. 463. For the religious association cf. the words of Isa. 55:1 inscribed on the fountain in the village square of Huntly, Scotland, and the annual well-dressing festivals in the villages of Derbyshire, England.

to the words of Jesus. This eternal promise to "those that love him" was implicit in the very concept of the kingdom (Ropes, p. 195). A closer parallel to the Hellenistic "faith-sight antithesis" (Dibelius) would be Jewish sayings about the reversal of poor and rich. But there is no doubt that James was directly inspired by a dominical word like Luke 6:20. J. Abelson shows that the kingdom (*malkuth shamayim*) and the Fatherhood of God are the twin concepts that lie "at the root of the mysticism and the *Shechinah*."[64] Bestowed exclusively on Israel, the chosen people (*'am segullah*), as a mark of God's election-love[65] the Shechinah now rested on the poor, who, as the new Israel, would inherit its splendor in the coming messianic kingdom.

6 The conduct described in vv. 1–4 is a violation of the Christian brotherhood of man, and it does not even give the sinners worldly security from oppression by this very same rich class to whom they are showing such conspicuous servility: and to all this oppression is added the persecution of Christianity by Jews, e.g., at first, by Paul. Here James not only shares with the prophets, from Amos to John the Baptist, their passion for social justice, but also declares emphatically his distinctively Christian loyalty and devotion to Christ.

You have had only contempt for[66] means not merely "disdain" (KJV "despised") but "actively treat with disdain." Since the reference here to *the poor* probably harks back to the poor worshipper of v. 2, we might almost translate "that beggar."[67] Clearly the discrimination against the poor took more active, serious, and even physical forms than being snubbed in church. The other verb,[68] whose literal meaning is "to act the potentate" and so *to oppress,* also has more violent, almost physical overtones. In the LXX, especially in the Prophets, both terms are used in denouncing social injustice, "the sighing of the poor," which banishes the Shechinah.

The distinction between criminal and private trials is not important here; a successful action for debt can be as vexatious and damaging to its victim as a fine for a traffic violation (if that is technically criminal), and v. 6 embraces both sorts. We think v. 6 at least chiefly contemplates the kind of oppression the poorer Jews had suffered for centuries before Christ, and v. 7 introduces the religious persecution of the Christians—not prosecution, for no law specifically prohibiting Christianity is known or is likely to have then existed. Thus Pilate's conviction of Jesus was on political grounds (see John

---

[64]*Jewish Mysticism* (1913), p. 85.
[65]Heb. *'ahᵃbāh*.
[66]For ἀτιμάζω in this sense cf. Prov. 14:21; 22:22; Sir. 10:23, of the poor; b. *Ber.* 43b; Mark 12:4; Luke 20:11; Acts 5:41.
[67]See Bl.-D., § 263; contrast "the poor," v. 5.
[68]καταδυναστεύω.

19:12). These "courts" were probably the local Jewish sanhedrin (Exod. 21:6; Judg. 5:10; Susanna 49) in every village, with a High Court in Jerusalem (Matt. 10:17; Acts 4:1; 13:50), to whom, within limits, Rome gave jurisdiction over Jewish cases.[69]

Drag[70] is used of the dragging of Paul from the Temple, Acts 21:30; so similarly another verb[71] is used in Acts 8:13; 17:6; and after such seizures the rich evidently found their claim or accusations endorsed by complaisant or venal judges.[72] The practice of the Pharisees throws light on the legal machinations of the rich: they too are accused in the NT (Matt. 6:15; 15:5f.; Mark 7:11–13). Elsewhere Christians are urged, if necessary, to accept even legal injustice, and be prepared to suffer rather than appeal to pagan justice (see Matt. 5:40; 1 Cor. 6:7).

They[73] stresses the responsibility of the rich. The grammarians suspect a Semitism. According to Moule, this and Luke 19:2 "are very curious."[74] "There is also in some cases an un-Greek frequency in the use of the possessive *autou* (his), etc.; and a Semitic idiom is *possibly* [emphasis added] behind the curious repetition of *autos* (he) in Luke xix.2 ..., and Jas. ii.6."[75] We do not deny this possibility; but we think there is another.

We have noted and discussed the similar use of "he"[76] in 1:18, where we have shown we believe it is a mistake to try to empty "this" and "that" (as well as "he") of all emphasis.[77] It is rather like *ille* (Silver Latin, *iste*) in its use: "*You* have *despised* the poor (as the Lord does not). Do not the *rich* (as contrasted with the poor) oppress you, and is it not actually *they* who drag you to court? Do not *they* blaspheme ... ?" Here *they* takes up *the rich* (emphatic as the Greek order shows) and has the emphasis of antithesis in contrast to the poor of Jas. 2:5 and 6a—the force which Moule appears to overlook in Luke 5:1. "The rich" has emphasis, as against "the poor"; "they," epanaleptic, takes up "the rich," with emphasis, as we think "he" in 1:18 takes up "the Father," etc.

Very often "he" in Greek implies a contrast with other persons, who may be either specific or undefined, as in (*a*) "Don't do that, James; I will do

[69]Found six times in the LXX and in the NT only in 1 Cor. 6:24, κριτήριον is common in papyri as "tribunal," and is used even in Plato *Laws* vi.767b, though the regular Attic term is δικαστήριον.
[70]ἕλκω.
[71]σύρω.
[72]For Jewish cases, see Bonsirven, *Le Judaïsme palestinien au temps de Jésus-Christ* I ([2]1934), p. 53.
[73]αὐτοί.
[74]*Idiom Book*, p. 121.
[75]*Ibid.*, p. 176.
[76]αὐτός.
[77]Moule, *op. cit.*, p. 122, §§ 2.ii and 3.

it myself"; and (*b*) "I like to type letters myself." This personal contrast is not always present: "He preaches temperance, but himself is a beer-brewer." Possibly he never comes within miles of his brewery: the "contrast" is in the supposed inconsistency. Where the other term in the contrast is only vague, "he" sometimes amounts to the English "actual" or "actually." "Let me see the actual will" is equivalent, and usually even preferable, to "Let me see the will itself."[78] In Jas. 2:6 and 7 we would translate *actually*.

7 Blasphemy is an attempt to injure a man by gravely malignant speech; against God, it is the sin of attempting to bring him into dishonor by such speech. In the OT blasphemy, in the last analysis, always refers to irreverence toward God; and besides speech certain actions, such as Gentile desecration of his name (Isa. 66:3; 1 Macc. 2:6) or molestation of his people (Isa. 52:5), constitute blasphemy, as sins against the majesty and power of God.[79]

To profane the name of the Lord[80] was a special type of blasphemy, punishable by stoning.[81] It included irreverence, insincerity, and some flagrant moral breaches forgiven only at death,[82] and also idolatry[83] and impudent disparagement of the Torah,[84] or putting shame on the name of Yahweh.[85] So at Lyons and Vienne the apostates are said by their apostasy to be bringing discredit on Christianity, "blaspheming the way."[86]

The *name by which you are called* probably indicates that the Antiochene name "Christians" for the believers was already current among other Jewish followers of Christ (see Acts 11:26). The death of James the brother of John is recorded in the next chapter (Acts 12:2) after Paul had

---

[78]Thus in Aristophanes *Eq.* 74ff., Cleon's straddle is so wide that he has one foot in Pylos (compare Sphacteria), the other in the ecclesia at Athens, and ὁ πρωκτός ἐστιν αὐτόχρημ' ἐν Χάοσιν ("among the Chaones," a native tribe near Ambracia, Thuc. ii.80.5). χρῆμα is often used by way of apposition or description even with a noun of another gender, e.g., τυραννὶς χρῆμα σφαλερόν (Herodotus iii.53); so here αὐτόχρημα, used adverbially, is almost the same as αὐτός, meaning "actually," and is given as one of the Greek words for "actual" in C. D. Yonge's old *English-Greek Lexicon* (1870); here LS translate "in very deed," "really and truly," and for both its other two occurrences, in Aelian and Lucian, both of the 2nd century A.D., give "just," "exactly." We suggest that in instances of weaker emphasis "indeed" might be adequate.
[79]See *JE* VII, p. 485; *TDNT* I, pp. 621ff.
[80]Heb. *hillul ha-shēm*.
[81]Lev. 2:10–16; Num. 15:30f.; Amos 2:7; Mishnah *Sanhedrin; ERE, s.v.* "Blasphemy" (I. Abrahams).
[82]b. *Yoma* 86a.
[83]S. Num. 112 on 15:31.
[84]S. Num. 112 on 15:30.
[85]b. *Pes.* 93b. Cf. Acts 26:11, where we think ἠνάγκαζον is no more conative than ἐδίωκον.
[86]Eusebius *Eccl. Hist.* v.1.48; cf. Tertullian *Idol.* xiv: *ne nomen blasphemetur*; 2 Clem. 13:1, ἵνα τὸ ὄνομα (of Christ) δι' ἡμᾶς μὴ βλασφημῆται.

spent a year at Antioch, which was in close contact with Jerusalem (Acts 11:27–30). The innovation of the name "Christians" would lend point to this verse in James (2:7). The phrase "the honorable name" (i.e., of Christ, from which the Christians got their designation "Christians") has been found at Pompeii;[87] and before the evangelization of Antioch, believers had spoken of "the only name under heaven by which we must be saved" (Acts 4:12; 5:41). *By which you are called* is not in Greek idiom but Semitic, a quotation from Amos 9:12, which James uses also in his speech to the Council (Acts 15:17).[88] The idea of a name being "called upon" someone is common in the LXX (e.g., Jer. 14:19), and here implies Christian profession (Matt. 10:22; Mark 13:13; Acts 9:16), possibly with reference to a baptismal formula (Acts 8:16).[89]

The consecration of Israel to Yahweh[90] is naturally extended to the new Israel, the faithful in Christ. To ill-treat the poor, therefore, was *ipso facto* to ill-treat Christ; for the Shechinah is said to suffer with those who suffer;[91] he who strikes the cheek of an Israelite strikes, as it were, the cheek of the Shechinah;[92] and in any case the Epistle is addressed at least primarily to the Jews.

In 2:8–11 James is meeting on their own ground those Christian Jews who, as they quite properly might, still clung to the old law; but he shows them what that involves, and he repudiates the rulings according to which too many sought to annul the rigors of the old law, and urges them to adopt the Christian attitude, and law of liberty (vv. 12f.).

8 The first crux here is the meaning of the Greek particle,[93] which KJV ignores; is it adversative, "however" (Ropes, Cranfield), or affirmative, "verily," "really" (Hort)? We prefer the latter alternative.

No sane man could have pretended even to himself that the conduct of 2:1–4 was a way of fulfilling the law of love. It is not quite so ludicrous to consider the unlikely possibility that "however" could be used in a tenor like this: "If, however, I am doing some of you an injustice, if in fact you do not all behave as in vv. 1–4, if in fact some of you are fulfilling the law of love, well and good: but if not, you are sinning and will suffer for it!" This possibility will be acceptable only if we believe that James is expressly recognizing that among the hearers of his Epistle an appreciable number are

[87]MM, *s.v.* ὄνομα.
[88]On the invocation of the name (Heb. *qārā' ba-shēm*) see K. Kohler, "The Tetragrammaton," *Journal of Jewish Lore and Philosophy* (Jan., Oct., 1919), pp. 19ff.
[89]W. Heitmüller, *Im Namen Jesu* (1903), p. 92.
[90]b. *Pes.* 54a; Gen. R. 11.
[91]Yalquṭ on Prov., 20.
[92]b. *Sanh.* 58b.
[93]μέντοι.

not in fact guilty of the sin he has been indicting. We think that James would concede that here, and in the host of other faults he censures in this Epistle (which confirms the picture Jesus gives of the too common insincerity of the contemporary established religion), not all his flock are in the same sad case; but even so we think the other translation is right. It is more apt for an Epistle hopefully, we are sure, intended for more than an immediate occasion; and the break thus made before the transition from the delinquents he has been rebuking to Christians in general, and to his statement of the vital choice to be made by us all, is by no means ineffective.

James has already looked at certain examples of spurious Christianity: "hearing" (1:22, 23, 25), ritual observance (1:26, 27), faith (2:1); here he deals with another, observance of law.

The phrase *sovereign law* (*nomos basilikos*)[94] has been interpreted in at least four different ways. "Sovereign" may be used:

i. For kings, who, unlike slaves, obey the law freely and gladly,[95] with a possible allusion to the Stoic idea of "supremely sovereign reason."[96] So Zahn, Dibelius.

ii. As king. The command to love, on which all others hang (Rom. 13:8; Gal. 5:14), is called "supreme."[97]

iii. Of the kingdom (*lex regina*); i.e., the law of love (*Liebesgebot*) in Lev. 19:18 (LXX), which governs the kingdom (2:5): so Mayor, Ropes, Windisch, Rendall.

For the most part these interpretations are merely derivative; we prefer:

iv. From a king, namely, Christ.[98] A sovereign law, *simpliciter,* might be the bad law of a bad king. Here is a law that is above all others *sovereign*, the law of the King of kings. Our heavenly King is a "king," and his realm is a "kingdom": so his law is "sovereign."

In his thought and idiom James is nearer to Classical Greek than most of the NT writers are. Just as anarthrous *sovereign law*[99] would suggest to an earlier Greek a law of the king of Persia,[100] who to him was not "the king," but "king" without the article, as if it were a proper noun, "The Great

---

[94]Found in Xenophon *Oecon.* xiv.7; see also Dan. 2:5; 1 Esdras 1:7; Tobit 1:20.
[95]Clem. Alex. vi.164; vii.73.
[96]λόγος βασιλικώτατος, Epictetus iv.6.20.
[97]For *lex rex* in Greek literature see Plato *Gorg.* 484B; Pindar fragm. 169: "Law, the sovereign of all, mortals and immortals" (νόμος ὁ πάντων βασιλεὺς θανατῶν καὶ ἀθανάτων); see C. H. Dodd, *The Bible and the Greeks* (1935), p. 39.
[98]Bauer, Deissmann, with K. L. Schmidt (*TDNT* I, *s.v.* βασιλικος, p. 591).
[99]νόμος βασιλικός.
[100]Xenophon *Oecon.* xiv.7.

King,'' so James, as John Wesley said, might well think of "sovereign law" as the Law of the Great (Heavenly) King. Law as originating from, and worthy of, a wise king is found in the OT (*Dominus regnavit*, Ps. 97:1), and also in Greek literature.[101] We venture to suggest that the curious omission of the article with *sovereign law* is an effect flowing from the adjective *sovereign,* which latter word in its Christian connotation is here influenced by the thought and anarthrous idiom of the pagan Greek noun "king." Or perhaps *sovereign law* without the article is just the same idiom as omits the article in the law of liberty in v. 12?

The comprehensive use of the term "the law of the Great King" is, we think, more likely here than the selective, which would indicate "the sovereign rule," without prejudice to other vital rules such as that forbidding idolatry: but the narrower interpretation is not altogether impossible; thus Paul, 1 Cor. 13:13, expressly ranks "love" even above faith. Nevertheless the emphatic exaltation expressed in the term "sovereign" is more apt for suggesting the law as a whole; so in the next verse (9) law is indisputably comprehensive, and the next verses (10–14) deliberately set to justify that comprehensive use. Even the law of liberty (v. 12) is no less comprehensive, in its own sense, than the OT notion of God's law.

We would translate 2:8: "If you fulfil the sovereign law (or? our Great King's law), according to the Scripture, 'Thou shalt....' " This interpretation also chimes with James's view of law as messianic Torah: "The Holy One, blessed be He, interprets to them the grounds of a new Torah which the Holy One, blessed be He, will give to them by the hand of King Messiah."[102]

The doctrine of this passage is found, if sometimes negatively, in almost all the world's religions. Though there are many expressions of neighborly love in the OT and later Judaism, it *is* inclined to be negative,[103] as well as predominantly egoistic and exclusive. "The Israelite," observed Stauffer, "loves his people with the same preferential love as is shown it by God."[104] It is easy to see how such a selective attitude fostered "respect of persons" even in Christianized Jews. Moreover, the standard of loving others "as yourself" is probably neither very clear nor inspiring;[105] in this matter, as in others, James brings us nearer to Christ and his words: "This is

[101]Ps.-Plato *Minos* 317c: "the right is sovereign law, and that which is not right, not" (τὸ μὲν ὀρθὸν νόμος ἐστὶ βασιλικός τὸ δὲ μὴ ὀρθὸν οὔ).
[102]Yalqut on Isa. 26; Gen. R. 98; W. D. Davies, *Torah in the Messianic Age* (1952), p. 74.
[103]E.g., Hillel: "whatever is hateful to yourself, do not to your fellow man" (b. *Shab.* 31a).
[104]*TDNT* I, pp. 38f.
[105]See A. E. Taylor, *The Problem of Conduct* (1901), pp. 43ff.

my commandment: love one another, as I have loved you" (John 15:12, NEB).[106]

9 *But* is in antithesis to "indeed" (v. 8); the verb[107] is found only here. "You are working sin": see "work" in Matt. 7:23; Ps. 6:8; 113:16, and see the notes on 1:2, 20 above. James sternly refuses to condone this grave sin as if it were a trivial peccadillo: the plain and unambiguous Greek word,[108] once only in Classical Greek and never in the LXX, "transgressor," explicitly condemns it as an offense against God's law. To the rabbis such transgression was "rebellion,"[109] and broke "the fence of the Torah,"[110] and the "yoke of heaven"—a most heinous sin, indeed effrontery toward the Shechinah.[111]

10–11 It is of paramount importance—throughout the Bible—to remember the distinction between God's attitude to sin and his attitude to sinners, between Law and Grace. The ruthless legalism of all passages like this pertains only to the former. Stricter rabbis taught that the Torah even in its separate statutes was immutable and indivisible: "If a man perform all the commandments, save one, he is guilty[112] of all and each; to break one precept is to defy God who commanded the whole."[113] On Augustine's discussion of the Stoic idea of the solidarity of virtues and its (unlikely) influence on James, see Ropes. A Jewish proselyte had to accept the Law without exception.[114] Aware of this tradition, James illustrates the Torah's basic unity by appealing to the seventh and sixth commandments on adultery and murder, both choice and order possibly dictated by local need (Hort), though more likely by the current LXX version.[115]

Even before the Incarnation, thoughtful Jews recognized that the Law was not the sole key to man's future before God. From all the possible references we cite only Neh. 9:4–31, for example, v. 9: "Thou art a God ready to pardon, gracious and merciful, slow to anger, and of great kindness"; v. 31: "Nevertheless for thy great mercies' sake thou didst not utterly consume them, nor forsake them." But many, though by no means all, of the

[106]See A. Skevington Wood, "Social Involvement in the Apostolic Church," *Evangelical Quarterly* 42 (1970), pp. 211f.
[107]προσωπολημπτεῖτε.
[108]παραβάτης (Vulg. *praevaricator*). See Menninger, *op. cit.*, pp. 18ff.
[109]Heb. *pesha'*.
[110]b. *Shab.* 11a; Eccl. 10:8.
[111]b. *Yoma* 36b; Schechter, *Rabbinic Theology*, ch. XIV; see our note on 2:1.
[112]Heb. *'āshēm*.
[113]b. *Shab.* lxx.2; cf. Deut. 27:26 LXX; Lev. 4:2, 13, 22ff.; Gal. 5:3; Schechter, *Rabbinic Theology*, p. 216; SB I, pp. 244ff., III, p. 755.
[114]Sifra on Lev. 19:34.
[115]Cf. Luke 18:20; Rom. 13:19; Rev. 22:15 (contrast 9:21); and see J. Moffatt, "Jesus on Sins," in S. J. Case, ed., *Studies in Early Christianity* (1928), p. 196.

rabbis made a fundamental mistake: they sought, in effect, to make grace part of the code of law, by glossing over the distinction between law and grace, by representing that in many matters a sin was not a sin, or, in small matters, that a law was not a law, and that even when it was a sin or a law a man could run a sort of credit and debit account with God, of good deeds and bad, and so need not try to do more than keep the balance on the right side. Some of the rabbis, too, held that, if the laws that were (sometimes rather arbitrarily) counted of prime importance were carefully observed, less or no respect *need* be given to the others: "light" (? easy) or nonessential,[116] for example, freeing a mother bird,[117] and "heavy" (? burdensome) or "weighty," essential,[118] *corpora legis,*[119] for example, honoring parents (Exod. 20:12), or observing the Sabbath: "The Sabbath weighs against all the precepts: if they keep it, they are reckoned as having done all."[120] Akiba and Hillel also held that to wear phylacteries was to observe the whole Torah;[121] that is, in effect sometimes a law is not a law.[122] All these were essentially subterfuges to escape having to admit the limitations of Law, to escape having to admit that God is not a tyrant whose law is all that counts for deciding whether a man is to be damned or saved. The essence of the contrast between Jas. 2:12 and 9–11 is that the Christian law of liberty gives a place both to law and mercy, with even more sympathy than that with which English Law gives a place to both Law and Equity.

What, then, is James's objection to the Jewish attempts to humanize their cherished legalism? We suggest it is in his righteous insistence that to say a law is not a law, or a sin is not a sin, can lead only to evil, for example, partiality. God, as the Jews always knew, is merciful to *sinners,* but not by any provision of the law. Those who seek to condone what they consider their excusable breaches of God's Law are *ipso facto* closing their hearts to repentance, for which God normally gives us time. No one can *claim* pardon for his sins; but, by his grace, if we sincerely repent, we may hopefully pray to be forgiven.

12–13 These verses clinch the argument for preferring the law of liberty, of which mercy is a part, just as strict law and also equity belong to the law (in the wider sense) of England. The strictness of law cannot be

[116]Heb. *qallāh.*
[117]Deut. 22:7; *Debarim* vi; b. *Qid.* 39b.
[118]Heb. *ḥamûrāh.*
[119]Heb. *gûphê tôrāh.*
[120]*Shemoth Rabba* xxv.
[121]*Aboth* iii.19.
[122]Mitton on 2:10, pp. 92ff.; I. Abrahams, *Studies in Pharisaism and the Gospels* I, p. 26; W. D. Davies, *Paul and Rabbinic Judaism* (1948), p. 120; Mayor; F. F. Bruce, *The Acts of the Apostles* (1951), p. 294; *Commentary on the Book of Acts.* NICNT (1954), p. 307.

humanized by subterfuges which pretend not to impair its integrity as law, but only, as in the law of liberty, by recognizing a distinct but not identical sister principle, at the same time recognizing that it is not identical with law in the narrow sense. James says in effect: "I advise you to *choose* the law of liberty as God's law of life for you: but remember this—just as the old law (which a Christian Jew may still choose as God's law for his life) requires infallibility within its scope, so likewise there is an indispensable requirement in the law of liberty." In England, if you can prove your debt, you can generally recover it from the debtor by process of law, if necessary. Equity, however, takes a wider view: one of its maxims, which we mentioned earlier, is "He who comes to equity must do equity." So in Christianity, as James points out in 2:13, he who seeks pity must show pity. Mercy and law are not really different principles. They are really the same in principle, both resting on God's justice; but they necessarily differ in administration, because it is not possible to frame rules (laws) completely covering all sorts of Christian duty (to God, and through him to our fellow men), such as Christian charity, gratitude, and kindness. Just as in England "the whole distinction between equity and law is not so much a matter of substance or principle as of form and history,"[123] so it is in the distinction between the earliest OT concept of God's law and the Christian concept of the "law of liberty." For anarthrous *law of liberty* compare "royal law" (2:8 and our note).

Here in *those who will be judged*, the Greek participle[124] has an ordinary meaning, "(men) who are going to be judged by the law of liberty," signifying not just a future event but a deliberate choice of the law of liberty (and mercy) in preference to the old ruthless rigor of the "Law." But if a man so chooses to hope in the law of liberty (and mercy) he must remember that he who seeks mercy must do mercy, and so must strive, with God's grace, to make mercy his own rule of practice in speech and act: otherwise he will come under the old ruthlessness of the "Law."

What seems a difficult ellipse (v. 13)—made even more difficult by the lack of particles—is not really hard: the thought and its sequence are clear enough. 2:10, 11 states the rigors of the law of ordinances; we have offered our interpretation of v. 12: "See that you so speak and act that (by showing pity) you will come under the merciful law of liberty"; v. 13 continues: "Otherwise (having been a merciless man), you will be judged without mercy, whereas (in the other case, the case of the merciful man) mercy triumphs over legalistic judgment."[125]

[123]E. H. T. Snell, *Principles of Equity* ([27]1973), p. 2.
[124]μέλλοντες.
[125]We read: (1) ἀνέλεος, "merciless"; *pace* ἀνίλεως, an obvious correction followed by TR and inferior mss. LS, *s.v.*, quote only this passage; ἀνελεής⫽ἀνηλεής (Menander) is

"To be judged" in v. 12 is judgment (consideration and decision) according to the law of liberty; in v. 13, twice, *judgment*[126] (consideration and decision) is according to the law of ordinances, without the intervention of mercy. Of course, it is the decision that is conclusive, but the meaning of "judgment" and "to be judged" is not necessarily to be confined to that. Against R. A. Knox, "give an honourable welcome,"[127] "true Christian pity,"[128] in neither occurrence in v. 12 does the word mean human judgment: dominating James's mind is the thought of *divine* judgment, with or without mercy, upon the merciful and the merciless respectively.

Man's duty of *pity* is a typically Jewish thought, with which goes the corollary that God will show mercy only to the merciful. "To him who is unmerciful to the created, Heaven is unmerciful."[129] Only obstinate legalism prevented the Jewish lively sense of God's love from leading sooner to the recognition of mercy[130] as an equal partner with ordinances in God's justice.[131] The Jews were long content to keep mercy (*ordinata*) apart from legalistic "justice" (*absoluta*), even declaring that God has two angels, Gabriel, the angel of justice, and Michael, that of mercy. He is also said to have two thrones, one of (legalistic) justice for the primeval God of justice, Elohim (Exod. 34:6), the other of mercy for Yahweh the God of mercy (Exod. 34:6), the world being created in accordance with both "justice" and "mercy," both being necessary for its continuance;[132] yet, see 2 Esdras 7:33f. for the emphasis on justice alone. "Rabbinic thought," writes M. Kadushin, "is dominated by the idea of God's love rather than by the idea of His 'justice',"[133] which is apt to connote chiefly things like the punishment of Adam or "visiting the sins of the fathers upon the children" (Exod. 34:7); and even in this chastisement the rabbis see the love of God. So Philo observes: "God not only pities after he judges, but he judges after he has pitied: for with him pity is older than judgment."[134]

Like the prophets, then, James resolves the tension between justice and mercy by giving precedence to mercy; so also Shakespeare:

"Attic" (Classical). (2) κατακαυχᾶται (B א), indicative, not the subjunctive of inferior Mss. κατακαυχάσθω, see Ropes, *ad loc.*

[126]κρίσις. Contrast κρῖμα, 3:1: "We shall receive greater damnation."

[127]*The NT . . . newly translated from the Vulgate Latin* (1947); Vulg. *superexaltat.*

[128]Comm., p. 100.

[129]b. *Shab.* 151b; D. Daube, *The NT and Rabbinic Judaism* (1956), pp. 254ff.; SB I, pp. 144ff., 203ff.

[130]*middat rahamim.*

[131]*middat ha-din.*

[132]A. Cohen, *Everyman's Talmud,* pp. 16ff.; A. Edersheim, *The Life and Times of Jesus the Messiah* I (1890), p. 242.

[133]*The Rabbinic Mind* (²1965), p. 219.

[134]*Unchangeableness of God* i.16; b. *Pes.* 161b; G. F. Moore, *Judaism* I, pp. 387ff.

And earthly power doth then show likest God's
When mercy seasons justice.[135]

This does not mean that mercy violates justice, for justice must be done.[136] As "judge" in the sense of "vindicator" or "champion," God extends his grace or "mercy" (*ḥesed*), that is, something more than justice, to the poor and oppressed.[137] So in his perfect righteousness, justice and mercy are both combined. In all this there is nothing that a Christian could not consider admirable. The bitterness of the Epistle of James must have been aroused by a dominant recrudescence of stark legalism (and corresponding insincerity) in Palestine in the time of Christ and James, especially, as the Gospels indicate, among the scribes and Pharisees (Matt. 5:7; 6:14f.; 18:21ff.; 25:4; Luke 6:36). Nevertheless, though sometimes regarded as antithetical, even antagonistic, law and mercy are really complementary, "for neither can have its perfect work unless it is combined with the other";[138] but, as James insists, men cannot *claim* lenience from God: for example, justice forbids mercy to the merciless.

Here James (as usual) is at one with Paul: *charisma* is the trademark of both their "gospels," as contrasted with the legalistic letter of the law. But he who wants grace or mercy (in such a context one may use either word, though *charisma* is peculiar to Paul, except once in 1 Peter) must show mercy. Regard for social status as paramount is a denial of "mercy." So James tells us to remember that we are to be "tried" not by a judgment that is the sanction of the (Mosaic) law, but, as Paul constantly, and James here, say quite clearly, by a judgment tempered by mercy. Since the advantage of a judgment tempered by mercy is offered us in Christ, the Christian must always so speak and act that by always showing mercy in this life, or trying so to do, he may have some color of hope with which to face that judgment. Not that we can do more than try: we cannot *earn* salvation; that comes only by mercy, or, in Paul's word, *charisma*, the gift of "grace" (*charis*).[139]

b. Christian faith expressed in Christian acts (2:14–26)

14 *What good is it, my brothers, if somebody says he has faith, but produces no works? Is faith enough to save him?*

15 *If a brother or sister is without clothes or in want of daily food,*

16 *and one of you says to them: "Go in peace, keep warm and eat well," but you do not give them what their body needs, what good is it?*

---

[135]*Merchant of Venice* IV.i.176f.; cf. *Hamlet* III.iii.45f.

[136]W. Eichrodt, *Theology of the OT* I (E.T. 1961), p. 124; A. Richardson, ed., *A Theological Word Book of the Bible* (1950), p. 119.

[137]Cf. W. F. Lofthouse, "The Righteousness of Jahveh," *ExT* 50 (1938–39), p. 343.

[138]R. H. Kennett, in A. S. Peake, ed., *The People and the Book* (1925), p. 390.

[139]See also the Introduction (pp. 31ff.) on the ethnic importance of the Jewish Law.

17 *So, too, faith without works is by itself dead.*

18 *Indeed one will say: "You claim to have faith, and I have works. Let me see your faith without your works, and through my works I will let you see my faith."*

19 *You believe that there is one God. Good. The devils also believe, and shudder.*

20 *But will you accept the truth, vain fellow, that faith without works is sterile?*

21 *Was not our father Abraham justified by works, when he offered his son Isaac on the altar?*

22 *Do you see that faith shared in his works and by his works faith was consummated?*

23 *And the scripture was fulfilled that says, Abraham put his faith in God, and it was reckoned to his credit for righteousness, and he was called God's friend.*

24 *Do you see that a man is justified by works and not by mere faith?*

25 *Similarly, was not Rahab the prostitute also justified by works, for receiving the messengers and sending them out another way?*

26 *For as the body without the spirit is dead, so faith without works is dead also.*

14 *What good is it . . . ?*[140] still heard apparently today (*shū il-faida*) in Jerusalem,[141] and common in some earlier Greek but not in the Bible (Job 15:3; 1 Cor. 15:32), is quite Socratic (Platonic) in this application of the test of "good." The meaning is clear. To paraphrase: "What is the use of a man claiming[142] to 'have faith' in our Lord Jesus Christ (2:1) if it is without works? Can this kind of faith save him?" *Save*, clearly *not* "unreflective" (Blackman), has the full soteriological sense to be expected in an argument for the soteriological significance of *works* in faith, and the soteriological examples of Abraham and Rahab.[143] The aorist[144] signifies "achieve salvation for him," not merely "promote it."

In the first question *faith* is personal and partial, as when a man says, "I have money"; the second *faith*, which has the article of previous reference,[145] is generic, as in "Faith can remove mountains," "that kind of faith"; so Bede, "that faith which you say you have."[146] The Greek interrogative[147] expects the answer "no" to the question: "Is faith enough to save him?" This latter kind of *faith* is impotent, unable to save, without

---

[140]τί τὸ ὄφελος;
[141]Bishop, *Apostles of Palestine*, p. 185.
[142]λέγῃ.
[143]See also the Introduction, "Faith and Works," pp. 35ff.
[144]σῶσαι.
[145]ἡ πίστις—see Moule, p. 111.
[146]*Fides illa quam vos habere dicitis.*
[147]μή.

works and *ipso facto* without worth. Such *works,* like feeding and clothing the poor as described by James (1:25, 27; 2:8), are "works of love" (*Liebeswerke*) similar to rabbinic *gemiluth ḥasadim,* [148] but essentially different from the ceremonial *mitswôt* attacked by Paul. [149] Whereas "Paul's contrast was a novel one, viz., between the works of an old and abandoned system and the faith of a newly adopted one, James is led to draw the more usual contrast between the faith and works which are *both* deemed necessary under the *same* system" (Ropes, p. 205). "Works of love" are one of the three pillars upon which the world, i.e., the social order, rests, [150] and are associated, and even identified, with the Shechinah itself: "How great is the virtue of charity? If a man gives only one coin to a poor brother, he becomes worthy to receive the face of the Shechinah." [151] Similarly, "the Shechinah is charity." [152] Significantly James also associates the Shechinah with "good works" (2:1ff.).

15 A simple analogy illustrates the issue. Suppose a fellow Christian, *brother or sister,* possibly husband and wife (but see 1:27, "widows"), is found, perhaps even in church (2:2f.), in rags and starving. Literally "naked" (*nudus*), e.g., Gen. 2:25; 3:7, the Greek word[153] usually indicates a lack of clothing (see Job 22:6; Isa. 20:2, 3; 58:7; 2 Macc. 11:12), sometimes a total lack (Mark 14:52), but other times "without an outer garment" (John 21:7; see Matt. 25:36). The meaning of *daily,* [154] only here in the NT, not in the LXX, and occasionally in Classical Greek, [155] is difficult to determine, depending on whether it is taken as "that which is on day," or "that which has day upon it." Instead of *daily food,* we could translate "the day's supply of food." [156] The choice of a less usual verb for "is"[157] (without clothes) may be a delicate and intentional touch, suggesting continuity with a previous state, not merely a temporary condition—"a

---

[148]Cohen, *op. cit.,* pp. 224ff.; SB IV, pp. 559ff.

[149]Schechter, *Rabbinic Theology,* p. 214. On the three (Greek, Jewish, and Christian) types of "good works," especially with his caveat on the General Epistles, see W. C. van Unnik, "The Teaching of Good Works in I Peter," *NTS* 1 (1954–55), pp. 984ff.

[150]*Aboth* i.2.

[151]Yalquṭ on Ps. 17; b. *Baba Bathra* 10a.

[152]R. Samuel b. Mai on Cant. 3:10.

[153]γυμνός.

[154]ἐφημέριος (Doric and Aeolic ἐπάμερος). LS 9 (1940), p. 606.

[155]E.g., Diodorus iii.32; Dion. Hal. viii.41.5. See Mayor, *ad loc.;* F. Field, *Notes on the Translation of the NT* (1899), pp. 236f.; H. Fränkel, *Transactions and Proceedings of the American Philological Association* 77 (1946), pp. 131ff.

[156]On the possible Aramaic behind "daily bread" in the Lord's Prayer (Matt. 6:11; Luke 11:3), see F. H. Chase, *The Lord's Prayer in the Early Church* (1891), p. 48. Cf. also B. M. Metzger, "How Many Times does *epiousios* occur outside the Lord's Prayer?" in *Historical and Literary Studies* (1968), pp. 64ff.; W. Mundle, *s.v.* "Bread," *New International Dictionary of NT Theology,* ed. L. Coenen, C. Brown, *et al.,* I (1975).

[157]ὑπάρχω for εἰμί.

backward look to an antecedent condition which has been protracted into the present,''[158] although this sense was lost in later Greek.[159] That such poverty and neglect could occur apparently in the Christian Church is hard to believe, but is clearly documented in Christian literature.[160] Apparently the Jews had a similar problem in the matter of feeding the poor in the synagogue.[160a]

16   Instead of caring for the poor—to do this is to "walk after the Shechinah''[161]—this "Christian" contents himself with mere words, a curt, colloquial "Good luck to you," literally *Go in peace.*"[162] The idea, as Moule correctly observes,[163] is not a *progressive* entering into peace, but departure in a state of peace. "Keep warm and eat well"—the form of the original[164] is important: imperative, not indicative (Plumptre), passive not middle,[165] present rather than aorist. This failure of Christian love was not accidental, but sustained and deliberate. The irony is unmistakable. To *warm* is frequent in the OT, especially of warm clothes, e.g., Hos. 7:7; in the NT see Mark 14:54; John 18:18, 25.[166] To *eat well* is a vulgarism, literally "gorge oneself," like a ravenous beast, especially of cattle,[167] as in early Greek.[168] "Go in peace,"[169] addressed to beggars, may still be heard today in the streets of Jerusalem,[170] and it has the same effect. It signals the end of the encounter. The speaker does nothing and goes off, leaving the beggar still cold and hungry, with the law of love unfulfilled.

The rabbis advised those unable to provide relief at least to speak words of comfort: "My soul goes out to you because I have nothing to give

[158]See M. R. Vincent, *Word Studies in the NT* I (1887), p. 743.

[159]MM, *s.v.* ὑπάρχω for the papyri; Bl.-D, §§ 114f.

[160]E.g., *Gospel according to the Hebrews*, in M. R. James, *Apocryphal NT*, p. 6.

[160a]See *Jewish Encyclopaedia* (1901), 3, pp. 667ff., "Charity" (W. Nowack), especially noting the charity box (*kuppah*) and bowl (*tamhoi*), which provided food and money for the poor.

[161]b. *Soṭah* 15a.

[162]ὑπάγετε ἐν εἰρήνῃ. The form with εἰς, sometimes futurive (cf. Mark 5:34; Luke 7:50; 8:48), was probably influenced by the LXX: cf. *lᵉkhu lᵉshālôm*, e.g., Judg. 18:6 and often; Luke 2:29 *Nunc Dimittis;* so *pax vobiscum* (J. H. Moulton, *A Grammar of NT Greek* II [1919], p. 463; SB I, p. 138).

[163]*Idiom Book*, pp. 70ff.

[164]θερμαίνεσθε καὶ χορτάζεσθε.

[165]Ropes, *ad loc.*, notes correctly that the middle "warm and feed yourselves" would need the reflexive pronoun.

[166]For secular use, see Galen *de Vir Med. Simpl.* ii, cited by Wettstein, which differentiates between that which warms and that which merely wards off the cold; also Plutarch *Quaest. Conviv.* vi.6.

[167]χορτάζω, cf. χόρτος.

[168]E.g., Plato *Republic* IX, p. 286, and particularly the comic poets; cf. LS, *s.v.* χορτάζω.

[169]*rūh ma'-as-salami*.

[170]Bishop, *op. cit.*, p. 185.

you.''[171] Apparently this "Christian" seems to be well able to provide relief: his ability is not in question, only his faith. He is in the same class as those condemned by Christ in the Parable of the Last Judgment (Matt. 25:41ff.). This parable, like the Lord's Prayer ("daily bread": compare *what their body needs,* and v. 15), seems to have deeply influenced James. This scene gives us a glimpse into the Church's earliest efforts to implement the social teaching of Jesus. For example, the Church at Jerusalem adapted the Jewish system of poor relief, and cared for the poor, notably the widows, at its daily services.[172] In such a setting it is not hard to imagine some bureaucratic church official dismissing this deserving case with a smug cliché: "Go in peace." "The sight of distress is unpleasant to these dainty Christians. They bustle out the wretched-looking brother or sister with seeming kindness and what sounds like an order for immediate relief, but without taking any step to carry out the order" (Mayor). These "dainty" Christians are full of words but empty of works.[173] But words in themselves without clothes and food are worthless: hence the reiterated, unanswerable question: "What good is it?" (v. 14).

17 See vv. 20 and 26. This verse is just a vivid way of stating that without *works* faith is no faith at all any more than a corpse is a man. Having form, this faith lacks force—"outwardly inoperative, because inwardly dead."

By itself does not qualify *dead* (RV) but *faith*: so KJV "faith alone," or better RSV "faith by itself,"[174] taking the phrase[175] as equivalent to *per se.* Faith, therefore, is considered "not merely in relation to other things, not merely in its utility . . . but in its own very and inherent nature" (Hort).

Note the vicious circle: Faith that produces no works is dead; and dead faith cannot produce works.

18 One may put it like this (by way of challenge that the challenger knows cannot be met): "You claim to have faith: I have works. I can prove my faith by my works. But I defy you to prove to me the existence of your faith without works: for, of course, you cannot do it."

i. The Greek[176] for *Indeed* is adversative, "Nay" when following an expressed or implied assertion that is not itself an expressed or implied

[171]Lev. R. xxxiv.15; Cohen, *op. cit.,* p. 224.
[172]See J. Jeremias, *Jerusalem in the Time of Jesus* (E.T. 1969), pp. 130ff.
[173]"In the magnificent cathedral, the Honorable and Right Reverend . . . High Court Preacher . . . steps forth, the favorite of the fashionable world. He appears before a chosen company and preaches *with emotion* on a text chosen by himself: 'God has chosen the base things of the world, and the things that are despised'—and nobody laughs" (S. Kierkegaard; translation adapted from Kierkegaard's *Attack Upon "Christendom" 1854–1855,* trans. and ed. W. Lowrie [1944], p. 181).
[174]ff. *sola;* Vulg. *in semetipsa.*
[175]καθ' ἑαυτήν.
[176]ἀλλ'.

negative, "Yea" when following an expressed or implied negative. Here it is "Yea" after the cumulative implied negatives.[177]

ii.   *One* is conceived as a supporter of James's view at least on this point, and most probably as a fellow Christian Jew rather than as a latter-day Aristotle or Rabbi.

iii.   *You* is addressed by this *one* to the prevaricator of v. 14.

iv.   *I* is the *one* of v. 18, the supporter of James's view.

In effect, James says here: You claim to have "faith" and I claim to have "works," actions, behavior. I can prove the existence and quality of my "faith" by my "works" (actions and behavior), but I defy you to prove (to me or any of the rest of mankind) the existence and/or quality of your "faith." For I do not believe that without "works" (actions and behavior) you can possibly have any genuine "faith."

James, we must remember, is contemplating a normal man, not, for example, a helpless paralytic, whose faith, if any, is perceptible only to God.

Here (2:14–26) "faith" is used sometimes to mean mere intellectual belief in God's existence, a faith which even the devils share (v. 19), a dead (vv. 17, 20, 26), useless and fruitless (vv. 14, 16) faith; and sometimes it has the ordinary Christian meaning of faith as the *activity* of a believer seeking to obey God. So also Paul, 1 Cor. 13.

"I have works," or "I have faith," does not here mean, "I have only works," or "have only faith," nor "I have mainly" works or faith. James, like all Christians, believes that Christian works can proceed only from Christian faith and that (except in stricken health) Christian faith cannot fail to produce Christian works: in the activity of Christian belief there can be no distinguishing bias between "faith" and "works."[178]

19   The words *You believe* are not, we think, here addressed to anyone specifically identified in James's mind; and not, we think, a question (Westcott, Hort, von Soden, Nestlé, and others); but, like "Well done," *ahsant,* a familiar Palestinian phrase, ironically affirmative (Mayor, Ropes, Oesterley, and others).[179] The verbal construction "to believe that God exists"[180] instead of "to trust God"[181] emphasizes intellectual acceptance, indicating that faith here is the *fides qua creditur* of orthodox Judaism.[182]

---

[177]τί τὸ ὄφελος . . . ; μὴ δύναται . . . ; (v. 14), τί τὸ ὄφελος . . . ; (v. 16), νεκρά ἐστιν . . . (v. 17).

[178]See further Excursus F, pp. 135ff.

[179]See Bishop, *op. cit.,* p. 186.

[180]πιστεύειν ὅτι.

[181]πιστεύειν with the dative.

[182]See C. H. Dodd, *The Bible and the Greeks,* p. 66; SB III, pp. 189f.; A. Meyer, pp. 123ff. Likewise "there is a world of difference between learning to repeat 'God is an omnipotent being' and learning to address oneself straight to God saying: 'Thou art my rock'" (cited from Régine Pernoud, *Heloise and Abelard,* by William Barclay, *A Spiritual Autobiography* [1975], p. 35).

This ability to assert belief in the existence and uniqueness of God was one—not the sole—indispensable requirement of the Jewish religion;[183] and it did not excuse, much less justify, repudiation of conduct conformable with that faith: on the contrary, the rabbis insisted that the *Shema'*, the pious Jew's daily confession of faith (Deut. 6:4, here quoted by James), was an express acceptance of the yoke of the kingdom (or Kingship) of God,[184] an act embracing, as they said: (1) that acceptance, and (2) commitment to the commandments (*mitswôt:* Deut. 11:13–21) and (3) to the study of the Torah. Indeed, the Shechinah was said to stand in the synagogue when the Jew entered to read the *Shema'*.[185] A midrash on Mic. 6:3 designates *qeri' at Shema'* as a divine edict, and tells how it should be read;[186] another stresses the need for awe: "terror and fear and with trembling and with trepidation."[187] Unfortunately the necessary and salutary emphasis on ritual too often led, as perhaps with us, to its perversion, that is, to insincere ritualism, as if you could guarantee your ultimate salvation merely by reading a passage of the Bible every day and attending worship every Sunday and other day of obligation. The pious Jew even attached merit to the way the *Shema'* was said: "Whosoever prolongs the utterance of the word One[188] shall have his days and years prolonged unto him."[189]

The idea of demonic terror[190] before the holiness of Yahweh (*mysterium tremendum et fascinans*) was familiar in Jewish apocryphal literature;[191] and so was the belief that the *Shema'*, credal recitations, and the charms of magic names and prayers gave protection from the demons.[192] Originally the numinous *shudder*[193] means "to bristle up," with an allusion perhaps to particular OT demons, "hairy ones" or *śe'irim* (Isa. 13:21; 34:14); but Jewish demonology is a vast subject and beyond our scope here.

Against Dibelius, E. Peterson contends that the order of B[194] may well be that of the apotropaic formula, not that of the Christian Kerygma.[195] He also thinks (although we are not sure why) that the "terror" theme,

---

[183]See T. W. Manson, *The Teaching of Jesus* (²1935), p. 192; M. Kadushin, *Worship and Ethics* (1964), p. 86, *The Rabbinic Mind*, pp. 57ff., 348ff.

[184]*malkut shamayim*; Deut. R. vi.4; SB I, pp. 177ff.

[185]J. Abelson, *The Immanence of God in Rabbinical Literature*, p. 123.

[186]Lev. R. xxvii.6.

[187]*Seder Eliyyahu Rabba*, p. 46; M. Kadushin, *Worship and Ethics*, pp. 83ff.

[188]Heb. *'ehād*.

[189]b. *Ber.* 13b.

[190]φρίσσω.

[191]E.g., 1 Enoch 13:3; 69:1, 14; see A. Deissmann, *Light from the Ancient East* (E.T. 1927), p. 260.

[192]Oesterley; J. Trachtenberg, *Jewish Magic and Superstition* (1939), p. 156.

[193]Lat. *horreo*; compare Heb. *śā'ar*.

[194]εἷς θεός (instead of εἷς ἐστιν θεός).

[195]*ΕΙΣ ΘΕΟΣ* (1926), p. 295, n. 3.

familiar in Judaism but especially associated with that of diaspora syn-
cretism which blended the One God with *Aiōn,* may be a pointer to this sort
of background. On the other hand, W. L. Knox notes that the theme is
inscribed on a certain amulet but ignored by Strack-Billerbeck; he thinks that
this may indicate Hellenistic—possibly even universalistic (Oesterley)?—
affinities, or "it may be due to the disappearance of the kerygmatic form of
exorcism from orthodox Judaism in the face of Christian competition."[196]
While it is possible that James is merely using a stock Orphic phrase for
casual illustration,[197] more likely the *Shema'* may well have been an integral
article in the creed of the Jerusalem Church, synonymous even with "taking
the yoke of the kingdom."[198]

The point James is now driving home is that a Christian creed without
corresponding Christian conduct will save neither devil nor man. So William
Tyndale, comparing James and Paul: "The devil hath no promise therefore
he is excluded from Paul's faith. The devil believeth that Christ died, but not
that he died for his sins."[199]

20 This brusque type of address, "Don't you realize . . . ?"[200] is
frequent in the Greek moralists, especially in the diatribe. The adjective
kenos (vain fellow)[201] means "empty," "hollow," "defective." This fits
the present context, where there is no hint of a contrast: e.g., "You are not a
demon, but a human being." The object condemned is not vanity, arrogance, or even doctrine, Pauline or Gnostic (Hilgenfeld, Weinel,
Schammberger), but rather insincerity. This emptyhead's "faith" is sham.
Faith lives by works; without works faith is *sterile*—not "dead," as in vv.
17, 26[202]; but literally "workless," "not at work"[203] (Matt. 20:3): so
"idle," "inactive," "ineffective," "untilled," "fallow," "unproduc-
tive"—clearly a play on the coming "works," "work together," v. 22. See
Milton *On His Blindness*:

> *And that one talent which 'tis* death *to hide*
> *Lodged with me* useless.

---

[196]"Jewish Liturgical Exorcism," *HTR* 31 (1938), p. 194, n. 25.
[197]Moffatt; E. Langton, *Essentials of Demonology* (1949), pp. 198ff.
[198]See Sifre Deut. 32:29.
[199]*The Obedience of a Christian Man* (n.d.), ch. XII: "The Duty of Kings."
[200]γνῶναι, punctiliar aorist conveying asperity.
[201]Rarely of men, it is here close to, if not the same as, NT *raca* (Matt. 5:22; Mayor, Knowling; *contra* Oesterley), OT *rēq* (e.g., Judg. 9:4; 11:3; 2 Sam. 6:20), and esp. Aram. *rēqā,* "empty," of persons "fool"; see T. W. Manson, *The Sayings of Jesus* (1949), p. 156. The Peshitta translates "weak" (Syr. *ḥalāshā*), Vulg. *inanis,* the Corbey ms. *vacue.* Cf. ἄφρων, 1 Cor. 15:36. With the vocative κενέ compare μωρέ, ὦ ταλαίπωρε, *stulte, miser.* See MM, *s.v.*; but also Mitton, p. 111; Epictetus ii.19.8, cited by Hort *ad loc.* See R. Bultmann, *Der Stil der Paulinischen Predigt* (1910), p. 14; Ropes, p. 14; also vv. 14, 19, 22.
[202]Here also TR, with A C K L P Boh. Syr. Eth.
[203]ἀργή, contracted from ἀ-εργής (perhaps by confusion with ἀργός, "shining").

127

Much more than a mere "quibbler" (NEB), the man who professes faith but does not exercise it is a "fool" (*Living Bible*); but while, as in later Jewish literature,[204] such foolishness may be partly intellectual, the prime stress here is ethical. "He who believes in the existence of God," writes John Baillie, "but who lives as if God were not, has fallen much further from God than he who has difficulty in believing in God's existence yet lives in such a way as often to put believers to shame. . . . The real unbeliever is not he whose life witnesses to a belief that he thinks he does not possess, but rather he whose life proves that he does not really believe what he thinks he believes."[204a] To have faith, and knowingly not to use it, is a sin (Jas. 4:17); so Hillel: "An empty man cannot be a sin-fearing man, nor can an ignorant person be pious."[205]

21 We offer this alternative translation to clarify the meaning: "Was not our father, Abraham, shown to be in the right by works, when he offered his son Isaac on the altar?"

"Søren Kierkegaard sank down at the thought of Mount Moriah. None was so great as Abraham. Who can understand him?"[206]

James's choice of Abraham was likely prompted by his opponent (2:19), who would be well aware of the Jewish traditions concerning this supreme type and the true hero of faith.[207] "Our father" has been taken as possible, but not conclusive, proof of the Epistle's Jewish-Christian origin. Paul, for example, extends the phrase to those who were children of Abraham, not by physical but by spiritual descent; and this later became a prime article of Jewish-Christian catechisms.[208] The alternative (but less well-attested) reading "your father" could better point to a Jewish-Christian origin.

The sacrifice of Isaac[209] was regarded as Abraham's greatest trial of faith, in which he glorified the divine name, and to some extent it was the Jewish equivalent of the labors of Hercules.[210] In rabbinic thought Abraham

[204]G. Dalman, *Jesus-Jeshua* (1929), pp. 76f.
[204a]*Our Knowledge of God* (1939), pp. 65, 66.
[205]*Aboth* ii.56; *Aboth de-Rabbi Nathan* version II, xxxiii.36b; also Midrash on Ps. 87:2. On the present verse see Augustine *De diversis quaestionibus* 76; *Enchiridion* 117 (J. P. Migne, ed., *Patrologia Latina* XL, 87, 286).
[206]W. Vischer, *The Witness of the OT to Christ* I (E.T. 1949), p. 20, referring to Kierkegaard's *Fear and Trembling* (1843, E.T. 1941).
[207]See W. Eichrodt, *Theology of the OT* I, pp. 49, 56ff.; SB III, pp. 186ff.; Dibelius, pp. 157ff.; Meyer, pp. 135ff., for Philonic and rabbinic references.
[208]Gal. 3:7ff.; Rom. 4:11f., 16; Justin *Dial.* 134; Clem. Rom. 31:2.
[209] *'aqedat Yitsḥaq*, lit. the "binding of Isaac."
[210]See Gen. 22; *Pirqe Aboth* v.3; 1 Macc. 2:52; b. *Sanh.* 9b; Tanḥuma *Wayyera*, in answer to Ps. 8:5; H. J. Schoeps, "The Sacrifice of Isaac in Paul's Theology," *JBL* 65 (1946), pp. 385ff.; M. E. Andrews, "Peirasmos: A Study in Form Criticism," *ATR* 24 (1942), p. 235; A. C.

is reckoned righteous on account of works of merit.[211] Though important, his "faith" is itself actually a kind of meritorious "work," to be equated with monotheistic belief and faithfulness to the Torah.[212] This is the kind of "faith" and "works" which James seems to be combatting. The "binding of Isaac" shows that Abraham's faith, in this instance, is as unquestioning, untheological, and unsophisticated as the trust of a little child; hence his readiness to sacrifice Isaac. "When Abraham," declared the rabbis, "without any questioning obeyed God's order to sacrifice his son, he was inspired by his love to God."[213] This is why Abraham was *justified*. The Greek verb *dikaioō* means "to declare righteous" or (passive) "to be in the right relationship," and while the forensic and moral are both present in James, the latter dominates. The works by which Abraham, according to James, is justified are not "works of law" (*mitswôt*) but what the rabbis called "works of loving-kindness" (*Liebeswerke*); his readiness to sacrifice Isaac was proof of his faith and revealed the basic relationship of obedience. His justification therefore was based on merit, not of law but of love.[214]

22 James next shows that *faith*, instead of being merely one particular work in Abraham's justification, is indissolubly linked to *works*, neither being unduly stressed at the expense of the other.[215] The clear deduction from the previous verse is that faith and works are indivisible. "Abraham's works were the product and expression of his faith," writes Cranfield (p. 12), "and they were also its completion—in the sense that without them it would not have been real faith." That faith and works seem to be "two magnitudes" (Dibelius, p. 167) in our Epistle is true only in the sense that there was a kind of "faith"—so-called and known to the "emptyhead" of v. 20—that had no works, a dead, fruitless tree (Mayor). They are one or two in the same way as a tree may be regarded as one or two (see, somewhat similarly, v. 26). Body and spirit are one and two just as one happens to consider them. Body without "spirit" is body in the sense of corpse (or *corpus*), but not alive. Body as seen in action is vivified only by "spirit."[216]

Clearly then—taking the sentence as a definite statement rather than

---

Swindell, "Abraham and Isaac: An Essay in Biblical Appropriation," *ExT* 87/2 (1975), pp. 50–53.

[211] SB III, pp. 186–201.

[212]Midr. *Tehillim* lxviii.17; Meyer, p. 133.

[213]See A. Buechler, *Studies in Sin and Atonement* (1928), pp. 126ff., with references.

[214]See also the Introduction, "Faith and Works," pp. 34ff.

[215]Ropes; SB III, pp. 186ff.

[216]James is actually using συνήργει as such, and as the Greeks used ἐνεργεῖ (ται): the συν-element explains the reference to "friend" in v. 26, while the remaining -ήργει is a play on ἀργή (v. 20).

(with KJV and RV mg.) as a question, though the sense is not affected[217]—
"faith" *shared in* or cooperated with (or in) *his works*.[218] The EVV
"wrought with" is not really satisfactory as it fails to emphasize the idea of
cooperation, for this idea of a partner, not instrument, is vital for bringing
out the real force of the passage: namely, that the writer is not pleading "for
faith plus works . . . but for faith at work" (Hort). The force of the imperfect
tense of "cooperated" (*shared in*), rather than the present,[219] stresses the
continuous nature of this cooperation: "was continually cooperating."

And by his works faith was consummated, that is, was realized, made
perfect, or expressed itself, fulfilled itself. This does not mean either (*a*) that
a faith previously defective was made perfect by works as a kind of addition
from without (for the works themselves were inspired by faith, and faith
cooperated in them), or (*b*) that a faith already perfect is revealed by its
works. The force of the statement seems to be that faith is fulfilled,
strengthened, and matured by exercise. Faith then operates in conjunction
with works, and not otherwise.

23 Abraham's action is now said to "fulfil" the text in Gen. 15:6:
"And Abraham trusted God, and it was reckoned to him as equivalent to
righteousness." The LXX wording should be compared with the Massoretic
Text.[220] Essentially James follows the LXX. The important word "reckon"[221] is often used as a *terminus technicus* in the LXX to express one
thing as being equivalent to or having the same force and weight as another.
Consider the following comments: "The habit of belief in Yahweh He
reckoned to Abraham as 'righteousness.' "[222] "That is transferred to the
subject in question, and imputed to him, which in and for itself does not
belong to him; . . . something is imputed to the person *per substitutionem*.
The object in question [here, Abraham's faith] supplies the place of that for
which it answers; it is substituted for it."[223]

---

[217]RV, RSV *that* with reference to *the fact* is to be preferred to KJV emphasis on method,
"how."
[218]συνήργει (Vulg. *cooperabatur* impf.). Common in Classical Greek, συνεργεῖν is found in
the LXX only in 1 Esdras 7:2; 1 Macc. 12:1 (but see Test. Iss. 3 and Test. Gad 4), and in the NT
at Mark 16:20; Rom. 8:28; 1 Cor. 16:16; 2 Cor. 6:1.
[219]So some mss. and Schlatter, due possibly to a desire to conform with the opening *you see*.
[220]A (א B missing) reads καὶ ἐπίστευσεν 'Αβραὰμ τῷ θεῷ, καὶ ἐλογίσθη αὐτῷ εἰς
δικαιοσύνην (LXX), containing (against the MT) 'Αβραάμ and the passive ἐλογίσθη, to
avoid the name of God (even by implication), for the active Hebrew with *lo* ("to him"). Apart
from the opening ἐπίστευσεν δέ, James follows the LXX version. See Rom. 4:3; Gal. 3:6;
Clem. Rom. 10:6; Justin *Dial.* 91; Philo *On the Change of Names* 33; for the same phrase, see
1 Macc. 2:52; also for Phinehas, Ps. 105(106):31.
[221]λογίζομαι.
[222]BDB, *s.v.* ḥashab.
[223]H. Cremer, *Biblico-Theological Lexicon of NT Greek* (E.T. ⁴1895), *s.v.* λογίζομαι. See

We have already noted the essential unity of James and Paul (2:21). This is not to deny differences of emphasis, even of intent and interpretation. Whereas Paul employs the example of Abraham to demolish the notion of salvation by merit, James uses him to illustrate the futility of a dead faith. There is also, as Dibelius shows (p. 168, n.1), a difference of interpretation: *Gen. 15:6:*

i.	Judaism	*Abraham believed God*	and this belief was counted to him as a work "for righteousness."
ii.	Paul	*Abraham believed God*	and this belief was reckoned to him "for righteousness" instead of works.
iii.	James	*Abraham believed God*	and his faith and works were counted to him "for righteousness."

James is more traditional than Paul in his treatment of Gen. 15:6: Paul isolates it from Gen. 22:1ff., whereas James combines them in regular Jewish fashion.[224]

The sacrificing of Isaac, recounted in Jas. 2:21, is the acid test of Abraham's faith and completely fulfils Gen. 15:6 both in relation to Abraham, who promises to believe, and to God, who promises to accept Abraham and his posterity. It is significant that the order James follows—Gen. 15:6 quoted in Jas. 2:23 *precedes* the events of Jas. 2:21—is not purely chronological. For James, as Martyn says, "true faith is always a beginning which looks beyond itself," and is related to "works" as "promise" to "fulfilment."[225] The Talmudic root *qwm* (in the Piel) indicates that this "fulfilment" is not an isolated "prophecy" (Mayor, Ropes), but rather, as A. Guillaume suggests, "an establishing by obedience to the spirit as much as to the letter."[226] In the sense, therefore, that it *established* and *interpreted* Gen. 15:6, the event was a "fulfilment," i.e., a divine suprahistoric (*überhistorisch*) verdict delivered on Abraham's entire life (see Dibelius, p. 153).

As "a co-partner with the Holy One,"[227] Abraham is reckoned "to

---

also Deut. 24:13; 6:25; Prov. 27:14; Isa. 40:17; Wisd. 3:17; 9:6; SB III, pp. 199ff.; *TDNT* IV, s.v. λογίζομαι (H. W. Heidland), pp. 287ff.

[224]See Ps. 106:30, 31 (Phinehas) and W. R. Farmer, "The Patriarch Phinehas—A Note on 'it was reckoned to him as Righteousness,'" *ATR* 34 (1952), pp. 26ff.

[225]J. L. Martyn, *Notes for Use in Studying the Letter of James* (1962), p. 10.

[226]In his discussion of *l^eqayyem mah she-ne'emar* ("to make to stand that which is said"), "The Midrash in the Gospels," *ExT* 37 (1925–26), p. 394.

[227]b. *Shab.* 10a; Mekilta on Exod. 18:14.

be righteous" because of his faith; such righteousness is to be construed neither in the narrow classical nor purely Pauline sense, but rather "in the right Covenant relationship."[228] In the LXX the meaning of the verb *dikaioō* is not "to make righteous," but "to declare righteous" (Deut. 25:1; 1 K. 8:32; Sir. 13:22; 42:2), while in Exod. 23:7 it means "acquit." So it has a judicial or forensic meaning which might not even go beyond observing the law. The same use is found in the NT (e.g., Matt. 12:37; Luke 7:29; Rom. 2:13). Here in the Epistle of James, Abraham is declared to be righteous, i.e., in a right relationship, because his faith led him to cooperate with God: this cooperation meant that he was even willing to sacrifice Isaac. Apparently Paul's problem, viz., the admission of Gentiles and justification of "sinners," has not yet arisen. The key to James's idea of justification appears to be the covenant relationship, a relationship which for Abraham at least ripened into friendship, for he was called "the friend of God"; and this title was indeed, in the full sense of the word, a verdict (*ein Spruch*) of justification.[229]

24 The author turns again to the Christian brotherhood, leaving the "vain man" (v. 14) aside.[230] He affirms that *both* faith and works are necessary for justification, faith alone (emphatic adverbial "only," with KJV, against RV; see "by itself," v. 17) being useless without works! Though neither ignored nor belittled, faith is regarded as complementing works, with which it must be combined (see 2 Esdras 13:23). The contrast is between faith minus works, and works minus faith—not between faith and works. For the Jews faith itself was a work,[231] and James preserves the distinction between them. But he does not teach justification by works: contrast 2 Baruch on "salvation by works" (51:3, 7; 67:6).

The Covenant, as the trial of Abraham showed, involves not only a necessary, initial act of faith, but also its continuous, confirmatory expression (Ropes, p. 218), i.e., each man has his *Recht* and *Pflicht*. Nor is this position—without perhaps the deeper Pauline insights—"false" (*falsum*: Luther) to Paul's position. We may say that Abraham was justified by faith (Paul) in that he trusted God and obeyed his voice in respect of his son Isaac; he may be said to be justified by works (James) because his trust and

---

[228]*Rechtspflichts-Verhältnis*. On the Hebrew idea of *tsedeq* as relationship (*Verhältnisbegriff*), see *TDNT* II, *s.v.* δικαιοσύνη (G. Schrenk), p. 195; C. H. Dodd, *The Bible and the Greeks*, p. 45.

[229]On "friend of God" see *TDNT* I, *s.v.* 'Αβραάμ (J. Jeremias), p. 8; SB III, p. 755.

[230]Elsewhere in the NT ὁρᾶτε—contrast βλέπεις, v. 22—is used in the imperative and has the significance "beware, see to it"; but here it means "fully understand." In the popular speech ὁράω was gradually being displaced by βλέπω and θεωρέω; but the suggestion that the process had become complete by the end of the 1st century A.D. is disproved by the papyri.

[231]SB III, pp. 187ff.

obedience led him to take Isaac—that is, to do something. John Calvin summarizes well this relationship between faith and works: "Faith alone justifies, but the faith which justifies is not alone."[231a]

25 We offer this alternative translation to clarify the meaning: "In the same way, too, was not even Rahab, the prostitute, shown to be righteous by what she did, when she cared for the messengers and sent them forth by a different route?"

For his next, and very different, example of vital faith James selects Rahab. The contrast is deliberate and provocative, carefully designed for maximum effect: compare Philo's mention, in parallel fashion, of Tamar after speaking of Abraham.[232] Any attempt to soften the contrast by suggesting, for example, that she was an innkeeper and not a prostitute should be rejected.[233] Bereft of all the obvious advantages of Abraham, the father of the faithful, this typical heathen Gentile (Canaanite) woman (not man) proselyte, once prostitute, by her conduct and example offered even more compelling proof that faith expresses itself in works. Her faith is assumed but not elaborated, in a way that affords comparison with Hebrews and Clement.[234] The point James effectively makes is that by itself her "faith," like Abraham's, was worthless apart from deeds, for both were necessary; so Cassiodorus: "Cases that are recognized as leading toward justification on a basis of works (expressive of faith), not on a basis of (absolutely unworking and unpracticed) belief" (Dibelius, p. 157, n. 1). Whereas Abraham was ready to sacrifice his son, Rahab helped the "messengers" escape[235] after apparently giving them hospitality (Heb. 11:31; 1 Clem. 12:1). Rahab's faith was consummated and vindicated by her deeds:

[231a]See W. H. Griffith Thomas, *The Principles of Theology* (1963), p. 61; also John Baillie, *Invitation to Pilgrimage,* pp. 66ff.

[232]*On Nobility* 6; see Matt. 1:5.

[233]See, e.g., Rashi, Targ. Jon. to Josh. 2:1. G. Kittel says in his footnote to the German translation of Num. R. iii.2: "Rahab is a kind of saint for later Judaism," and he cites Heb. 11:31; Jas. 2:25; 1 Clem. 12:1; also Matt. 1:5. According to the rabbis she was a woman of surpassing beauty, whose name inspired lust (b. *Meg.* 15a; b. *Taʿan.* 56), and who, having had the chance of approaching God, was debarred through unworthiness (Num. R. iii.2); but she was also said to have been converted through the report of the miracles (Exod. R. xxvii.4; compare Josh. 2:9–11), married to Joshua, and welcomed into a Jewish family (Midr. Ruth, ed. Wünsche, pp. 14ff.). She became ancestress to eight prophets (b. *Meg.* 14b and c), perhaps but not probably even of the Messiah, and was visited by the Holy Spirit (Sifre Deut. 1:24 [par. 22, 69b]); see SB I, pp. 20ff.; Montefiore and Loewe, *Rabbinic Anthology,* p. 563. A modern archeological argument for regarding her as one who provided lodging for alien visitors is presented by D. J. Wiseman, "Rahab of Jericho," *Tyndale House Bulletin* 14 (June 1964), pp. 8–11.

[234]As suggested by, e.g., B. W. Bacon in *JBL* 19 (1900), pp. 12ff.

[235]"Sent forth" (ἐκβαλοῦσα) is used here, not pejoratively (compare John 9:34), but simply to emphasize the difficulties of escape, e.g., the different route, possibly by "a window instead of by a door"; compare Josh. 2:5 (Mayor).

so she was shown to be righteous. According to Jewish tradition, she risked everything because she repented, and believed in the true God of Israel of whose mighty deeds she had heard; and in pleading for forgiveness, she cited her treatment of the messengers, and was declared righteous.[236] Rahab's "justification" was the sparing of her life when the town fell (Josh. 6:17, 23). It could be argued that Rahab was self-serving in that she regarded only the safety of herself and her family; but while there is no need to approve all the moral implications of Rahab's act (done in admittedly difficult and extenuating circumstances), the modern critic of James ought to allow a different biblical view of history: Paul was ready to admit that many who did not know the Torah acted in accordance with its dictates. This may well explain why James chose this example of works to justify Rahab. In any case she presents a striking contrast to formal religion (though Judaism curiously regarded her as a forerunner of the later proselytes), whether practiced by monotheists or others. Her "moral standard was faulty." Yet sarcasm may lurk in James's words, for he calls the two men not "spies" but *messengers* (see Ropes).

By his choice of Abraham and Rahab, therefore, James shows not only that the acid test of faith is works but also that this principle has universal application, embracing both patriarch and prostitute. Of necessity, too, such proof will always be clear and convincing; witness, for example, the simple eloquence of a Salvationist servant lass: "My missus says she believes I am saved because I sweep beneath the mats, and I didn't before!"[237] The indisputable point is that true faith operates in, cooperates with, and is vindicated by works. Like Abraham, Rahab was justified through faith and works—and not by faith alone.

26 In his usual circling fashion James by analogy[238] reiterates and clinches his basic thesis, "faith without works is dead" (v. 17). The omission of "for," inserted by some manuscripts and most versions, is correct and in keeping with James's brusque style.

Faith is compared to the body, works to the spirit—an apparent inversion which has caused some to question the soundness of the text (so Spitta). The exact details of any comparison should not be pressed. In this case the comparison may well be his opponent's, and its elements should be carefully considered in context. Thus *faith* is used in the non-Pauline, especially Jewish sense of a body or *corpus* of opinion; "body" represents the Hebraic monistic (rather than Greek "body-tomb" dualistic) view of the

---

[236]Eccl. R. v. 1; Pes. R. 167b; S. Schechter, *Rabbinic Theology*, p. 26; *JE* X, *s.v.* "Rahab" (M. Seligsohn), p. 309; see also her own words, Josh. 2:9–11.
[237]W. Clark, *The Soldier's Armoury* (July–December 1972), p. 11.
[238]ὥσπερ, used not for exact similarity but as ὡς, which is not found in James.

total, essential person (see 1 Cor. 15); that is, "the body is the soul in its outward form";[239] and the primary effect of "spirit" or "breath," like OT *ruaḥ*, is life, and this makes the body a living soul (*nephesh*) from which it departs at death (see Mayor). The *tertium comparationis*, therefore, is the essential deadness of both "body" and "faith" apart from the vital principle of "works," which is equivalent to the spirit.

EXCURSUS F
JAMES 2:18: A FURTHER EXPLANATION

This verse, as it stands, is exceedingly difficult to interpret[1]—indeed Dibelius[2] deems it one of the most difficult of the whole NT—for it seems a reversal of what one might expect. Nor is it clear that the discussion is confined to v. 18: if it is extended over to κενέ (v. 20), we have a similar pattern to 1 Cor. 15:35f., ἀλλὰ ἐρεῖ τις . . . ἄφρων.

Among the attempted explanations of this text we note the following:

i. It is possible to give up in despair on the grounds that the text has suffered and that something is missing. Alternatively we may take the bull by the horns and emend the text,[3] and this is particularly tempting in the middle of straight, unpunctuated prose. All difficulty might be avoided, for example, by inserting σὺ πίστιν ἔχεις after ἀλλ' ἐρεῖ τις[4] and adopting ἐκ τῶν ἔργων (κτλ) for the correctly attested χωρὶς τῶν ἔργων or the secondary, corrupt Latin Codex Corbeiensis (ff): *tu operam (opera) habes, ego fidem habeo*, reading[5] σὺ ἔργα ἔχεις κἀγὼ πίστιν ἔχω.

ii. Hort[6] lets τις, an objector, ask: Σὺ πίστιν ἔχεις; κἀγὼ ἔργα ἔχω, implying that, while James has only faith, the objector for his part (κἀγώ) has works. In reply, James stresses that faith and works are inseparable: δεῖξόν μοι κτλ. Against this ingenious theory—and in such an *impasse* any fresh way out is

---

[239]See J. Pedersen, *Israel* I–II (1926), pp. 170ff.; for the Greek view, see E. Käsemann, *Leib und Leib Christi* (1933), pp. 23–59.

[1]See H. Preisker, "Zum Verständnis Jak. 2:18 f.," *Theol. Blätter* (1925), pp. 16f. For a conspectus of the various interpretations, see Ropes, pp. 211–14, and Marty, pp. 96–100.
[2]*Ad loc.*
[3]R. A. Knox, comm. *ad loc.*
[4]Spitta, Hollmann.
[5]Also Hincks, Pfleiderer, Baljon.
[6]Also, practically, Von Soden, Moffatt.

welcome—we note that the Greek requires WH mg.'s interrogative πίστιν ἔχεις; as well as an introductory μή expecting the negative answer, μὴ σὺ πίστιν ἔχεις;[7] which, apart from destroying the sentence's parallelism, makes the καί of κἀγώ extremely awkward. It is also doubtful if κἀγώ could bear the meaning: "I, for my part," which, as Mayor points out,[8] would need ἐγὼ δέ.

iii.   B. Weiss[9] on inferior ms. evidence links this interpretation with Rom. 14:22: "Someone will say: 'Thou (the opponent) hast faith; and I (James) have only works'; show me, etc." Weiss, however, confuses direct and indirect speech, for any reference to James would require to be in the third person; and, further, if the ἐγώ or κἀγώ really meant James, it would not have been left so extremely ambiguous—not to say misleading—as it is bound to be when set so near a σύ.

iv.   Similarly, Ropes,[10] whose view is adopted by NEB, which has:

"But someone may object: 'Here is one who claims to have faith and another who points to his deeds.' To which I reply: 'Prove to me that this faith you speak of is real though not accompanied by deeds, and by my deeds I will prove to you my faith.' "

Ropes argues that τις is properly an objector, and that σύ and ἐγώ do not represent the objector and the speaker respectively but merely εἷς . . . ἕτερος, ἄλλος . . . ἄλλος, or some such expression. It is impossible, however, to divide these words thus between two speakers: "To which I reply" cannot thus be thrust into the Greek. Ropes does this because he frankly admits that there is no other way of making τις an objector. But the first part of v. 18 is just a sort of preliminary to the second half, and the two are inseparable; the asyndeton (lack of conjunction) in its own way marks the connection. The "ideal" second person[11] is another matter, as any Grammar will show. Besides, if I am a Christian, but am arguing for *live and let live* (or some such parity of esteem) in religious matters, then, even if I want to speak quite generally and impersonally, I would not put it like this: "Never mind; you are a Christian, I am a Muslim; let us get on with it." For the same reason, an objector, who is supposed to be shouting for *faith* against James who is shouting for works, would not say: "Never mind; you have faith, I have *works*; let us get on with it." Surely it is obvious that even if he meant merely to point out the existing variety of opinions and beliefs in religion, the man who is keen on *faith* will put it thus: "All right; *I* have *faith,* you have works," or, which is the same thing: "You have works, *I* have *faith.*"

It may be said that this form, "But someone will say," is used regularly to introduce an objection. We think that, properly understood, this *is* an objection. The verses before this have had, ". . . if one (of you) *say* . . . . . . if . . . . . . one of you

[7]Ropes, *ad loc.*

[8]"Further Studies," p. 32, in 3rd ed. of his commentary (1913).

[9]See, too, O. Kuttner, *Zeitschrift für Wissenschaftliche Theologie* (1888), pp. 36ff., cited by Dibelius, p. 146.

[10]Also Dibelius, Marty, based originally on Pott and Bouman.

[11]Ropes, p. 209 *ad fin.*

say . . . . . . what good is it? So, too, faith is dead." "Yea, one will say . . ." here has the meaning, (thus faith is dead) yea, one will *object* (ἀντερεῖ):[12] i.e., in reply and contradiction to the man who says, "I have faith" (v. 14) or "Be ye filled" (v. 16), one will object, thus: "You have faith, I have works (let us suppose): show me, etc."[13] The quotation from Teles[14] proves nothing. "Thou art a ruler" begins a quotation from Bion, and the preceding words are not part of the same "speech," but are merely illustrated by the words of Bion.

"Yea" is quite good for the Greek ἀλλά (*immo vero*)[15] when the preceding sentence has a negative quality, as "dead" carries the suggestion of "worthless" or "lifeless" or "unreal." In fact, in this sentence older English—like Arabic *bal*— might translate, with much the same effect, ἀλλά by the ascensive "Nay" or "Nay more." So the phrase could be translated: "Indeed, I might put the matter like this," or "We could go further and say."[16]

To sum up: It is difficult to understand why Ropes should think that James should adopt this impenetrably obscure expression when the straightforward ἄλλος . . . ἄλλος would have done. "To tell the truth," writes C. F. D. Moule in a personal note, "I cannot think of a *less* likely way to express what J. H. Ropes wants the James passage to mean than what there stands written." He points out that there would surely need to be some word expressing (on his showing) that it is *possible* for one man to have (virtually) nothing but faith, and another (virtually) nothing but works! As it stands, then, this is the last thing one would expect the words to mean, were it not that the ἀλλ᾽ ἐρεῖ τις crux drives one to desperate measures.

---

[12]ἀντερεῖ (fut. of ἀντιλέγω) is not used in the text here: we only mean that, in reply to the "say" (λέγῃ and εἴπῃ) of vv. 14 and 16, ἐρεῖ in v. 18, "one will say," does in fact here introduce the reply to such statements.

[13]It is difficult to see why Gebser as long ago as 1828 carried the contribution of one ally down to v. 23, very strangely cutting out any reference to Rahab. The ironical use of δείκνυμι, very frequent in Epictetus, is further evidence of the method of the diatribe, unique in the NT: Philip's request (John 14:8) is obviously sincere. The reading δείξω σοι (A C K L minn. Vulg.) for σοι δείξω was probably due to the preceding δεῖξόν μοι. We prefer to translate χωρίς as *apart from* rather than "without" (KJV), which may have been suggested by Vulg. *sine*. As in Classical Greek (but not LXX, e.g., Job [10]; Sir. [6]), χωρίς is more common than ἄνευ (only Matt. 10:20; 1 Pet. 3:1; 4:9). Ropes (*ad loc.*) rightly calls the TR ἐκ (following K L and great majority of minn.) "an unfortunate conformation to the following clause, which spoils the sense."

[14]Ropes, p. 209.

[15]Cf. Luke 17:8; John 16:2; Phil. 1:18; 2 Cor. 7:11; Heb. 3:16. See Mayor, *ad loc.*

[16]See R. A. Knox, *New Testament, ad loc.*, although in his later *Commentary* he favors a corrupt text.

CHAPTER 3

The instruction offered in the first half of this Epistle includes mention of the Christian's duty to guard his tongue (1:26); in ch. 3, however, we have not just a lament over a constant weakness of mankind: 3:5–12 deliberately leads up to an indictment (3:14–16) of contentious heresy by which the Christianity of the converts is itself being threatened. There is no suggestion that among the members of the body the tongue is unique in its ambivalence for good or evil, but it is probably unequalled among the members in the harm (intentional or unintended) that it can do in some vital fields, especially in politics and religion; in the latter Paul found some very grave examples among his converts in Galatia and Colossae. This menace was plainly no less serious among some of the Jewish Christians for whom James was writing, and in this chapter he treats it no less severely than Paul, who in Col. 2:23 denounces it as a "mere *show of wisdom*," with this warning in Col. 2:8: "Beware lest any man spoil you through philosophy and vain deceit, after the tradition of men, after the rudiments of the world, and not after Christ." This language and situation are clearly paralleled in Jas. 3:14–16, for example, in v. 15: "*This wisdom* is not one descending from above, but is of the earth, of this life, of the devil."

In ch. 3 James turns to wisdom, and begins with a salutary and sympathetic caution to sincere Christians, warning them of the higher standards expected of leaders in wisdom, and the greater risks involved, since in speech, in which most of the teacher's work is done, it is even harder than in bodily action to avoid the sin of error, wilful or involuntary. All men commit many sins (including—but not only—teachers): that is precisely why men should be chary about incurring the risk of greater punishment, as we shall if we become teachers, entrusted, as teachers are, with increased knowledge.

So James, thinking first and always of sincerity, in his usual "rondo" manner returns to the theme of speech (1:19, 26) and warns his true Christians of the dangers of the tongue, which he calls (in effect) "a demon of insincerity (or inconstancy)'' (3:8); the thread of the thought is clearest if we accept the better text.[1] We notice how "unstable" and "doubleminded" occur together in 1:8, "unstable" or "treacherous" in 3:8, and "doubleminded" (plural) in 4:8.

Chapters 3 and 4 develop the thought of 1:5-8, the *sincere* seeking for God (literally, God's wisdom). He starts, as in 2:1 where he deals with *sincere faith,* with a preliminary warning which is developed on somewhat divergent lines, for he deals with one aspect only of the matter. The tongue is represented as the acme of insincerity, a lie against that consistency and constancy of nature which should sound in the nature of everything that is uninfected (as, alas, "the world of iniquity" and unregenerate man, including the tongue, are infected) with sin.

Chapters 3 and 4 are so closely allied as to form almost a unity. It is one mark of James's style, as of much other oratory, to round off a paragraph by coming in full circle to the point with which it began: 3:13–18 is an obvious example, beginning and ending with the duty of good works in meekness and peace as part of true wisdom. So here James begins the former and ends the latter of these two allied chapters with the same warning, namely, of the responsibilities of advancement in knowledge (3:1 and 4:17).

Jas. 3:1, 2, is an application of 1:19, "slow to speak"; 3:13–18, of the same verse, "slow to wrath"; and 3:3–12 is related to 1:26 on the duty of bridling the tongue. 3:13, 15, 16, indicate the special application to teachers of the directions against wrath (in 1:19, as already mentioned) and to humility and good works, as in 1:21ff. In 3:17, on *pure* see 1:21; on *peaceable, gentle, easy to be intreated* see 1:19; on *mercy* see 1:27 and 2:13; on *good fruits* see 1:22; on *unwavering* see 1:6; and *without hypocrisy* is close to 1:22, 26.

This third chapter drives home the lesson of 1:5. Even with faith in God and in righteousness, I still constantly need his guidance in the daily problems of life.

VERSE:

Who would be a teacher? (3:1)

> 1 *Seek not many of you to be rabbis, my brothers, knowing that we shall be adjudged more severe punishment.*

1   If I am a teacher, I am at least likely to receive greater condemnation. Why? Is it because God expects a higher standard from teachers than

---

[1]ἀκατάστατον (see 3:8).

from others? If so, why? James does not say. Is it because the damage done to others by my sins is greater? Possibly; but James does not say so. Is it because my sins are apt to be more numerous?

We think that here *many* (v. 2) indicates that teachers sin particularly often, and ''all'' has an emphasis evoked not by universal human fallibility but by the universal susceptibility of teachers to sin, in fact (as he proceeds to underline), with the tongue: vv. 3–12 contain a bitter diatribe against it. James does not otherwise say why this is specially relevant to teachers, and if ''we all sin'' meant that all human beings sin, the logic of the passage would be *entirely* tacit: the relevance of the diatribe would be left entirely to the hearer to gauge. We have shown in our Analysis[2] that this passage is part of the wider unity of the Epistle; there is no need to postulate an independent document like an ''adapted Hellenistic tract on slander'' (on such theories, see Ropes, p. 228). The logic of the passage is better preserved if we take James to be saying that teachers, all teachers, are prone, very prone, to sin; for the tongue is preeminently uncontrollable and a ''treacherous'' source of evil; only an ideal man would *never* sin with his tongue. Then, admittedly, James seems to think it needless to say *why* the tongue, a menace in every man's life, is particularly so to teachers: obviously among them it has particularly many opportunities for its sinister work, since, as we need not be told, it is one of the chief tools of their trade.

In the Jewish Diaspora congregations there was an order of ''teachers,'' which this passage suggests was in danger of being overrun by unworthy members and candidates (see Mitton, pp. 188ff.). KJV ''masters'' preserves the older meaning which has survived in ''schoolmaster.'' For ''teachers'' we prefer *rabbis* (see Ropes, p. 226). Apparently James himself was a member of the order: ''*we* shall be adjudged . . . ,'' though a few minuscules and versions emend to the second person to soften this inclusiveness.[3] This chapter, though not formally addressed to this order, is specially aimed at them: vv. 1–12 caution the sincere against the constant danger of sinning with the tongue, a danger inseparable from the teaching profession; the rest of the chapter is a warning to the others against the professional insincerity, jealousy, and contention of which the Gospels speak (Matt. 23:8). We must distinguish the two sets of unfit candidates—here as always—in James's circle: first, the sincere who nevertheless are not likely to be able to approach the high standards required of the teacher; and second, the insincere who are pretenders not fit to be counted as Christians, much less teachers. Milton castigates these pretenders as ''blind mouths'' in his famous poem *Lycidas*.

[2]See p. 45; also Summary, p. 16.
[3]E.g., Vulg. *sumitis;* m *accipetis;* so also Boh.

The main thought in vv. 1–12 is the greater responsibility of teachers and the extremely dangerous character of the instrument which they have to use. This passage naturally connects with 1:19f., 26; 2:12 (Ropes, p. 226). Greater responsibility brings greater judgment. If every idle word will be weighed at the Judgment (Matt. 12:36f.), how much more the utterances of the teacher?[4] We may be tempted to think the diatribe on the tongue approaches too near to exaggeration; but it goes no further than James's deep feeling for his vocation would justify. Any attempt, therefore, to emend or to evade its plain meaning is not only inapposite here but also ruinous to the passage, as a whole, on the tongue. Among the Jews the desire for the office of teacher and title of Rabbi was prevalent,[5] and "teacher" may have been the earliest description of Jesus;[6] but, then and later, men claiming to be teachers without due authority or qualification abounded (Matt. 23:8; Acts 15:24; 1 Tim. 1:6f.; 3:2). The desire to teach may be a sign of youth or immaturity: because of inexperience such teachers may be ignorant of the peculiar temptations of the office, and self-assertion, acrimony, and impatience often accompany their efforts. It is possible that in the present case a situation similar to that described in 1 Cor. 14:26ff. (contrast Heb. 5:12) was threatening to develop. Of course, in teaching as in other careers it is not the profession that does honor to the man, but the man to his profession.[7]

When James warns the genuinely faithful against "an undue influx of teachers" he reminds us of the zealous pastor who tells his (quite admirable) young people today: "To many of you I say: Avoid entering the Christian Ministry. The standard of righteousness is one that few can hope to approach, and none can hope to reach."

V. SOME CHRISTIAN ADVICE (3:2–18)

a. The power and treachery of the tongue as a menace of evil (3:2–12)

> 2 *For we are all guilty of many sins. Only if such a man there be as never sins in what he says, only there would be a perfect man, able as with a bridle to control his whole body also.*
>
> 3 *See, we put bits in horses' mouths to make them obey us, and so we are able to turn their whole body this way and that.*
>
> 4 *See also how ships, so great as they are, and driven by fierce winds, are*

---

[4]Wisd. 6:5; *Aboth* i.11; see Mark 12:40.
[5]F. W. Weber, *Jüdische Theologie* (1897), pp. 125ff.; *TDNT* VI, *s.v.* ῥαββί (E. Lohse), pp. 961f.
[6]*TDNT* II, *s.v.* διδάσκαλος (K. H. Rengstorf), p. 153.
[7]So Thomas Aquinas *Contra Impugnantes Dei Cultum* ii.

turned this way and that by a very small rudder in whatever direction the steersman's desire may choose.

5 *So, too, the tongue is a little member of the body vaunting great powers. See how much brushwood a little fire sets alight!*

6 *The tongue, also, is fire; the sinful world (is) wood. Thus the tongue stands among our members, defiling the whole body and setting fire to the circling course of creation, and being set on fire by hell.*

7 *For every genus of beasts and birds, reptiles and sea-creatures, is subdued and stands subdued to mankind.*

8 *But the tongue no man can subdue; it is an evil irreducible to order, full of deadly venom.*

9 *With it we bless our God and Father, and with it we curse men, who have been created in the likeness of God.*

10 *Out of the same mouth come forth blessing and cursing: it is wrong, my brothers, that this be so.*

11 *Does a fountain from the same outlet spout forth both sweet and bitter?*

12 *Can a fig tree, my brothers, produce olives, or a vine, figs? So no fountain can produce salt water and fresh.*

2–4 James at once begins to justify the serious warning he gave in the previous verse, the explanatory *for* and the first person plural of the verb indicating the continuity of thought, in the temptations (of the tongue, as presently appears) to which the teacher is exposed, and inevitably often succumbs. For only an ideally perfect man would *always* be able to resist temptation: and, apart from Jesus, such a man never existed,[8] for "all have sinned" (Rom. 3:23).

We cannot debate the allegorical theories revived by B. Reicke (pp. 37f.); we have no common ground to go upon. The ships, winds, and rudders of which James speaks are real and literal: he is thinking of ships on the Sea of Galilee. The bridle and bit, the rudder and helm, are analogies, not allegories. Horses and ships and winds were familiar enough in James's world; the analogy in these, and in fire-kindling, is in the huge contrast between the size of the originating element and the magnitude of the effect achieved, as between the size of the tongue and its potency. In the case of horses and ships the Greek verb literally means, "We make the horses change their direction," and, "The ships are made to change their course," i.e., big as they are, we turn them this way and that by such little means.[9]

The bit, rudder, and tongue, therefore, are here mentioned as being alike in one thing, their *multum in parvo* power. Each is comparatively

[8]Eccl. 7:20; b. *Sanh.* 101a; SB III, pp. 155ff.; *TDNT* I, *s.v.* ἁμαρτάνω (G. Stählin and W. Grundmann), p. 291.
[9]See Rendall, p. 38, n. 2, on the "lakeside vernacular of the Sea of Galilee."

small, but each produces great effect; and in v. 5, in both halves, James emphasizes this *fundamentum comparationis* not once but twice: "the tongue is a little member . . . how much forest (or, growing timber) a little fire sets ablaze." With the correct text and interpretation, v. 6 (*q.v.*) explains the tongue's *multum in parvo* power again quite clearly.

Bit and rudder are useful inventions; the tongue is by nature pregnant with evil. This was a truism in Greek, and, more than in other oriental traditions, in the warnings that characterize practical Jewish wisdom,[10] where it is a scourge, a sword (Sir. 28:18), a bow and arrow (Jer. 9:3, 8), and produces both life and death (Prov. 19:21). Its unruly nature is betokened in the safeguards with which God has created it—horizontal, and enclosed within both bone and flesh.[11] "James is thinking," writes John Coutts, "not of foul language and the conversation punctuated with four-letter words, but of the reviling, slandering tongue. And when the wound is inflicted with politeness and polish it is no less sinful."[11a] We must remember that the Orientals give their tongues far more license in speech than we have generally done until quite recent years. But James does not mean to say that we can control our body *by* controlling our tongue; he means that if we can do the latter we shall be able to do the former, which is easier.

5–6   With the Peshitta reading, which parallels the immediately preceding Greek sentence, we translate: "The tongue also is fire, the world of unrighteousness is a wood: so stands the tongue among our members, a thing which defiles the whole body, and sets on fire the wheel of birth," i.e., the wheel (of a man's varying fortunes), which (wheel) each man's birth sets turning for him. This passage may be disagreeably sophistic in expression, though there is no question but that it is perfectly sincere. See Ropes, p. 235: "As a spark . . . the exaggeration is pardonable." It is Ropes who exaggerates here; James, we believe, does not carry the tongue's damage beyond human life—the whole body and, in effect, all the vicissitudes of every man's life from the cradle to the grave.

To be sure, the fire destroys the wood,[12] the tongue does not destroy sin: that need not bother anyone. Analogies need not be complete. When a man calls his wife a jewel, he need not mean that she is hard. We constantly speak of things that *inflame* the passions, meaning the evil passions. In that sense, words often inflame to sin; they rouse the quiescent innate passions latent in every man (the world of sin, i.e., all the potential evil present in us and the rest of the human race) and inflame them into ardor and activity, and

---

[10]*TDNT* I, *s.v.* γλῶσσα (J. Behm), p. 721.
[11]b. 'Arak. 15b.
[11a]*The Soldier's Armoury* (January–June, 1976), p. 113.
[12]See L. E. Elliott-Binns, "The Meaning of ὕλη in Jas. iii.5," *NTS* 2 (1955), pp. 48–50.

the man into sin; so even James had hinted in 1:14, 15: there lust "conceives"; here it is fired into flame.

So stands the tongue: i.e., the tongue in our body, with its (the body's) base instincts, is like a fire (e.g., an unguarded campfire) in a forest; any minute, there will be a conflagration (see Excursus G, pp. 158ff.).[12a]

7–8 James continues to justify his criticism of the tongue: *irreducible to order*[13] is preferable in itself (*lectio difficilior, lectio potior*) to the variant reading, the commonplace "unruly,"[14] and also as characteristically opening the "rondo" on the duplicity of the tongue, beginning here and closing on the same note in the question in v. 12. In 1:8 the word is used (with "doubleminded") to denote another aspect of "two-mindedness" which is the gravamen of James's charge against the tongue (3:8–12). Here we interject a suggestion that the reader might profitably notice James's recurrent detestation of precisely such insincerity and inconstancy in general: it is one of the main threads in his thought from 1:8 onward, like its corresponding opposite, "constancy," from 1:3 onward. In 1:6–8 the words "wavering," "doubleminded," "irreducible to order,"[15] and again in 4:8 "doubleminded," indicate doubt, damaging to the man so described; in 3:2–12 the damage is to others, e.g., in v. 6, by the tongue's duplicity (see vv. 9–12); hence we suggest "irreducible to order" or "treacherous."[16]

The complaint against the tongue then is its treacherous inconsistency—an evil irreducible to order, to a consistent character of disciplined obedience and to righteousness. It is the tongue itself, not only its misuse, that is condemned. His characteristically Hebrew emphasis on the mischief of the corporal tongue is not intended to minimize in any way the guilt of the man who is using it, any more than the versatility of the helm excuses the negligent or even malevolent steersman: the case is not parallel to corporal weakness beyond our control. To James the tongue is not merely a disease (see 5:13–19). In plain, and perhaps not really too free English: "the tongue is a monster of inconsistency"—or even better a "monster of caprice" *full of deadly venom*.[17]

The Greek noun here translated *genus*[18] does not mean "inborn qualities," like strength, ferocity, or docility, but KJV "kind," "every natural sort." James's list here is based on Gen. 9:2 and similar lists in Deut.

[12a]Cf. Shakespeare's observation in *King Henry VI*: "A little fire is quickly trodden out which, being suffered, rivers cannot quench" (IV.viii.7).
[13]ἀκατάστατον, which we prefer to the variant ἀκατάσχετον ("unruly").
[14]KJV; C K L minn. m Syr.
[15]διακρινόμενος, δίψυχος, ἀκατάστατος.
[16]"Fickle" is a recognized translation in general in LS, *s.v.* ἀκατάστατος.
[17]On "poison" as a metaphor for evil influence, see Mitton, p. 130; *TDNT* III, *s.v.* ἰός (O. Michel), p. 335.
[18]φύσις.

4:17f.; 1 K. 4:35; Acts 10:12; 11:6. The ancients even speak of tamed fishes:[19] not that fishes are notably savage, as a rule, but even the tongue can (treacherously) be as mild as a tame goldfish punctually awaiting its ants' eggs.

"Beast"[20] in the NT is used only of undomesticated animals.[21] Sea-creatures,[22] here only in the Bible, is common in Greek poetry and late Greek prose.[23]

Both pagans and Hebrews were proud of man's lordship over the animal world.[24] As in Ps. 8:6–8, the thought, in biblical and secular literature, of man's dominion over the animal world comprises both aspects of his power: (i) over what (not to particularize too much) he hunts and traps and perhaps eats; and (ii) over what he domesticates—perhaps for food, like sheep or hens, or perhaps for training and working, like horses and dogs.[25] "Tamed" (EVV) is slightly ambiguous and too strong: so we prefer *subdued* (Dan. 2:40), "subjected," or "domesticated."[26] The domesticating of wild animals is a sign of the Messianic Age (Isa. 11:6, 9). On the point of domesticated animals, it may be relevant to remark that the rich denounced by James regarded and treated the poor workers as cattle; we think that is a fair deduction from what James says of the rich.

James no doubt knew the current sophisticated treatments of this subject, involving man the trainer no less than man the hunter and killer. Whatever he borrowed we can be sure he, like Paul, made his own. Of all animals, says Aristotle, the human young is most intractable. Thinkers like James were understandably indignant when, as Isocrates protests: "Every year men see in the circuses lions that are more gently disposed toward their keepers than some men are toward their benefactors, and bears rolling and wrestling and imitating our skills";[27] but men are absolutely unable to discipline their own tongues. Man can bridle and break a horse, but he cannot reduce the tongue to discipline.[28]

9 We may find ourselves unsympathetic with James's attack on

---

[19]See Aelian *De Nat. Animal.* viii.4.

[20]θηρίον.

[21]*TDNT* III, *s.v.* θηρίον (W. Foerster), pp. 133ff.

[22]ἐναλίων (genitive plural of ἐνάλιος).

[23]E.g., Sophocles *Antig.* 345.

[24]Cf. Cicero *De Nat. Deorum* ii.151, 158f.; Seneca *Benef.* ii.29; Gen. 1:26ff.; see Mayor, pp. 115f.

[25]See Sophocles *Antig.* 332ff., cited by Mayor.

[26]See F. Field, *Notes on the Translation of the NT*, p. 237.

[27]*Antid.* 213.

[28]We think, *pace* Cranfield (p. 15), that ἀνθρώπων is not emphatic, and does not signify a contrast with God; we think it is unemphatic, οὐδεὶς ἀνθρώπων being merely a varied repetition of the reference in τῇ φύσει τῇ ἀνθρωπίνη. James is concentrating on his point—that mankind is unable to govern the tongue.

145

that little member, the corporal tongue: such a text as Prov. 11:13 or Sir. 5:9 seems to put the blame fairly on the speaker, not the tongue; but in Hebrew thought the distinction between the man and the guilty member, e.g., tongue or hand, is not so clear, wide, or rigid as with us. To them, my tongue is, as it were, a part of my ego, or an alter ego of me; see Sir. 5:14: "Be not called a whisperer and lie not in wait with thy tongue; for a foul shame is upon the thief, and an evil condemnation is upon the double tongue." Here we may note how "lie in wait" agrees with James's charge against the "treacher-ous" tongue, also called "double" here and in Sir. 5:9: "the sinner that has a double tongue," a phrase repeated two verses later (Sir. 6:1), as Sir 28:13 condemns "the whisperer and double-tongued." The transition from the man to the member is easy to the Hebrew; and even with us we sometimes hear the excuse, even in extreme cases, "My hand slipped," as if you were not to blame for what your hand did or caused. In our approach to James we should give due weight to this Hebrew custom of thought.[29]

To bless God is the sublimest function of the human tongue; thrice daily the devout Jew recited "the Eighteen Benedictions," with their ending "Blessed art Thou, O God."[30] But the tongue of blessing can also curse—a reference perhaps to the practice of imprecation but more probably to disputes and slanders within the community (4:1ff., 11ff.). "It is man's nearness (and even original likeness) to God, which makes the cursing of him a still greater offence to God who made him" (Mitton, p. 132). We note that James, like Jesus, knows nothing of what is popularly thought of as the doctrine of "total depravity": though impaired, the *imago dei* is not totally destroyed.[31] Ethically this doctrine is crucial for both Jew and Christian. "Since men are formed in the divine semblance," writes Cohen,[32] "they must keep that knowledge always in mind in their relationship with one another." Hence R. Akiba's saying: "Whosoever sheddeth blood, they reckon it to him as if he diminished the likeness." James is well aware of the moral and spiritual significance of this doctrine, especially as it touches man's speech.[33]

10 In the strongest possible Greek—only here in the NT[34]—James condemns the tongue's ambivalent defiance of any uniformity of law in its

[29]On their doctrine of speech, see Paul S. Minear, *The Commands of Christ* (1972), pp. 42ff., with important references.
[30]See A. Marmorstein, *The Old Rabbinic Doctrine of God* I (1927), pp. 93, 112ff.
[31]Or, as Calvin put it, a certain *sensus deitatis* survives. The true, classic doctrine of "total depravity" does not conflict with this: it does not mean that the divine image in man is so obliterated that every man is as evil as it is possible to be, but rather that there is no part of our being which is not in some degree infected by sin—or, as James says, "we are all guilty of many sins" (3:1).
[32]A. Cohen, *Everyman's Talmud*, p. 67.
[33]See Sifra on Lev. 19:18.
[34]οὐ χρή.

character and behavior (cf. 1:13 and 3:7–12). His phrase is rather like our "It's not *right*!" spoken with all the force of protesting condemnation. Bunyan's character "Talkative," described as "a saint abroad and a devil at home," is a good illustration of what James is condemning. Of the tongue's fundamental ambivalence the rabbis were also well aware: "From the tongue comes good and bad, the best and the worst."[35]

11   "Palestinians are very good water-tasters," says E. F. F. Bishop.[36] Here *bitter* may mean "brackish," "sulphurous," or more probably denotes a case where above the outlet good water has suffered contamination from a salty source. Of a river flowing into the Dead Sea T. K. Cheyne wrote: "The salt water and the fresh intermingle some way above the mouth of the river, and fish that are carried down are thrown up dead on the beach."[37] We observe the use of the article with *fountain*,[38] as twice in John 4:6, and once in v. 14, while another word[39] is used in v. 11, except that in v. 11—as in Rev. 9:2f., where it means "pit" from which comes smoke as of a fiery furnace—the "picture" is of a deep cavity containing water, not springing water. It is of springing water[40] that James is here thinking and writing, and we suggest it is relevant to remember that among country folk "the spring" or "the well" has a prominent individuality (see the latter half of Eccl. 12:6). Here James is speaking of springing water, and of its being drunk or unfit to drink: "Does a spring from the same fountainhead gush with both salt and fresh?" *Outlet*[41] is, as often, a hole in the ground, or, it may be, in the rock.[42]

12   The fig tree is not guilty of duplicity in its production of fruit, but observes the rule of Gen. 1:11. The uniformity of nature is a well-known concept in Greek philosophy. Ropes (p. 243) quotes enough classical parallels. These three fruits, fig, olive, and grape, found in all the Near East, are particularly associated with Palestine.[43]

Jas. 3 is related to the Sermon on the Mount and the similar passage

---

[35]Lev. R. xxxiii (130b).

[36]*Apostles of Palestine*, p. 187.

[37]Cheyne, *Encyclopaedia Biblica* II (1901), 1292.

[38]πηγή.

[39]φρέαρ. πηγή is a spring; but, as in John, both πηγή (twice in 4:6 and once in 4:14) and φρέαρ (4:11) can be used for "well": in the former the "picture" is of springing water, in the latter it is of a cavity, deep in John 4:11 and in Rev. 9:2f. bottomless and filled with fire. Jacob's well (John 4:6, 11, 14) could properly be called by both nouns: it was dug by Jacob, and was therefore a φρέαρ, but was also fed by an underground spring, and is therefore a πηγή.

[40]βρύει—here with cognate accusative, as in Justin Martyr *Dial.* 114, πέτρας . . . ζῶν ὕδωρ βρυούσης, and elsewhere; see Mayor, *ad loc*.

[41]ὀπή.

[42]See Shakespeare's *A Midsummer Night's Dream* III.i.66, 73.

[43]οὔτε—we should expect οὐδέ, but they are interchanged so often in the mss. that some suspect the Greek practice on this point was less strict than our grammarians' rule. The text of Scholz has οὕτως οὐδεμία πηγή.

in Luke 6:12–49. We note how Jas. 3:7–12, olives from figs, uses the fruit analogy of Luke 6:44, 45, figs from thorns. In Luke this analogy belongs to the mote and beam passage, and expressly refers to speech. In Matt. 7:16 "figs from thistles" relates to false prophets, ravening wolves. Luke and Matthew have in mind rabbis who, rather as in Jas. 3:14, are living lies, and false prophets who are really seeking to prey on God's flock. The antecedents of Jas. 3 possibly and perhaps probably are not Matthew and Luke as we have them, but personal experience or first-hand accounts at the beginning of the traditions from which Matthew and Luke are variously derived. These are not merely the trivial variations in the fruits and trees named. The most interesting variation is in James. In discussing the rabbi he makes two divisions of the topic: first, the difficulties of even the sincerely well-intentioned rabbi (3:1–12); second, the impostor (3:14–16), in direct contrast with the sincere (3:13, 17, 18). Since he had used the analogy of fruit in the first (3:12), it was not indeed necessary but it certainly was natural, especially for a writer of James's literary culture and skill, to use another expression, "his works," in the second (3:13). We need not enumerate the instances of this word in James. It would be hard to exaggerate its importance in his thought. It accords also with the passage in Matt. 5 with which James, we think, has strong affinities. We have said that in "let him show" in 3:13 James is urging the duty of doing something to show for your wisdom. That is just what we find in Matt. 5:13–16: "Let your light thus shine (like a lamp on a lampstand) in order that men may see your *good works*."

b. The contrast between the self-conceited controversies of the tongue and the fruitful peace of true wisdom (3:13–18)

13 *Who among you is a man of wisdom and knowledge? Let him by his way of life show his works accordingly in meekness of wisdom.*

14 *But if[44] there is bitter jealousy and faction in your hearts, glory not in your lies against the truth.*

15 *This wisdom is not one descending from above, but is of the earth, of this life, of the devil.*

16 *For where there is jealousy and faction, there is confusion and every evil.*

17 *But the wisdom from above is first pure, then peaceable, humane, yielding to persuasion, full of mercy and good fruits, undivided in mind, untainted with hypocrisy.*

18 *And the fruit of righteousness is sown in peace by those that cultivate peace.*

Having addressed the sincere, James proceeds to warn the insincere. He does this by expounding the nature of true wisdom, first negatively and

---

[44]Gk. εἰ δὲ . . . , not a continuation of the previous verse—"And if . . ." (Ropes), but an obvious contrast: "But if . . ." (KJV, RV, RSV, NEB, etc.).

then positively. His consideration of this subject follows naturally on the evils of unwise speech—to suggest that the link is merely verbal ("bitter," vv. 11, 14) is inadequate—and chimes in with James's characteristic insistence on practical reality in religion. In the natural world trees produce their own fruits. Man, too, has natural capacities, but these may be fruitful for evil as well as for good. Fruitfulness is still the test (v. 18).

The opening words at once challenge the readers who profess wisdom, but by their conduct show that they have not grasped its true character. James is still thinking—although not exclusively—of teachers, especially of those whose motives are suspect. The genuine Christian will always exhibit wisdom by the kind of life he lives, especially in human relationships. He will control his tongue and shun strife and controversy. The ideal of wisdom, then, is essentially Hebraic, moral rather than intellectual. This insistence on the need of true wisdom is typical of the practical aims of the Epistle: "faith without works is just a corpse."

13 Having given sincere teachers a warning to beware of the ever present dangers of the tongue, dangers notably great in their work, James now tries to awaken insincere teachers to a proper sense of their vocation.

Of teaching the Jewish ideal was high, as is shown in the Jewish use of the term "wise" for the teacher: it signifies "in Jewish usage one who has a knowledge of practical moral wisdom, resting on a knowledge of God" (Ropes, p. 244). Since the Fall no man, except Jesus as man, of any time, past or present, can be absolutely innocent of sin, in his nature and behavior: it is the *effort* that distinguishes between those who seek and those who do not seek righteousness, i.e., between those on the one hand who genuinely believe that there is such a thing as right distinct from wrong, and believe that God exists, and those on the other hand who do not make the effort to serve him.

We must therefore realize the difference between worldly and genuine wisdom, between self-seeking and genuine prophets (see Matt. 7:16–20). Worldliness is the negation of true wisdom ("from above"), and James uses the strongest possible language in condemning it (3:15). Here, as constantly in his Epistle (e.g., 2:1–9), he is condemning not just a possible but an actual and present evil. Sincerity is a *sine qua non*: worldly self-seekers *cannot* receive true wisdom (2 Tim. 3:7). That is the doctrine that sounds in James's terms, already mentioned, "wavering," "double-minded," "undivided," "anarchic,"[45] which last recalls "traitors"[46] in 2 Tim. 3:4.

The first step in genuine wisdom is to know God: he that would come

---

[45]διακρινόμενος, δίψυχος, ἀδιάκριτος, ἀκατάστατος.
[46]προδόται.

to God must believe that he exists, and that his reward, not the world's, is the reward we must seek. Upon this knowledge and conviction follows the task of applying his principles and rules to our life: that is the Jewish religious ideal of practical moral wisdom (1:12ff.; 3:15ff.). W. D. Ross wrote:

> Practical wisdom cannot exist independently of virtue. The power to attain one's end, be it good or bad, is not practical wisdom but cleverness. . . . Let the wrong end be aimed at, and it becomes mere clever roguery. And just as practical wisdom implies moral virtue, moral virtue in the proper sense implies practical wisdom.[47]

Now, if all true wisdom is the servant or ally of our aim to live according to God's will, it is self-evident that the attributes and qualities of true wisdom will be the same as those of the godly life. It is therefore not surprising but inevitable that James's panegyric of true wisdom should largely be word for word identical with the vocabulary of the several NT descriptions of the Christian life. Of a host of passages we mention only Gal. 5:22f.; Eph. 4:2; Phil. 4:8; Col. 3:13f.; 1 Tim. 6:11; 2 Tim. 2:25; Tit. 3:2. "Undivided in mind" is James's characteristic way of reprobating the man "of divided mind" and insisting on the well-known prime essential of Christianity, faith: his other adjectives seem to raise no question at all.

"Wise man"[48] is used of the genuine teacher (see headnote, pp. 138f.). False pretenders abounded then as always. "Who is . . . ?" is used as a vivid alternative for: "If there is a. . . ." The test is sound: *in meekness of wisdom*[49] is a Hebrew idiom for "in wise meakness" or "in meek wisdom," but here the Hebrew is preferable even in English. This is not "a paradox" (Hort) but almost a genuine Christian truism.

The doctrine here is: "If anyone of you is, or claims to be, a man of wisdom and knowledge, let him see that he makes his virtuous life show the peaceable temper of wisdom." This is the only train of thought that can logically lead to James's verses 16, 17, and 18. We must not be misled by Ropes here, "prove not his wisdom but his meekness." There is no question of his "pointing to his good works," but of his behavior, by its quality pointing to his wisdom. *Works* will be done in the spirit of meekness, and this—not arrogance or argument—is the mark of true wisdom. R. Eleazar ben Azarya asked: "He whose wisdom is greater than his works, to what is he compared? To a tree the branches of which are many, but its roots are few."[50] We must not think the evidence is more important than what it proves: my arrogance would be a danger (at least principally) to my own

---

[47]*Aristotle* ([5]1949), pp. 217–221.
[48]σοφός.
[49]πραΰτητι σοφίας.
[50]*Aboth* iii.18.

soul; my false doctrine, heresy, and schism are a menace not only to me but in fact principally to the whole Christian religion. Moreover, true wisdom always produces wisdom in its possessor, but meekness often goes with hypocrisy: "by their fruits you shall know them" (Matt. 7:20).

14 Not, "Do not let such passion come to expression," but, "Do not *continue to give it* expression, as you have been doing in glorying in false wisdom, but repent." *Bitter*, "contentious" (or, here, "controversial"), is not at all a bad literal translation[51] ("contentious," as contrasted with the peaceable and gentle and "unquarrelsome" Christian). We take *glory not ... against the truth* as a (not difficult) hendiadys. Ropes explains his preference for "zeal," a word with a good or evil sense, rather than *jealousy*, i.e., *personal* jealousy, noting the LXX equivalent,[52] "jealous devotion to a cause," "fanatical ardor" (see Num. 25:11, of Yahweh).

Both in politics and religion zeal can degenerate into mere partisanship: men are prone to transfer to a party the zeal that should be devoted to society, and the notorious zeal of the Jews (Acts 21:20) sometimes produced particularly harmful results. Faced with this kind of situation, James, like Paul (Gal. 5:20), links "zeal" with *faction*,[53] the latter, "a curious word with an obscure history," meaning "to show a factious or partisan spirit."[54] Aristotle[55] speaks of political constitutions changing for various reasons: they may change without any reason as at Heraea, where apparently they changed from election to lot. Before this change, they had been in the habit of electing candidates by political bribe.[56] The picture in this word and its cognates is of unattached workers who go round seeking a day's work (e.g., helping with the harvest or clipping your hedge), or politicians who, more or less like them, e.g., by canvassing, solicit support for themselves or their faction while advancing their own glory, pride, profit, pleasure, personal interest or ambition: such also are these careerist religious pretenders who may have been, as in Paul's case (Rom. 2:8; Phil. 1:17), Judaizers and possibly even those visitors to Antioch who claimed to come from James.[57]

15 This wisdom is condemned in three carefully chosen adjectives, signifying respectively, godless, subhuman, and devilish.[58]

Of the earth,[59] six times in the NT, sometimes in the literal sense (e.g., contrast "marine" biology), does not occur in the LXX, but it is found

---

[51]πικρόν.
[52]Heb. *qin'āh*.
[53]ἐριθεία, cf. cognates ἔριθος, συνέριθος (LS, *s.v.* ἐριθεία).
[54]J. B. Lightfoot, *The Epistle to the Galatians* (1865), p. 211.
[55]*Polit.* v.2, 3.
[56]τοὺς ἐριθευομένους.
[57]Gal. 2:12; 2 Tim. 3:6; Hort, pp. 81–83; *TDNT* II, *s.v.* ἐριθεία (F. Büchsel), pp. 660f.
[58]Viz. ἐπίγειος, ψυχική, δαιμονιώδης.
[59]ἐπίγειος.

in other sacred literature, often in a pejorative sense.[60] Thus here, in contrast to true wisdom, the spurious wisdom is godless in its source and sphere, and is of the earth only, without art or part in the works of Christian faith: so Phil. 3:19 denounces such sectarians, "whose glory is in their shame, whose aims are earthly." Its entire operation bears the stamp of "the world."

Of this life,[61] it appears, had not previously been used as a technical term of Jewish ethics.[62] Whereas the noun,[63] which occurs over a hundred times in the NT, may mean life, soul, mind, or heart, the sophisticated adjective, *psychikos,* comes in only four places in the NT (1 Cor. 2:14; 15:44 [*bis*]; Jude 19), each time in express or (in James) implied opposition to "spiritual,"[64] in the highest sense of that word, implying spiritual insight and aspiration. We do not necessarily find here an allusion to the Gnostic division of men into "natural" (*psychikoi*) and "spiritual" (*pneumatikoi*). It is hard to find a satisfactory translation for the adjective (*psychikē*). "Psychical" transliterates but certainly does not translate it. KJV, RV, NEB "sensual" seems not to have been bettered. Vulgate *animalis,* with a derivation parallel to that of *psychikē*, tempts one to substitute "animal," which now in modern psychology has reached connotation a little more free from the thought of quadrupeds. It certainly chimes with the condemnation so often applied to the lusts of the flesh. The Greek word seems to go back to one of the earliest uses of the noun *psychē,* denoting, like *spiritus* at first, little more than life: compare the Latin adjective *animalis,* literally "breathing."[65] Insofar as some translations stress the flesh they are surely misleading. The man whose wisdom is *psychikos* is in a different category from, say, the libertine. He may well be compared to the morally good, yet non-Christian, modern sophisticated intellectual, who—in a word—is "unspiritual" (RSV).

James goes on to say that false wisdom is not only godless and subhuman but positively "devilish."[66] The false wisdom is not merely neutral, spurious, or inadequate—but positively demonic: see 1 Tim. 4:1. After pointing out that the ending of this Greek adjective denotes (1) fullness, (2) similarity, Hort (p. 84) suggests "inspired by demons" is too strong. But his interpretation of the word as meaning no more than "shared by the demons" (see 2:19) cannot be maintained. In the NT demonic forces

---

[60]E.g., Hermas *Mand.* ix.11; Marcion on 1 Cor. 15:40; 2 Cor. 5:1. See LS, *s.v.*

[61]ψυχικός, RSV (here) "unspiritual."

[62]SB III, p. 329; R. Reitzenstein, *Die hellenistischen Mysterienreligionen* (1910), pp. 42ff.

[63]ψυχή.

[64]πνευματικός.

[65]AG, *s.v.* ψυχικός.

[66]δαιμονιώδης, found only in the NT, and in a scholium on Aristophanes *Frogs* 295 and in Symmachus' translation of Ps. 91:6.

were responsible for inspiring evil thoughts and even overt hostility to God in fulfilment of the will of Satan.[67]

Ropes (p. 248) says that "it is not the substance, but the temper, of the 'wisdom' that makes it false. James is not attacking systems of false teaching." We would not quibble about what is or is not a "system"; but it must now be clear that he, like Paul, is attacking both what the "sect-propagators" are saying and the personal vanity and ambition that Ropes calls "temper" (2 Tim. 3:8, 9). These three adjectives are all associated with the contemporary situation, "the sect-propagators." In 1 Cor. 2:13 man's wisdom is contrasted with "the spiritual": and, we observe, 1 Cor. 2:14 uses the same term as James to describe the professor of man's wisdom, i.e., "unspiritual" (*psychikos*). Here again *psychikos* describes the false wisdom and is clearly linked with the contemporary situation, the "sect-propagators." "Devilish" also is part of the campaign against the "sect-propagators." Unlike "the wisdom from above," which comes from God, *this wisdom,* which is arrogant and partisan, comes from the devil. It is the negation of the true wisdom, and to mark the contrast James uses the strongest word possible, the almost unique "devilish" (Ropes, p. 248). His vehemence, in our view, is proof that he is condemning not mere possibilities or probabilities but actualities, even perhaps in the Church of Jerusalem itself.[68]

16 That the evil was actually rampant is shown by the case at Corinth (1 Cor. 1:10–31, esp. 12–15), where Paul thanks God he baptized there only Crispus and Gaius, and the household of Stephanas, so that it could not be truly said of him that for self-glory he had in his own name baptized any others. The fruit of false wisdom, says James, is "confusion and every evil"—a phrase that might admirably sum up the activity of the Corinthian teachers. It is not hard to see these people at Jerusalem, too. Divorced from its usual political associations,[69] "anarchy"[70] may best sum up James's idea here. Elsewhere Paul uses the same word to describe the disorders arising from the disputatious discussions in his churches (1 Cor. 14:33; 2 Cor. 12:20). Produced by jealousy and rivalry, this kind of unsettlement is the very antithesis of the peace of true wisdom.

The aim of the propagator of a party view, religious or political, is not only to accumulate adherents but also to infect them with the greatest possible sectarian or partisan zeal—though such zeal naturally cannot be quite the same in the mere adherent as in the leader. In both instances,

---

[67] 2 Thess. 2:9; 1 Tim. 4:1; Rev. 6:13f.; *TDNT* II, *s.v.* δαίμων (W. Foerster), p. 19.
[68] W. L. Knox, *St. Paul and the Church of Jerusalem* (1925), p. 21, n. 44.
[69] See E. Hatch, *Essays in Biblical Greek* (1889), p. 4, cited by Ropes, p. 249.
[70] ἀκαταστασία.

however, theirs is "base self-seeking," or simply "baseness," "the nature of those who cannot lift their gaze to higher things."[71] Probably James's rebuke then is primarily aimed at upstarts who, though not leaders, are scarcely less self-regarding: their arrogance would often be greater than that of their leaders (see Phil. 2:1–11). Hence the proverb: "More royalist than the king."

17 This eulogy is composed with the skill that pervades the Epistle.[72] Note the balance, and the similarities and variations—first the pair with similar endings,[73] then a pair with another ending, chiming together in rhythm and sound,[74] then not straight adjectives nor a rhyming pair of nouns but a rhythmical balance, "full of compassion and good fruits":[75] note the effect of *good*, coming with the second noun, and finally the pair of twin adjectives,[76] and the clinching three-chord cadence (3:18).[77] Note here the art of this nine-word sentence—the three three-word phrases, the first suspending the other two, these two themselves being united by "peace" at the beginning and end respectively.

Let us here briefly consider the relation of each element to the Epistle as a whole, to the situation to which it is addressed, and to the whole true wisdom from above. The motif of wisdom introduced in 1:5 pervades the Epistle and reaches its climax in this great Hymn of Wisdom. The unity underlying the seven adjectives is the ideal of the character of Christ; compare 1 Cor. 13,[78] which calls not for an accumulation of virtues but for the submission of the entire personality to God (cf. Jas. 4:7). Wisdom like love is not just a fact but a spirit. First mentioned are the inner characteristics; then follows the outward evidence of Christian wisdom. The wisdom from above is *pure*,[79] a term, infrequent in both LXX and NT, which here describes not only freedom from ceremonial or corporal defilement but sincere moral and spiritual integrity, associated especially with Christ, as in 1 John 3:3.[80] The wise man will copy Christ and keep himself "unspotted from the world" (1:27). Thus "purity" is not just one quality among others but the key to them all.

The next three adjectives describe the qualities denied in the jealousy

[71]*TDNT* II, *s.v.* ἐριθεία (F. Büchsel), p. 661.
[72]See the Introduction, "Author," pp. 18f.
[73]ἀγνή . . . εἰρηνική.
[74]ἐπιεικής . . . εὐπειθής.
[75]μεστὴ ἐλέους καὶ καρπῶν ἀγαθῶν.
[76]ἀδιάκριτος, ἀνυπόκριτος.
[77]καρπὸς δὲ δικαιοσύνης ἐν εἰρήνῃ σπείρεται τοῖς ποιοῦσιν εἰρήνην.
[78]*TDNT* II, *s.v.* ἐπιείκεια (H. Preisker), p. 590, n. 4.
[79]ἀγνή.
[80]See *TDNT* I, *s.v.* ἁγνός (F. Hauck), p. 122; and on the papyri, MM, *s.v.*

and faction of the wisdom that is false. *Peaceable*[81] (elsewhere in the NT only in Heb. 12:11) may be used to cover the narrower classical "freedom from strife with others" and the distinctively Hebraic meaning of inward peace, *shalom*, i.e., "well being," especially "salvation," not altogether unlike the Latin use of *Salve* as a greeting.[82] Contrast vv. 14–16. The neighborly virtues in the remainder of v. 17 suggest the social rather than the introspective force of the word:[83] the good Christian not only prefers to be peaceable but also does his best to spread peace among his fellows. True wisdom is not disputatious but conciliatory, exemplifying the spirit and teaching of Christ, which was the very antithesis of censorious self-seeking.[84]

The word translated *humane*[85] is essentially Greek and without any single equivalent in English: compare Latin *clementia*.[86] Matthew Arnold's definition "sweet reasonableness" is good if it includes the man who is fair, considerate, and generous rather than rigid and exacting in his relations with others: thus in Aristotle it is contrasted with "strict justice,"[87] and is used of judges who do not press the letter of the law.[88] Thucydides also speaks of men of moderation who listen to reason.[89] It was also highly prized by the rabbis.[90] This quality Christ constantly exhibited especially toward his enemies.

Yielding to persuasion,[91] only here in the NT and once in the LXX (4 Macc. 8:6), is the opposite of "disobedient," and is used both of military discipline and for observance of legal and moral standards in ordinary life.[92] We may conjecture that the dissension in the church was caused not only by the conduct of the leaders but also by the rank and file. They are reminded of a quality notable in the character of Christ, in his obedience to his Father's will.

Characteristically James returns to the practical quality of wisdom (cf. 1:8, 22, 27; 2:13, 15, 16); it is full of *mercy*[93] rather than "venom"

[81]εἰρηνική.

[82]*TDNT* II, *s.v.* εἰρήνη (W. Foerster), p. 418.

[83]*Ibid.*, pp. 405ff.; E. D. Burton, *Galatians*. ICC (1921), p. 424.

[84]For the possible influence of the Beatitudes (Matt. 5:8, 9) see F. B. Clogg, *The Christian Character in the Early Church* (1944), p. 28, n. 5.

[85]ἐπιεικής.

[86]L. H. Marshall, *The Challenge of NT Ethics* (1946), p. 306; Preisker, *art. cit.*, *TDNT* II, p. 588.

[87]ἀκριβοδίκαιος—*Eth. Nic.* v.10, 14.

[88]*Rhet.* i.13; xiii.17.

[89]See viii.93; i.7.

[90]b. *Yoma* 23a, 87b; b: *Ta'an.* 25b.

[91]εὐπειθής.

[92]For examples see MM, *s.v.*; Mayor, p. 127; Clogg, *op. cit.,* p. 28.

[93]ἔλεος.

(3:8), in the broader sense of "loving kindness" and *good fruits* (see Matt. 4:7). The Jews believed in mercy, though it was often restrictive, certain classes being excluded from its benefit.[94] Here James is closer to Jesus, and notably his beatitude on the merciful. Such mercy is all-embracing, without "respect of persons," and triumphs in the Day of Judgment (2:13). The use of *good*[95] (fruits) here emphasizes, not of course exclusively, the benefits to others (e.g., 1:27; 2:15) and not only credit to the benefactor.

Undivided in mind[96] (here only in the NT, and in the LXX only in Prov. 25:1) repeats the truth of Jas. 1:6 and 2:24, condemning the waverer, the negative form implying the opposite, namely, singlemindedness (see Mitton, p. 141); and the rare final adjective,[97] a reference perhaps to the "Pharisaic leaven" lingering among Jewish Christians (Hort), indicates the essential sincerity of the wisdom from above, *untainted by hypocrisy*.

18 A brief, typically "capping" sentence brings this section to a close. Though its general meaning and connection with what has gone before is clear enough, its exact meaning is difficult. For example, how do we interpret the phrase *fruit of righteousness*? (See Prov. 11:30; Isa. 32:17; Amos 6:12; Phil. 1:11.) If the genitive is objective, *fruit of righteousness* must mean "the fruit that righteousness produces." If subjective, it means "the fruit that is righteousness." Hort, in a well-argued note, claims that "the latter alone suits this sentence." Mayor concurs, and we agree with both. Ropes's interpretation (p. 250), "i.e. the reward which righteous conduct brings," is quite wrong; nothing here suggests the (not in itself unbiblical) sense: "righteous conduct brings a reward" (Ps. 58:10, 11; Isa. 32:17 with "works" rather than "fruit"). This passage (3:13–18), and this verse, are related to a message that Hort admirably emphasizes: "St. James cannot too often reiterate his warning, founded on our Lord's, against anything that bears no fruit, an unfruitful religion, and unfruitful faith, and now an unfruitful wisdom." The righteous mind must *be* a peace-loving, peacemaking mind (v. 17), and must also work in and for peace (v. 13), fostering peace (v. 18). Having already said to the so-called "righteous" that "a man's wrath does not express in action the righteousness of God" (1:20), he now shows them positively how this righteousness is really achieved. "It is not," Hort continues, "the product of angry vindications: but it grows slowly up as the corn from the seed, the seed which is inevitably and always sown by those who make peace." Clearly, too, the mind of vv.

[94]*Aboth* i.2; SB I, p. 205; IV, pp. 536ff.; *TDNT* II, *s.v.* ἔλεος (R. Bultmann), p. 483.
[95]ἀγαθός rather than καλός.
[96]ἀδιάκριτος.
[97]ἀνυπόκριτος.

14–16 is necessarily neither righteous nor wise, and, as such, is inevitably unable to behave with righteousness or wisdom.

We have chosen (with most commentators) to link *in peace* with *is sown*, translating: "the fruit of righteousness is sown in peace." Hort alone (and no one seems to have accepted his view) tried to connect "righteousness" with "in peace." On this point we think he is wrong. Sense, rhythm, and (in our view) emphasis all connect "in peace" with "is sown." It is true that righteousness and peace are closely linked (e.g., Ps. 85:10; 72:7), sometimes righteousness being regarded as the basis of peace (e.g., Ps. 73:3; Isa. 32:17), at others peace the condition of righteousness (e.g., Luke 1:74). See, too, and compare Heb. 12:11. But James is not (in our view) telling us how "peaceable righteous conduct" is sown and fostered: he is telling us how righteous conduct is sown (i.e., in peace-loving minds) and fostered to fruition (i.e., by and for those who continue to further peace), and *fruit*, though grammatically only a noun, is a quasi-predication as informative as *is sown*. Strictly speaking the seed, not the fruit, is sown; or, we may say, if *is sown* denotes origin, *fruit* denotes the result, the intervening stages being omitted. For similar pregnant expressions, see 2 Bar. 32:1; 2 Esdras 8:6; also Job 39:12; Hag. 2:19, where the figure is reversed and the seed stands for harvest. Fruit is both an end and a beginning, the crown of one process and the germ of the next being present in the seed. So Tertullian: *fructus omnis in semine est*.[98] The figure here is essentially Hebraic, suggesting that righteousness is no sudden growth, but the product of seed sown in peacefulness. The expression suggests the sphere—"mental state" (Mayor)—rather than the instrument, implying that the condition of peace is the prerequisite for the conception of righteousness. The idea of "peace" is also thoroughly Hebraic, meaning much more than a mere absence of disquiet. The prime notion is positive, embracing prosperity, contentment as well as security. Mayor comments (p. 133): "the difficulty of the expression here consists in the prolepsis which regards the seed as already containing in itself 'the fruit'." We interject here: this word for *fruit*[99] in old Greek quite regularly can mean "grain."[100] We have already indicated that we understand "full of good fruits" in the same proleptic way: the true wisdom (in the mind, of course) is potentially full of good fruits (to be performed in conduct) as the seed sown is *potentially* the fruit (to be grown therefrom). That is how we can speak of the *fruit* being *sown*.

---

[98]*Apol.* ix.8.
[99]καρπός—see LS, *s.v.*
[100]See also A. C. Jennings on Ps. 97:11 (cited by Mayor, p. 128), "light is sown for the righteous."

To change the metaphor, the pacific mind (and no other) can conceive a righteous notion and, remaining steadfast in the habit of peace, can in due course bring it to birth.

EXCURSUS G
JAMES 3:5, 6: A FURTHER EXPLANATION

In James the expression τὸν τροχὸν τῆς γενέσεως, termed by Hort "one of the hardest phrases in the Bible," can have no meaning repugnant or irrelevant to his never forgotten faith in the imminent end of "these last days." Κόσμος and τροχός, the latter equivalent to κύκλος, circle or cycle, are Greek terms; from Greek comes "that conception of the circle itself which is probably the basis of James's use of τροχός";[1] but as Ropes says, γένεσις in James means κτίσις, "creation" (not "becoming" as opposed to "perishing").

"It is very difficult to believe that we have the text as St. James wrote it," comments R. A. Knox.[2] We do not believe it. As for the wheel, he continues, "we do better to refer it to the whole cycle of creation." We agree. "But the whole verse runs so awkwardly that it suggests the effort of a copyist to make some sense out of an indecipherable original." Yes, indecipherable as it stands:[3] Ropes, in effect, agrees. "We should have expected him to speak of the spark or tinder which carries the fire, *so as to complete his metaphor,*" says Knox. Nothing could be more apt than these last six words; but we would not say "spark or tinder." We have the spark (fire), that is, the tongue; what is wanted to complete the metaphor is the timber or what not that is set alight by the fire, the πῦρ/γλῶσσα. We think the correct text is that of the Peshitta: "The tongue is fire, the sinful world, wood,"[4] accepted, says Mayor, by Morus, Bassett, and others:

See, how much brushwood how little fire sets alight (i.e., sets on fire, kindles); the tongue, also, is fire (and) the sinful world (or world-order) (is) wood. Thus the tongue stands (καθίσταται) among our members, defiling the whole body and setting fire to the circling course of creation, and being set on fire by hell.

[1]Ropes, p. 238.
[2]R. A. Knox, *NT Commentary* III, pp. 104f.
[3]The text has several variants which are neither convincing nor helpful, being obvious attempts at clarifications; e.g., to insert οὕτως before the second γλῶσσα is, as Hort said, "spurious and misleading." The reading of ff is interesting, where *lingua ignis seculi iniquitatis* = ἡ γλῶσσα πῦρ τοῦ κόσμου τῆς ἀδικίας.
[4]Ropes, p. 234; Mayor, p. 111.

We cannot believe that James or anyone would say that the tongue is, or stands for, the world of sin (the sinful world) in the body. Even Ropes (p. 234) calls this interpretation "awkward and unsatisfactory," though he thinks it "the best sense of which the passage seems capable," and it seems to be that of the NEB ("it represents among our members the world with all its wickedness").[5]

Unlike Mayor, we see no inconsistency in our view, following Morus and Bassett. After the metaphor of defiling in ἡ σπιλοῦσα, the word φλογίζουσα "returns to the figure of fire and completes the interrupted application of that comparison.... As a spark can set a great forest afire, so the tongue kindles the whole world into flame" (Ropes, p. 235). With the Peshitta text we find not only that James returns to the figure of fire, but that he repeats explicitly in other words what he has just now implied in the statement above that the tongue sets fire to the sinful world/wood; for after ἡλίκον . . . ἀνάπτει that obviously implies that the tongue sets fire to the sinful world. Such repetition is characteristic of James, and is common in the NT and elsewhere.

How then does James come to use "the round of creation" as at least an approximate equivalent for "the sinful world"? We are sure the phrase is the analog of ὁ κόσμος τῆς ἀδικίας, as in the Peshitta. Surely there is no difficulty. Here τροχός denotes not an infinite interminable process but a definite, finite course, in space of time; this meaning, as of a rounded period or a closed circle, is well authenticated (Ropes, p. 237); it is inherent in περίοδος and in some uses of the word αἰών, especially in the eschatology of Virgil, as well as in the NT, notably including James. ὁ κόσμος τῆς ἀδικίας is the ordered world, sinful, in James's view: ὁ τροχὸς τῆς γενέσεως is the circling course of creation, rapidly circling to its close, as James believes.

By this interpretation, we think, we restore the simple lucidity and force that are the strongest and most constant characteristics of the Epistle; and what the commentators offer oftentimes could scarcely be feebler or more obscure.

Gehenna, as Ropes remarks (p. 240), is a purely Jewish idea,[6] a "sudden intrusion . . . into a notably Greek context." But sudden ὁ κόσμος τῆς ἀδικίας is also non-Greek. This phrase, taken by some to be corrupt (Spitta and others would omit the whole passage from ἡ γλῶσσα to ἀδικίας), is hard to interpret. Bearing in

---

[5] The NEB actually seems to adopt the notion in small print at the very end of Ropes, p. 239 (there rejected).

[6] The Targum on Ps. 120:2 similarly speaks of the tongue being affected by "hot burning coals" from Gehenna. In *Apoc. Abraham* 31, the wicked are to be burned with the fire of the tongue of Azazel, earlier described (14) as "the burning coal of the furnace of the earth." Gehenna (Heb. *gê ben-Ḥinnōm*), which occurs in the LXX only in Josh. 18:16 (b) of the actual locality; elsewhere in the NT only in Matt. 5:29; 18:9; 23:33; Mark 9:43, 45, 47; Luke 12:5 (see also Rev. 20:14f., λίμνη τοῦ πυρός), was the valley of Hinnom, west of Jerusalem, where rubbish was burned. It came to mean the abode of apostate Jews and the place of eternal perdition for the Gentiles (e.g., 2 Esdras 7:36f.; 2 Baruch 59:10; 85:13). Though James does not hint at any such punishment, the work strikes a sinister note, for Gehenna seems to be a symbol of the devil, the source of evil deeds (cf. John 8:44; 1 John 3:8–10); the periphrasis is probably due to a desire to keep up the metaphor and to connect with "fire."

mind such parallels as Luke 16:8 (cf. next verse), the uses in the LXX,[7] also 1 Enoch 48:7, and especially Rom. 6:6 τὸ σῶμα τῆς ἁμαρτίας, rendered by Sanday and Headlam[7a] "the body of which sin has taken possession," most commentators translate as a genitive of quality, namely, the world consisting of ἀδικία,[8] the sinful world, "die gegenwärtige, gottlose Welt" (Hauck).[9] Following the early Greek Fathers, some favor the Greek spatial idea of "order," "adornment" (1 Pet. 3:3), so "that which puts a fair outward show on injustice" (Dibelius); even "a place of assembly" (Prov. 17:6) (Meyer). To take it spatially, however, especially in the sense of the universe, would suggest something vast, a reversal of the previous idea of the tongue as a small member. But the term is essentially Hebraic and eschatological, referring to that period of time, τὸν αἰῶνα τοῦ κόσμου τούτου (see Eph. 2:2 for that "combination of synonyms" [J. Armitage Robinson]), at the end of the age. "The whole period preceding the final Messianic revelation," writes G. Schrenk,[10] "is viewed as a time of unrighteousness." In 2 Esdras 4:51ff.; 1 Enoch 48:7; 91:5ff., we find the same expression "the world of unrighteousness," which the Messiah will destroy (see 1 Enoch 91:8; Ps. 17:29, 36). So *kosmos* means the world in an evil sense, "human society in a corrupt and perverted state. . . . The tongue is to the rest of the body what the corrupt society is to mankind, and especially to the Church as the representative of mankind in its true state" (Hort). The term then is non-Greek. Paul, James, and others in the NT and Qumran believe that the world, or the flesh, is devilish: not so the Greeks. Far from being sudden, therefore, Gehenna, or some such Jewish expression, is the expected complement of "the world of sin" (Hebraic, as we have noted, in the very form of the expression); here, too, our interpretation of this whole passage is vindicated.

Now we will summarize, with a few comments, Ropes on 3:6 (τὸν τροχὸν τῆς γενέσεως): "γένεσις is here to be taken (cf. 1:23 and note) as substantially equivalent to κτίσις, 'creation' " (p. 236). But even in 1:23 the creation is that of a man by generation and birth: so long as we remember this there is no danger in calling it creation. We are now ready for the rest of Ropes's paragraph:

> The description of nature as a "wheel" is made comprehensible by some of the parallels given below under 2 (a). Here it is used to suggest the continuousness, and so the far-reaching vastness, of the damage done, but the whole phrase is native to other contexts, and the writer's idea is not to be too precisely defined. Of course, what is actually enkindled by the tongue is

[7]E.g., Hos. 12:7; Ps. 143:8, 11.
[7a]*The Epistle to the Romans.* ICC (1905), p. 158.
[8]For Aristotle the whole of vice, as δικαιοσύνη was the whole of virtue (*Eth.* v.1.9 (1130a)). Ἀδικία is found frequently in the LXX (the adjective often means "false," Deut. 19:16; Jer. 5:31, or "valueless," Job 13:4), only in Luke of the Synoptics, fairly common in Paul and in a few other places. Defined by Lightfoot on 2 Thess. 2:10 as "any act which disturbs the moral balance," ἀδικία here is conceived eschatologically (see *supra*).
[9]Cf. *universitas iniquitatis* (Vulg., so also Erasmus, Calvin, *et al.*). Other noteworthy parallels are the Freer Logion Mark 16:14 ὁ αἰὼν οὗτος τῆς ἀνομίας καὶ τῆς ἀπιστίας, and *Corp. Herm.* vi.4 ὁ γὰρ κόσμος πλήρωμά ἐστι τῆς κακίας.
[10]*TDNT* I, *s.v.* ἀδικία, p. 155.

mankind and human society, in which the evil results of wrong speech are manifest and universal; the actual phrase is more inclusive, but in such a rhetorical expression the exaggeration is pardonable. (p. 235)

Inter alia, Ropes here has "wheel" for τροχός, and says that the phrase suggests continuousness, and so the far-reaching vastness of the damage done, i.e., that the damage stops never and nowhere yet; that the phrase originates in other contexts, from which it has been taken by James without any idea "to be too precisely defined"; he says further that the expression is, pardonably but nevertheless, a rhetorical exaggeration. We may never know just what James means here; but we reject the gratuitous assumption that James himself did not know precisely what he meant.[11]

"The phrase," says Ropes (p. 236), "cannot be accounted for from Jewish modes of expression and implies contact with (though not understanding of) Greek thought." Kittel,[12] on the contrary, thought there was no need to connect it with Orphism or other similar systems, and cited evidence for Palestinian belief in a wheel of fate. Philosophic in origin, it may then have become part of common speech, employed with no thought of its original meaning. So Bauer, for example (AG, *ad loc.*), thought that the original idea of "wheel of origin" has been replaced by the "course of life." Certainly it must have been well known in Jewish circles, for there is no attempt to explain it to the readers. Nor (*pace* Ropes) do we find any evidence of misunderstanding. Ropes draws attention to "the occurrence in Greek writers of the exact phrase ὁ τροχὸς τῆς γενέσεως and its equivalent ὁ κύκλος τῆς γενέσεως." It should be noticed, he adds, that "wheel" (τροχός) and "circle" (κύκλος) are "frequently used with little or no distinction."

Ropes continues: (1) The revolving wheel may be used as "a symbol of the changeableness of human fortune, now up, now down." Change might concern human fortunes; and thinking of the wheel used in irrigation, the rabbis[13] sometimes used it in this way.[14] Ropes quotes Anacreon iv.7, "life runs rolling on like the wheel of a chariot" (τροχὸς ἅρματος γὰρ οἷα βίοτος τρέχει κυλισθείς), and Ps.-Phocylides 27 (= *Or. Sib.* ii.87): κοινὰ πάθη πάντων· βίοτος τροχός ⟨life is a wheel⟩ ἄστατος ὄλβος. The latter refers merely to the vicissitudes of fortune in a

---

[11]A collection of parallels and suggested theories may be found in H. Heisen, *Novae Hypotheses interpretandae Epistolae Jacobi* (1739), pp. 819–880 with shorter treatments in Mayor, Hort, Ropes, Dibelius, *et al.* In spite of careful research, G. H. Rendall (pp. 59f.) confesses to be baffled, and as an expedient of despair, proposes to read for τροχός, ὀπός, a nonbiblical word meaning "juice," "sap," which might have been read as ὄχον, and then turned into τροχόν. Another, simpler emendation would read τρόπον (cf. Heb. 13:9).

[12]τὸν τροχὸν τῆς γενέσεως, *Theologisches Literaturblatt,* Beilage I, pp. 141ff.

[13]See SB III, p. 756; G. Kittel, *Die Probleme des palästinischen Spätjudentums* (1926), pp. 140ff.; C. G. Montefiore, *Rabbinic Literature and Gospel Teachings* (1930), pp. 277f.

[14]So Exod. R. on 14:25 with reference to Ps. 75:8: "God . . . brings down one and lifts up another." They also often speak of "a wheel (*galgal*) that revolves in the world" (b. *Shab.* 151b) and the wheel of circumstance . . . "Because there is an ever rotating wheel in this world, and he who is rich today may not be so tomorrow" (Exod. R. xxxi.3).

man's life, and is useless here for James.[15] (2) It may be used to denote rounded completeness, as in Rhetoric: see any composition book on the Latin period.

Before considering Ropes 2(a), p. 237, we must remember to distinguish the use of circle or wheel or the like to symbolize the rise and fall of one man's life, or the rise and fall of a single sentence of periodic construction, from the other use rather confusingly obscured by Ropes's mention of the finite use in the middle of his first paragraph under 2 (p. 237); by "the other use" we mean the use of the circle to denote infinity and eternity. It was from the ring that the Greeks got their notion of infinity: ἄπειρος is applied to a circle, a ring, and in Aeschylus to the seamless robe in which Clytemnestra entangled Agamemnon when he was to be murdered. The seamless robe mentioned in the crucifixion story (John 19:23f.) would, we are sure, be felt by many ancient readers to be a symbol or at least a reminder of immortality, and eternity.[16] The Euripides fragments 415 and 419 (from *Ino*)[17] rest on the notion of eternal succession of generations; so does the passage from Simplicius (quoted by Ropes, p. 238), which actually has the word "infinite"—τῷ ἀπεράντῳ ... , "the infinite or endless circle of becoming." In Orphism and Pythagoreanism the idea is also found in connection with the transmigration of souls (metempsychosis) and the circle of necessity, "a long and weary circuit of birth and death which must be traversed before we can return to the place whence we came."[18] W. L. Knox[19] thought that James was indebted to the Hellenistic Hermetic writings;[20] but he did admit that James could not have accepted a "cyclical" course of destiny, pointing out, however, that Philo, who would likewise have rejected it, can speak of Pharaoh's necklace given to Joseph as a symbol of κύκλον καὶ τροχὸν ἀνάγκης (*On Dreams* ii.44).[21]

For the understanding of James, therefore, we must begin where Ropes leaves off. Who can suppose that James is thinking of an infinite eternity of creation? His dominant thought in this Epistle is not of endlessness but of an imminent end; and it is a thought which in and around his lifetime was evidently widespread through the then known world, from Virgil in Rome to the Wise Men from the east, with their hope of a new age and a new King. Virgil's Fourth Eclogue represents a combination of two ideas.[22] The first is that of the several ages (golden, silver, bronze, etc.). We

[15]See also Herodotus i.207; see *TDNT* I, *s.v.* γένεσις (F. Büchsel), pp. 683f.

[16]So Ocellus Lucanus (Ropes, p. 237 *med.*) says the circle is without beginning and without end.

[17]Ropes, p. 237 *ad fin.*

[18]J. Adam, *The Religious Teachers of Greece*, p. 100. See, e.g., Plato *Phaedo* 72B. See Büchsel, *art. cit.*, p. 684 for a discussion, with references, of the wheel in Buddhism. He concludes: "there may be connections between Buddhism and Orphism, but they cannot be shown, and it is hardly likely that they will be. . . . For the wheel of Buddhism rolls through the world, whereas that of the Greek and Jewish proverb rolls through our own lives."

[19]"The Epistle of St. James," *JTS* 46 (1945), pp. 15f.

[20]E.g., *Corp. Herm.* xvi.8 (I, p. 266): "It is the revolution of the heavenly bodies that determines the fate of men."

[21]For an earlier view, however, see his *St. Paul and the Church of Jerusalem*, p. 91, and his discussion there of Psalms of Solomon 12:2, 3.

[22]See W. A. Heidel, "Vergil's Messianic Expectations," *American Journal of Philology* 45 (1924), pp. 205–237.

are living in the last, the iron age, the approaching end of which is thus prophesied by Hesiod.

For James, as for the Jews and for Christians,[23] the circle of existence was a wheel of divine purpose, for all things come from God and return to him. While we cannot agree with Schlatter's attempt (pp. 221ff.)[24] to link the phrase in James with the rabbinic *galgal ḥammah* (*Sonnenkugel, Sonnenrad*)—the rabbis taught that the sun would burn up the sinner on the Day of Judgment—we do believe it is thoroughly eschatological, and must be interpreted in the light of James's doctrine of the imminent End. This does not mean that James is saying ($\varphi\lambda o\gamma\iota\zeta o\upsilon\sigma\alpha$, etc.) that the sins of the tongue, or any sins, have hastened the end of the present dispensation.[25] Illustrating the tongue's *universitas iniquitatis,* Mayor (p. 115) selects the following from a multitude of rabbinical examples:

> Life and death are in the hand of the tongue. Has the tongue a hand? No, but as the hand kills, so the tongue. The hand kills only at close quarters: the tongue is called an arrow as killing at a distance. An arrow kills at forty or fifty paces: but of the tongue it is said (Ps. 63:9), "they have set their mouth in heaven and their tongue goeth through the earth." It ranges over the whole earth and reaches to heaven. (b. *Ber.* 15b)

Considering some NT remarks about hell-fire, not least the words of this actual verse (Jas. 3:6), we think James is visualizing the world of iniquity, sin, or whatever we care to call Satan's world, as a world consisting of fire. The tongue is fire, the world of sin, set on fire by hell (*Gehenna*)[26] and setting on fire the cycle of our mortal birth (and life; or our mortal creation), being set among the members of the body, which frames a man's mortal existence. The present all-pervasive evil influence of the tongue, therefore, is uppermost. But we do believe that τροχός is eschatological, as signifying the course (of time) ordained by God for the present era, now (as James thinks) in its last days.

To conclude: We are not by any means sure that we are right in our interpretation of τροχός, but, quite separately, some of these remarks are relevant to such a verse as Jas. 5:3, "last days." Mayor (p. 117) has:

> The clause [about ὁ τροχὸς τῆς γενέσεως] is evidently meant to be distinct

[23]Cf. Rom. 11:36; 1 Cor. 15:28.
[24]Cf. W. Bieder, "Christliche Existenz nach dem Zeugnis des Jak.," *Theol. Zeitschrift* 5 (1949), p. 109; see also Büchsel, *TDNT* I, p. 684.
[25]Such an idea is indeed paralleled in the Bible, and prebiblical material, e.g., the Flood stories; but we think that here James is contemplating only the pervading extent of the evil done by the tongue.
[26]Some Greek philosophers (e.g., Heraclitus) thought that the substance of the κόσμος was fire. The Stoics (see Cicero *De Nat. Deorum* ii.41) also taught that the fire which was the creative and restraining principle of the universe differed from common fire. According to Jewish tradition, the fires of Gehenna go back to the creation, but differ from ordinary fire, being created on a different day (b. *Pes.* 54a) and sixty times more intense (b. *Ber.* 57b). See A. Cohen, *Everyman's Talmud,* pp. 380ff.; Bonsirven, *op. cit.,* I, pp. 529ff.; and "Gehenna" in *Encyclopaedia Biblica*; Hastings' *Dictionary of the Bible.* The use of "Gehenna" itself, however, seems to have been restricted. Danby's index to the Mishnah has only five references, three in *Aboth.*

from and stronger than that which precedes: it cannot therefore be anything confined to the individual [i.e., the life of the individual man]. . . . On the other hand it cannot be referred to the material world. . . . James speaking here of the tongue's power of mischief in its widest extent can only refer to the world of human life, the sphere of the worldly spirit, ὁ κόσμος, of which the tongue is always at enmity with God.

All the commentators would agree in this, at least, that κόσμος refers somehow to all (or perhaps only all men) brought into being, from Adam to the end of this era of creation, not to something about the life of an individual man from the cradle to the grave. Not far from our view is J. B. Phillips' translation "all that is included in nature," though we are inclined to confine the reference to mankind. Besides nonliving things, non-animal living things, nonhuman animals, *genesis* may—and here does—mean mankind; the cognate verb is applied so in 3:9. We think our suggestion, ". . . sets afire all that revolving time brings to birth," fits fairly well the other references of *genesis*, in 1:23, "the face that he was born with." If, as we think, James has *mankind* only (or almost only) in mind when he speaks of *genesis* and *kosmos* in 3:6, we suppose we should say, to be clear, "all whom revolving time brings to birth." Strictly, we suppose, it should be "brings or has brought"; we could say . . . whom revolving time has brought to birth: in English "has brought" can bear a retrospective present, and prospective meaning. The Peshitta, though perhaps rather a paraphrase than a translation, having started right is good and seems to keep at least near the truth: *the successions of our generations which run like wheels*.

CHAPTER 4

VI. LOVE OF THE WORLD AND LOVE OF GOD (4:1–10)

1 *What is the source of wars and fightings among you? Is it not in this, in your lusts, which make war in your members?*

2 *You lust, and have no satisfaction; you covet and you envy, and you cannot get your desire; so you fight and war: you have not, because you do not ask.*

3 *When you ask, you do not receive, because of your corrupt asking, in order that you may spend it on your lusts.*

4 *Adulteresses, do you not know that friendship with the world is enmity with God? Anyone who has chosen to be a friend of the world becomes an enemy of God.*

5 *Or do you suppose it is an idle saying in the scriptures that the spirit that has taken its dwelling in us is prone to envious lust?*

6 *But he gives grace that is yet stronger: and so it says, God sets himself against the haughty, but gives grace to the humble.*

7 *So enlist under God: fight the devil, and he will flee from you.*

8 *Draw near to God, and he will draw near to you. Clean your hands, sinners, and purge your hearts, you double-minded.*

9 *Repent, and mourn and weep; let your laughter turn to mourning and your rejoicing to dismay.*

10 *Humble yourselves before God, and he will exalt you.*

James 4 continues the same topic of strife, and addresses now not only the teachers of 3:14 but also the rest of the brotherhood who are in similar sin: strife springs from within (vv. 1–3) and is fostered by worldliness; love of the world and love of God cannot coexist (vv. 4–6); Christians must resist the devil and draw near to God (vv. 7–10).

This passage is closely akin to ch. 1. Thus 4:6 and 1:5 both speak of God's liberal grace to the meek and humble; see also 1:21. The second half of 4:8, on purity, harks back to 1:21, 27, and *sinners* and *double-minded*, in the same verse, to 1:15 and 6–8. The humble repentance of 4:9f. is akin to

165

that of 1:21, and the concluding promise of 4:10 is not far from that of 1:21, "which is able to save your souls."

1 Having declared at the end of ch. 3 that true wisdom is peace, and false wisdom, strife, James naturally begins ch. 4 with some remarks on the genesis of strife: it springs, he says, from our lusts. We fight, we even pray, for the means of gratifying those lusts: no wonder those prayers are not answered. The twofold "whence . . . whence" in the Greek[1] without the customary "brothers" (see v. 13) reveals the intensity of his feeling, as does the duplication in *wars* and *fightings*,[2] one broader and the other narrower in meaning without any sharp distinction here, like our "trouble and strife" (Ger. *Streit und Hader*), and in the regular sense of the plural *fightings*,[3] i.e., of battles fought without actual weapons—fightings, quarrels, strife, disputes in church and society. In later Greek "fightings" was used of philosophical contests and in disputes about words (Prov. 25:10; 2 Tim. 2:23; possibly 2 Cor. 7:5) and personal quarrels (Prov. 15:8; Sir. 28:8); but there is no reference here to doctrinal disputes, political or literal warfare between rival religious Jewish factions in Samaria and Galilee.[4] The whole tone of the Epistle suggests a period of quiet stability; even the "confusion" of 3:16 does not suggest politics or violence (see too 1:8; 3:8).

These battles arise from the lusts within your body which fight against righteousness. Despite its philosophic guise,[5] *lusts* is to be taken in a practical and bad sense (see, e.g., 4 Macc. 1:22; 5:23), probably, against Ropes, equivalent to "desires" of 1:14 (RV "lusts"; see Dibelius, p. 198, n. 3): here *members*[6] is used collectively as the abode of the passions. We have already noted (Jas. 1:2, 12ff.) that James owes his doctrine of desire to the Jewish *yetser*, and, like the rabbis, associates the passions with the physical body—a point made explicit by the present verse, where the bodily appetites are said to reside in the flesh. But particularly in view of the Pauline use (e.g., Rom. 7:23; 1 Cor. 6:12–18), it is possible that *members* should not be understood literally. James has already used the expression in a natural and more individual manner of the tongue as one of the members, 3:6. Here

---

[1]The pleonastic ἐντεῦθεν, which corresponds to πόθεν (*contra* TR and following ℵ A B C ff² m we insert the second πόθεν), here prepares the way for the true explanation to which it gives added force; there is no need for James's readers to look far for the cause. The further question shows that such conflict has its source in "the pleasures" (ἡδοναί) which lie entrenched in their members (τὰ μέλη), i.e., "flesh" or, better, "personality."

[2]πόλεμοι, μάχαι.

[3]As W. Bauer shows, AG, *s.v.* μάχη.

[4]H. Grotius; Rendall; Josephus *Jewish War* ii.13.2. See M. J. Townsend, "James 4:1–4: A Warning Against Zealotry?" *ExT* 87 (1975–76), pp. 211ff.

[5]See for ἡδοναί Plato *Phaedo* 66c; Dibelius, p. 199, n. 1.

[6]τὰ μέλη.

the use is more figurative. According to C. A. Anderson Scott,[7] Paul uses *members* (and "body") "not so much in their physical connotation as in their function of giving expression to the personality." This suggests that like Paul, especially in his doctrine of the "flesh," James traced all sin neither to pleasure nor desire, but ultimately to the core of disordered personality.[8]

A good commentary illustrating this passage is 1 Cor. 1:10–16. "You ask," etc. (v. 3) suggests not abandoned sinners but false Christians: and it is Christians James is addressing.

2–3   James characteristically comes round to where he started, with a delicate variation in the order, from "wars and fighting" to "you fight and war." Then he proceeds to explain *why* they achieve no satisfaction: "You fail to receive satisfaction because. . . ."

Every attempt to make sense of "you kill" (*phoneuete*) as it stands in the traditional text produces an intolerable climax, for example: (i) as a reference to Zealotism (Rendall); (ii) as hendiadys, "You murderously covet," *occidĭtĭs per odia et zelum* (Bengel); (iii) as a rendering of the Aramaic for the Arabic use of "kill," *qāṭala,* in a milder sense, "quarrel";[9] and (iv) by the psychopathic analog, "hate" (Oecumenius, Theophylact).

For this reason Ropes,[10] Mayor (provisionally), Knowling, and many others change the punctuation, making "you kill" belong to the first element in the sentence as "you fight and war" belongs to the second. Ropes (p. 254) claims that this punctuation "alone . . . preserves the perfect parallelism between the two series of verbs, which is fatally marred by the usual punctuation." In fact it deforms both the structure and the thought of vv. 2 and 3.[11] It does not appear here (in vv. 1–3) in the simple additive sense exemplified in the conjectural punctuation of Ropes, etc., which also disrupts the thought of these two verses, where the sequence is, in brief:

> *Whence come your wars and whence your battles?*
> *From your* lusts *warring in your members.*
> *You desire,*

---

[7]*Christianity According to St. Paul* (1927), p. 208.
[8]Cf. C. S. Lewis, *Surprised by Joy* (1955), p. 213. On "members," an abstract quality, see C. F. D. Moule, *Colossians and Philemon.* Cambridge Greek Testament Commentary (1957), pp. 115ff. Cf. Menninger, *op. cit.,* pp. 148f.
[9]E. F. F. Bishop, *Apostles of Palestine,* p. 182.
[10]Following WH mg.
[11]In these καί occurs only six times, i.e., three times with coupling force, in the three pairs, πόθεν . . . καὶ πόθεν, φονεύετε καὶ ζηλοῦτε, μάχεσθε καὶ πολεμεῖτε, and three times with antithetical force, almost equal to "but," in three similarly bisected sentences, viz., . . . καὶ οὐκ ἔχετε, καὶ οὐ δύνασθε ἐπιτυχεῖν . . . καὶ οὐ λαμβάνετε.

and have not:
You are envious and jealous,
and you are not able to obtain.
   so you battle and war!
   [that is, scilicet, *from the causes he need not*
   repeat again, viz., frustrated desires].
Why do your desires fail?
Because you fail to pray.
You ask, and do not get,
Because your prayer is corrupted—
By the desire only for what you mean to spend on your lusts.

It is obvious that the form is shattered by the proposed punctuation, and the thought is ruined by the word for "you kill" with any punctuation. The word goes far beyond the limits of the metaphorical or modified use of "wars" and "battles" and "campaigning" in vv. 1–3. In spite of all the arguments to the contrary, it is still very difficult to take it literally, as Mitton admits (pp. 148f.), citing 1 John 3:15 and John Wesley's commentary, which to the word "kill" adds "in you heart"; and it is no less difficult to give it any meaning to fit this passage.

In these difficulties, therefore, it seems best to change the text from "you kill" (*phoneuete*) to "you are envious" (*phthoneite*) with the meaning shown in the above summary of vv. 1–3, a meaning parallel to "you are jealous" as in the next sentence "you battle" is parallel to "you war." Thus we may truly claim to be restoring the parallelism of this passage. This emendation was long ago suggested by Erasmus and possibly Oecumenius, and has been accepted by (among others) Moffatt, Phillips, Spitta, Windisch, and Mayor, who preferred it to the provisionally approved placing of a colon after *phoneuete* (see above). Besides the harmony in meaning and formal pattern between "envious and jealous" and "battle and war" we may mention that "envy" and "strife" come together in Rom. 1:29; Phil. 1:15; 1 Tim. 6:4; and the verb "to envy" comes in a suggestively similar passage in Gal. 5:26: "Let us not be desirous of vain glory, provoking one another, envying one another" (KJV); see also Jas. 4:5, in our present context.

At Gal. 5:21, as Mitton points out (p. 149), there is a like confusion, some manuscripts having "envyings" (*phthonoi*) and others "murders" (*phonoi*); and at 1 Pet. 2:1 Dibelius cites two which read "murders" (*phonous*) for "envyings" (*phthonous*).

"Your praying is corrupt." The meaning of the Greek[12] is not

---

[12]κακῶς.

simply "amiss" (KJV) but "corruptly" with a probable reference to the *yetser*.[13]

No certain distinction has been established between the middle and the active voices of *aiteō* ("pray"), both of which are found here, in the order middle-active-middle.[14] The variation has been called "hypothetical" (Dibelius), "interchangeable,"[15] "arbitrary,"[16] "an extinct subtlety,"[17] on the basis of: (i) loan and gift;[18] (ii) personal and business (official) affairs;[19] (iii) asking a person and for a thing.[20] (iv) Mayor regards the middle as "subjective" or "dynamic," "prayer of the heart," the active suggesting "prayer of the lips," "outward action" as opposed to "inward feeling."[21] (v) Liddell and Scott (*s.v.*) define the middle as "to ask for one's own use," "claim," i.e., "claim as one's own, appropriate";[22] cf. Mark 6:25, where Salome *claims*[23] (not only asks for) the head of John the Baptist: it is said that, like Salome, James's readers claimed "evilly."

In our opinion, no certain distinction has been established between the middle and the active here; the middle, however, both times seems to contemplate *prayer* more specifically than the active, which has a broader connotation as in Matt. 7:7–11. Simply to make our point clear let us for the moment translate: "You have not, because you do not petition (God). You ask and do not get (just as you seek and do not find, and knock and nobody opens), because your prayer is corrupted by the desire only for what you mean to spend on your lusts." The alternative is to say that here in meaning there is no difference between them at all, only a difference in form adopted to balance the two active forms.[24] We think we may safely assume that something like Matt. 7:7–11, together with the stock Jewish teaching on misguided prayer, was already familiar to James and his flock.[25]

4 Here *adulteresses* (*moichalides*), a Greek vulgarism, is used not literally but in the common OT sense of unfaithfulness to God. KJV follows

[13]See W. F. Lofthouse, "*Poneron* and *Kakon* in Old and New Testaments," *ExT* 60 (1948–49), p. 264; Wisd. 14:29, 30; 4 Macc. 6:17; John 18:23; also Jas. 1:5; 5:16.
[14]Of αἰτέω, as in αἰτεῖσθαι and αἰτεῖσθε on the one hand and αἰτεῖτε on the other in v. 3.
[15]AG, *s.v.*
[16]Bl.-D., § 316.2.
[17]J. H. Moulton, *A Grammar of NT Greek* I (1906), p. 160.
[18]Ammonius, 4th century A.D.; Thomas Magister.
[19]*TDNT* I, *s.v.* (G. Stählin), p. 192; MM, *s.v.*
[20]See Hort; also the solution of Didymus, noted in Dibelius, pp. 201f.
[21]Favorinus, for αἰτοῦμαι as the request (μεθ' ἱκεσίας or μετὰ παρακλήσεως) of an inferior to a superior. See also Thucydides iii.59, 2ff.; iv.18.
[22]Like the Latin *sibi vindicare*; so Cicero *Rep.* i.17, 27; see Lewis and Short, *s.v. vindico.*
[23]ἠτήσατο.
[24]αἰτεῖτε and οὐ λαμβάνετε.
[25]See, e.g., *Sanh.* ix.3; *Ber.* vi.3; and Montefiore and Loewe, *Rabbinic Anthology,* on "Prayer."

a later Byzantine gloss, "adulterers and adulteresses."[26] "In the OT all sin and apostasy are spoken of as adultery" (Hort; see, e.g., Hos. 2:9, 19, 20; 9:1; Exod. 34:15). The marriage metaphor was taken over by Jesus in denouncing Israel as an "adulterous generation" (Matt. 12:39; 16:4; Mark 8:38), by Paul of the Church as the Bride of Christ (2 Cor. 11:1, 2; Eph. 5:22f.; see Rev. 19:7; 21:9), and in this verse by James of the new covenant with Israel. Here, as the context shows, *adulteresses* is figurative of idolatry, and the false god is *the world*. We do not assume any quotation (Spitta); the knowledge to which James appeals, *do you not know?* is empirical, for he is challenging their conscience and harking back to 1:27; see 2:5. Citing the case of Empress Poppaea, Hort (inadequately) defines "friendship with the world" as "conformity to heathen standards of living." In his concept of the "world" Dibelius believes James closer, not to Paul, as in 1 Cor. 1:20ff., but to the radical dualism of John, as in the farewell speech in his Gospel, or in 1 John, especially 2:15ff. This distinction, however, cannot be maintained: James would have thoroughly agreed with Paul's diagnosis of Demas (2 Tim. 4:10), and with the Johannine definition of "the world" as "the lust of the flesh, and the lust of the eyes, and the pride of life" (1 John 2:15ff.), briefly epitomized by James as "the world of iniquity" (3:6).

In no man can love of God coexist with love of the world: "you cannot serve God and Mammon" (Matt. 6:24). The genitives in the two delicately balanced phrases, *friendship with the world* and *enmity with God,* are both objective, conveying strongest ethical contrast. On *friendship* and *enmity,* with the distinction between states and feelings, Hort says: "To be on terms of friendship with the world involves living on terms of enmity with God. It is neither simply hatred of God nor the being hated by God; but being on a footing of hostility." From "friendship" and "enmity" in general, James shows precisely[27] how choosing the world constitutes deliberate enmity toward God. Like Abraham's friendship with God (Jas. 2:23) and the Christian's friendship with Christ (John 15:14), friendship with the world is the result of deliberate choice; as in 1:18, the Greek[28] means "not mere will, but will with premeditation" (Hort). He who "determines" to be a friend of the world becomes an enemy of God, not because God hates him but because he hates God.

5 The source of the *saying in the scriptures* is totally unknown to us. It has been traced variously to:

i.   LXX: Gen. 6:3–7 and Exod. 20:5; Gen. 6:3–5; Zech. 1:14, etc.
     (Mayor, Knowling, Ropes);

[26]μοιχοὶ καὶ μοιχαλίδες (K L P *et al.*).
[27]οὖν.
[28]βουληθῇ.

ii.   NT: mixture of Matt. 6:24; Rom. 8:7; 1 John 2:15 (de Wette);

iii.   a lost Hebrew Gospel (Resch) or apocryphal book like *Eldad and Modad* (Moffatt, Spitta, Dibelius);

iv.   a quotation or paraphrase of a passage in the Qumran Rule of the Community (1QS 4:9ff.), listing the sins to which the spirit of perversity incites a man (T. H. Gaster); or

v.   a corrupt text, demanding the "desperate hypothesis" of emendation by way of minor changes in punctuation or drastic excision and transposition.[29] To James and his readers the "saying" was obviously familiar and in his opinion indisputably valid. The meaning, however, is disputed, four main versions being offered:

(a)   He yearns jealously over the spirit which he has made to dwell within us;

(b)   He yearns jealously for the spirit he set within us;

(c)   That spirit which he made to dwell in us yearneth for us even unto jealous envy;

(d)   The spirit which dwelleth in us lusteth to envy.[30]

The questions arising include: Does *the spirit* mean the Spirit of God or the spirit of man? Can the Greek word *phthonos* possibly be imputed to God? Notwithstanding Mayor and Mitton, we think the question answers itself. The root idea of *phthonos* is "malice" or ill-will and ought to be distinguished from *zēlos*. Trench writes: "*Zēlos* is a *meson*, . . . while *phthonos*, incapable of a good, is used always and only in an evil, signification."[31] Significantly the jealousy ascribed to God in Exod. 20:5 is not *phthonos*, but the milder *zēlos*, which James has already condemned in man (Jas. 3:14). Yet this we would expect, for what Jew could attribute *phthonos*, in the true Greek sense of a god's spiteful envy of man, to Yahweh?

What then of "the spirit of man"? It is intelligible here as the force of good, the spirit of truth and longsuffering, which in every man wages a constant battle against the spirit of anger, bitterness, and lust.[32] Dibelius (pp. 205ff.) postulates a pre-Christian, probably Jewish, "demonological ethic." This spirit of good, the rabbis taught, is given by God to each man when he is born (Gen. 2:7); it is pure at his birth, and his duty is to keep it pure throughout his life: "The soul I have given thee is pure; if thou givest it back to me in the same state, it is good for thee; if not I will burn it before

---

[29]E.g., πρὸς τὸν θεόν, "to God" (Wettstein, Kirn); πρὸς τὸν φόνον, "to murder" (J. A. Findlay; see Ropes, *ad loc.*).

[30]The Arabic versions generally support (d), but the most recent accepts (a), inserting "God" for "He." There is little difference among the first three; the main difference is between them and the fourth, which alone among them is essentially right.

[31]*Synonyms of the NT*, p. 34; cf. Ropes, p. 263; LS, *s.v.*

[32]For almost identical wording compare Hermas *Mand.* iii.1, 2; v.1, 2.

thee."[33] But the rabbis also taught that not only a good but an evil spirit dwelt in man.[34] Idolatry and adultery were the two great passions on which this *yetser* fed,[35] and both were in James's mind in writing 4:1ff., making it all the more likely that the idea of the *yetser* dominates 4:5, 6 also.

After James's usual circling manner, 4:1–12 revives the theme of 1:9–21, both passages based on the notion of the "doubleminded man" of 1:7f., repeated in 4:8; so 1:9, 10, 21 are renewed in 4:6, 8, 10. Now "adulteresses" (4:4) refers to defection from God, as the commentators rightly concur: in fact, this stringent apostrophe balances in 4:8. But the Greek "desires jealously" or "is prone to lust"[36] cannot bear the odd interpretation adopted by Ropes (p. 264) that "God is a jealous lover." The phrase reverts not to the "adulteresses" of 4:4 but to the lusts of 4:1–3, human covetousness, envy, and the like, the appetites for food, drink, sex, etc., which in themselves contain no, or no sufficient, controlling gauge of right or sufficiency; for it is not right for me always to eat or drink as much as I can hold; as James roundly asserts (1:13, 14), it is false to say that God made appetites to be indulged in *ad libitum*. Appetites are necessary for life; but so, for good life, is discipline; and, like every other virtue, according to James and all Christian teachers, the mastery of appetites comes only by God's grace (4:6). Envy usually combines grudging spite (*phthonos*) with covetous (and vv. 4, 12, pugnacious) desire: the verb "desires" (*epipothei,* lit. "yearns") in the Vulgate is (rightly) *concupiscit,* the word also at the beginning of the Tenth Commandment, "Thou shalt not covet," *non concupisces* (Exod. 20:17). So *phthonos* states the natural, proud, unregenerate mode of human yearning; compare 1 Pet. 2:2, where the same verb *epipotheō* ("long for," RSV), and its truly Christian object, are contrasted with *phthonos,* "envying," etc., as in Jas. 4:5, i.e., spitefully or covetously, in the spirit which leads men to envy their neighbors, and so rouses strife (as in Jas. 4:1ff.) in vain.

These considerations, therefore, lead us to conclude that James is here referring not to the yearning of God nor that of his Spirit, but to the sinful propensities of the spirit implanted in man. This interpretation gives clear cohesion to vv. 5 and 6. The opponent, envious desire, that is overcome by God's conquering grace is named immediately before that grace. An apparently old quasi-apocryphal scripture would hardly be the place to find the supposed reference to the Spirit of Christ, or of God, as the Father of Christ. After v. 4, enmity with God, enemy of God, is it not a bad anticlimax

[33]Eccl. R. xii.7; b. *Shab.* 32b, 152b; b. *Niddah* 30a; W. Hirsch, *Rabbinic Psychology* (1947), pp. 150ff., 215ff.
[34]Gen. R. xiv.7; b. *Ber.* 61a; Schechter, *Rabbinic Theology,* p. 264; Jas. 1:14; 4:1ff.
[35]Schechter, *op. cit.,* p. 250.
[36]πρὸς φθόνον.

to continue in v. 5: "Besides, you are breaking his heart with his jealousy of your earthly addictions"? We think *dwelling*[37] refers to the creation of man in Gen. 2:7, who was, however, at least after the creation of woman, prone to forbidden desires. So NEB correctly translates: "The spirit which God implanted in man turns to envious desires."

In addition to its inherent merits, then, this interpretation has the added advantage both of fitting in the preceding verse and also of furnishing an easy transition to the following verse: thus Mitton (p. 155) well says: "If this verse is an affirmation of the corruption which infests the human heart, the reference to God's still more abundant supply of grace to counter this prevalent evil [in v. 6] is very appropriate." We therefore translate: "Or do you suppose it is an idle saying in the scriptures, that the spirit that has taken its dwelling in us is prone to envious lust?"[38]

6 *He gives grace that is yet stronger*, literally "greater,"[39] that is, greater in comparison with the strength of the evil spirit in man, in short, the devil of v. 7, not the "envy" falsely attributed to God in, for example, the RSV, nor "the grace of the world," as with Bede: *maiorem gratiam dominus dat quam amicitia mundi*. Here James is once more close to good rabbinic doctrine. To the humble, and not to the proud, God gives his grace, which is stronger than the evil *yetser* (Prov. 3:34). R. Lakish said: "Every day the *yetser* strives to overpower a man and kill him. Were it not for God's help, it would not be possible to withstand him."[40] But in James, as in Paul, *grace* has not the limited meaning of Proverbs, "acceptance and favor," but, as Mitton observes (p. 156), one "similar to that which is characteristically Pauline, of God's generous, active, effective help to man, far beyond anything the man deserves or can rightly expect." The sublime word *grace* has one of its fullest meanings here: that is the point of "greater," that is, "conquering," "grace manifested in victory." James (need we say?) here and in the next verse views life as a battle for good against evil.[41] *Haughty*[42] signifies especially the arrogant rich (4:16; 5:1ff.), contrasted in 1:9 with the humble poor. "God," said the rabbis, "cannot live in the same world as the proud and arrogant";[43] thus the text James quotes from Proverbs contains both a promise and a threat.

[37]We prefer to read "dwells" (κατῴκησεν), KJV, TR, rather than "caused to dwell" (κατῴκισεν), א A B WH; see Ropes, p. 265.
[38]See further S. S. Laws, "Does Scripture speak in vain? A Reconsideration of James iv.5," *NTS* 20 (1973–74), pp. 210ff.
[39]μείζονα.
[40]b. *Sukkah* 52b; Hirsch, *op. cit.*, pp. 224ff.; Schechter, *op. cit.*, p. 278; G. F. Moore, *Judaism* I, p. 455, for texts and discussion.
[41]ἀντιτάσσεται.
[42]ὑπερήφανος (see further on v. 16).
[43]b. *Soṭah* 5a. "Over nearly forty years there comes back to me," writes Stephen Neill, "a beautiful description of a preacher returning from the University Church at Oxford with a bulky

7 *So enlist*[44]—this verb is regularly used of submission to human authority, for example, Luke 2:51; Rom. 13:1; Eph. 5:22; Tit. 2:9; 1 Pet. 2:13, but only here (and Heb. 13:9) of submission to God.[45] The notion here is of complete humble subjection (Calvin), modelled on the pattern of Christ.

Like other NT writers James regards the devil as an external power (see, e.g., Matt. 13:39; 25:41; Eph. 4:27; 6:11; 1 Tim. 3:7), and embodiment of the evil of his realm, the world. The Jews usually represented him as the enemy, accuser, slanderer. Here the devil and pride are mentioned together. The devil, unlike the Christian, observed Florence Allshorn, takes pride seriously, knowing that as long as he can control human pride he can frustrate God's purposes, if but temporarily. There may be many kinds of pride, but, she adds, "for the devil's purpose a proud Christian is of much more use than an atheist or a pagan."[45a] Nevertheless it is not the devil that James takes most seriously but our own lusts (1:14), with which the devil's relation is not clearly defined.[46] *Fight the devil, and he will flee from you*, described by Bengel as a "happy word" (*laetum verbum*), is perhaps a proverb[47] or even a lost *verbum Christi*, which recalls our Lord's own example, especially his humility, in his successful fight with the devil (Matt. 4:1ff.; Luke 4:1ff.).

8 Originally *draw near*[48] was used of the Jewish priest drawing near in worship (Exod. 19:22; Lev. 10:3; Ezek. 43:19; 44:13), and then by a natural transition, of any approach to God. "God goes out," as the rabbis taught, "to those who approach him."[49] On the other hand, the NT emphasis on God's moving even toward the undeserving is, as C. G. Montefiore perceived, without precedent in Judaism;[50] but "God loves," as St. Bernard said, "both more than you love, and before you love at all."[51]

The call to cleansing seems to be bound up with the call to God—two aspects of one action. Although the language is Levitical, it is used here, as often by the rabbis, of spiritual and moral cleansing: God himself was once compared to a purifying ritual bath.[52] Here *hands* and *hearts* symbolize

---

manuscript under his arm, bursting with pride because he had just preached so excellent a sermon on humility" (*Christian Holiness* [1960], p. 38). Cf. Menninger, *op. cit.,* pp. 135ff.
[44]ὑποτάγητε, aorist imperative passive of ὑποτάσσω.
[45]Passive with middle meaning and a verbal echo of ἀντιτάσσεται and ταπεινός, v. 6.
[45a]J. H. Oldham, *Florence Allshorn and the Story of St. Julian's* (1974), p. 126.
[46]On the *yetser* and the devil, see Schechter, *op. cit.,* pp. 244ff.
[47]See Test. Naph. 8:3; Sim. 3:4; Iss. 7:7.
[48]ἐγγίζω.
[49]Sifre on Num. 10:29; Midr. Psalms on Ps. 120.
[50]*Rabbinic Literature and Gospel Teachings* (1930), p. 337.
[51]*Sermons on Canticles* lxix.8.
[52]M. *Yoma* viii.9; see b. *Baba Mezia* 86a; Philo *Unchangeableness of God* 2, on the pure worshipper.

deeds and thoughts respectively. From David's prayer for a clean heart (Ps. 51:11) it was concluded that his *yetser* was unclean.[53] Repentance is the sinner's first step toward God; the Greek word[54] is the usual strong word for *sinners*,[55] and *double-minded*[56] indicates the fundamental defect of these professing Christians (see 1:8).

9   This is a stern call to worldly and frivolous Christians to grieve and lament for their sins (see 1 Clem. 23:3; 2 Clem. 11:1, 2). There is no hint of asceticism, suggested notably here by Erasmus, Grotius, Mayor, Blackman. The performance of weeping and wailing is worthless in itself; it is penitence[57] that matters—the sorrow of sincere penitence: given that, the weeping and wailing will take care of themselves. So the prophets demanded outward expressions of grief as tokens of penitence, not substitutes for it. In what Dibelius calls this "old prophetic warning of doom" (Isa. 32:11), James is not bidding these frivolous people never to laugh again, but instead of pursuing joy all the time let them be abashed and give some serious thought to God.

Found only here in the NT, frequently in Classical Greek and Philo, less often in Josephus, "dismay"[58] is the "downcast, even shameful look" of the publican, with no reference to "fasting" or "garb of mourning."[59]

10   *Humble yourselves*[60]—passive in form, reflexive in meaning. Self-abasement is a decisive act which James bids them do at once, *before God,* not Christ (see vv. 6, 7, 8). It is the necessary condition of spiritual exaltation and victory (see vv. 6f. and 1:12), not the vanity of the world's glory.

VII. CAUTIONS (4:11–17)

a. Against speaking ill of another (4:11–12)

11 *Do not speak ill of one another, brothers. He that speaks ill of his brother and passes judgment on his brother is speaking ill of the law and passing judgment on the law; but if you pass judgment on the law, you are not a servant of the law but a judge of it.*

---

[53]b. *Sukkah* 52a; Eccl. R. i.19: "The heart sees, the heart hears"; see Schechter, *op. cit.,* p. 255, n. 1, also pp. 313ff. on repentance.

[54]ἁμαρτωλοί.

[55]*TDNT* I, *s.v.* ἁμαρτωλός (K. H. Rengstorf), pp. 327ff.

[56]δίψυχοι.

[57]ταλαιπωρήσατε, "become wretched."

[58]κατήφεια, κατηφέω.

[59]Mayor; see Luke 18:12; Moulton, *Grammar* II, p. 317.

[60]ταπεινώθητε, aorist imperative passive of ταπεινόω.

*12 There is one dispenser of law and judge, he who has power of life and death.
And who are you, that you pass judgment on your fellow?*

James characteristically concludes the chapter as he began it, with
temptations of the tongue, here singling out the sin of censoriousness: "Who
are you to judge another?" Exactly as in 1:26, this failure to bridle the tongue
is a form of self-righteous pride: so is the self-confident boasting of 4:13–16.
4:17, as we said above, returns in full circle to the teacher and the responsibilities of his privileges in wisdom.

11 The triple repetition of *brother,* while no doubt influenced by
grammar (Mayor), signals primarily a change of tone and a fresh appeal. The
suggestion (Ropes, p. 273) that this is an appendix in which James, characteristically (2:25), and after the style of Rom. 14:10, neatly turns the tables
on hypercritical Christians, is attractive, even though there seems nothing to
show that the occasion of such criticism was "a supposed moral lapse." This
warning, an echo of 1:26; 2:12, 13; 3:10, applies not simply to allegedly
anti-Pauline (Schneckenburger) or Gnostic (Cerdon, Marcion: so Pfleiderer,
Schammberger) teachers, but to all, and especially the proud (4:10), who in
their speech truckle with the world (4:1ff.). The OT denounces evil speaking, both against God (e.g., Num. 21:5) and man (e.g., Ps. 49:20), oftener
than any other offense. Thus Miriam, who was punished because she spoke
against Moses, was a stock rabbinic theme.[61] Slander (as we have said on
1:19) was denounced as "the third tongue" (*lishan telitay*) because it slew
three persons: the speaker, the spoken to, and the spoken of.[62] "Slander not
thy neighbor. For whoever slanders his neighbor, there is no salvation for
him."[63] According to Dibelius, slander was almost a *terminus technicus* in
the early Christian vice catalog (*urchristliche Kataloge*); here James, like
Christ (Matt. 7:1), views it with the utmost gravity and even equates slander
of a fellow Christian with breaking the Christian Torah,[64] since the interests
of both are exactly identical. The addition of *his* (a brother . . . his brother)
stresses the unity of the Christian brotherhood, and in turn the heinousness of
this sin. Even if actual condemnation is not here involved, the habit of
judging others,[65] especially with the censorious spirit, is a sign of self-
righteousness and a breach of the brotherhood. So Hillel: "Judge not your
neighbor before you find yourself in the same situation."[66]

[61]Sifre Num. 12:1; Deut. 24:9.
[62]b. 'Arak. 15b.
[63]Derek Erets Zuta 1; Midr. R. Deut. vi.9; Cohen, *Everyman's Talmud,* p. 99; SB I, pp. 226ff.,
905.
[64]On this as Jewish Torah, see Oesterley, Knowling.
[65]Reading ἤ κρίνων (A B K Vulg. Syr. Sah. Boh.) instead of TR καὶ κρίνων.
[66]*Aboth* ii.4; see b. *Shab.* 127a; Matt. 7:1f.; John 12:31.

Not only is the law personified, but it is in some sense identified. The precise meaning is somewhat obscure. Possibly the brother may be said to personify law, if he is law-abiding; to speak evil of him therefore is to speak evil of the law which inspired his conduct. Judging and doing the law are delicately contrasted: man must obey the law, not judge it; to set oneself above the law is to usurp the divine prerogative. Indeed the rabbis taught that judging our neighbor logically leads to the graver sin of judging God: Rabbi Asi declared that the man who begins by disavowing his neighbor will end by denying God.[67] We must be careful to note the far-reaching consequences of James's teaching here: respect for law and order is necessary (as we are often told) for the health of modern society, but James goes on to remind us (v. 12) that, since God is the source of all law, what is ultimately at stake in a "permissive society" is respect for the authority of God himself.

The use of the present imperative in this verse does not indicate a less severe attitude in James, but his condemnation of a habit.

If we consider James 4:4–5:8 as a coherent message, we think that the paramount point is in 4:12, and that the analogous passage in Matt. 10:5–42 has the same permanent point, in vv. 15, 22, and 28. (By "analogous" we do not mean the analogy is exact in detail, but that it is there, and important.) See also the exposition of 5:9 (pp. 191f.).

12 If the Torah is so personified, any slander or judgment of a brother implies not only an active disregard of Torah but also an attitude of superiority reserved solely for God, who is the omnipotent Lawgiver and Judge. Read predicatively, the phrase is more expressive: "One is lawgiver and judge." God is the sole lawgiver:[68] "He gave the law. He is above the law. He alone has the right to modify or overrule it" (Mitton, p. 167). God is also the sole judge: unlike mortals, God *is* God, uniquely, divinely One, the original fountain[69] as well as the ultimate arbiter of law, who, unlike human judges (2:2ff.), is completely impartial. There are many passages that describe this characteristically Jewish monotheistic doctrine of God's supreme sovereignty. Of God as the final source of judicial authority, Rabbi Ishmael says: "Judge not alone; for there is none save One that judgeth alone."[70] Dibelius cites these two striking rabbinic parallels: "Truly, the Eternal destroys life and sustains," and "One he casts down and the other he raises up. . . ." In the OT the reference is to the power of God to rescue from mortal peril; here we have suggested the translation "whose judgment. . . ,"

---

[67]Midr. Debarim Rabba 6 on Deut. 24:9, cited by Dibelius.

[68]All mss. save B P have the article before νομοθέτης only here in the NT, but it is to be rejected as an insertion.

[69]K L wrongly omit καὶ κριτής.

[70]*Aboth* iv.8; see also Deut. 32:29; 1 Sam. 2:6; 2 K. 5:7; Ps. 75:8.

for we think James is referring to "salvation," or the opposite, at the Last Judgment (5:9).

The point is clinched with a devastating question.[71] The disjunctive pronoun is sarcastic, emphasizing the sheer folly of the world to judge, while the vigorous proleptic *you* serves to widen the gulf between God's judgment and man's. "And who are you that pass judgment on another?" To which John Wesley replies: "A poor, weak, dying worm." For James, as for us, however, the best answer is scornful silence.

b. Against presuming on tomorrow's program (4:13–17)

13 *Come now, you who say, Today or tomorrow we will go to some particular city, and stay there one year, and trade, and make a profit.*

14 *In fact, you know nothing of tomorrow. (For what is your life? A vapor that shows for a little and then vanishes.)*

15 *What you should say instead is, If the Lord will, we shall live and do this or that.*

16 *As it is, you vaunt yourselves in your bragging: all such vaunting is wicked.*

17 *If then a man knows how to do right and does not do it, he is in sin.*

13 The vigorous *come now*[72] is the signal for an attack, in good OT prophetic style, on the godless merchants, pictured planning future business ventures. There were three kinds of merchants: (i) the old Hellenistic mariners; (ii) sea and caravan traders; and (iii) those who combined domestic with foreign trade.[73] James is here rebuking a fault common to all these categories, but without the severity of his attacks on the farmers in 5:1–6.

These merchants were the materialist core of the contemporary bourgeois prosperity. In 4:11, 12 the sin of arrogance was in self-opinionated, self-righteous smearing of others; here it is in the equally godless self-assurance in the usual trader's mentality and prospectus. Whether the reference is to a definite city pointed out on the map (RV, Mayor) or general ("such and such a city or town," KJV, RSV) is immaterial: either case exhibits unwarranted presumption. With a flourish they announce that either today or tomorrow[74] they will travel for trade and profit. KJV "buy and sell" is too definite and obscures the original meaning,

---

[71]σὺ δὲ τίς εἶ . . . ;

[72]ἄγε νῦν (Latin *agedum*); see on 5:1.

[73]ναύκληροι, ἔμποροι, πραγματευταί.

[74]Reading ἢ αὔριον, B minn. ff Boh. Syr. Pesh., for TR καὶ αὔριον, A K L P minn. Syr. Harc.; see Luke 13:32; cf. Heb. 13:8. καί suggests greater presumption, but in either form the phrase being proverbial stems from the same Aramaic original: see M. Black, *An Aramaic Approach to the Gospels and Acts* (1946), p. 152. Futures πορευσόμεθα . . . κερδήσομεν are read by ℵ (except ποιήσωμεν) B P minn. ff Vulg. Boh.; the aorist subjunctive by K L S Ψ minn.; and ἐνιαυτόν, B P, instead of ἕνα ἐνιαυτόν, A K L.

which is "travel"[75] (sometimes of troops on the march), but the idea of trafficking came in very early.[76] James employs the verb intransitively in the sense of "carry on business, be a merchant." *Make a profit,*[77] unknown in the LXX though found in Aquila's version, is fairly common in the NT, where it is employed metaphorically of proselytizing (e.g., Phil. 3:8) or of avoiding injury or loss (e.g., Acts 27:21). James employs it literally, "to profit"; Ger. *verdienen, profitieren.*[78]

The skillful use of the repetitive *we will go . . . and stay . . . and trade . . . and make a profit,* and the mention of the year's stay, both suggest deliberate and calculated arrogance. They would go where they liked, and for as long as they liked. Their resolve, together with the refusal to reckon with death, has a modern ring. There is no proof and probably no presumption that here, any more than (obviously) in all the rest of the Epistle (except in the peculiarly bitter climax in 5:1–6), the offenders rebuked do not include some Christians, who (v. 17) ought to know better. The balance of evidence (e.g., omission of "brothers," parallels with 5:1, especially the *come now* with no call to repent) could point to a Jewish rather than Christian constituency; but none of these, singly or together, is decisive. The context gives no help: indeed it has a most modern ring and could well describe the conduct of the businessman today who is merely a professing Christian. Nor is this confined to "merchants," for we are all to some degree prone to the sin of presumption, which is a form of practical atheism. It is plain from v. 15 that there is no thought of sharp practice, an obvious possibility (see 2 Pet. 2:3; Prov. 3:14), with which James in this passage is not concerned, but only of self-assurance.

14 In essence this verse[79] means: The steam or smoke, which appears for a little and then vanishes, graphically depicts the transience of life—a common idea even among pagans,[80] and here used parenthetically to point the folly of planning without God. In his journal John Wesley wrote of his uncertainty while waiting at Chester for a favorable wind to sail to Ireland. "James would have approved the spirit of this entry," observes Coutts,[80a] "contrasting as it does with the presumption of those he re-

[75]πορευσόμεθα.
[76]E.g., Thucydides vii.13; Plato *Laws* 952E.
[77]κερδήσομεν.
[78]See AG, *s.v.* κερδέω.
[79]We note the following variants: *Contra* WH (cf. mg.), Nestlé, Souter, we place a stop after αὔριον. The mss. disagree on whether to omit τό or τά before τῆς αὔριον. We accept τό; to omit either (B omits both; so WH; Nestlé) emphasizes the conditions of life rather than its uncertainty. WH, Nestlé, Souter (wrongly) omit "for" (γὰρ); we prefer ἐστε to ἔσται or ἐστιν. The omission (B P WH) or retention (Nestlé; Souter; Mayor) is more difficult to decide but makes little difference to the sense.
[80]E.g., Seneca *Ep.* 101.4; see Wettstein for other examples.
[80a]*The Armoury Commentary: The NT Epistles* (1975), p. 271.

buked who planned the future without regard to the will of God or the uncertainties of life. What James urges is not a morbid preoccupation with possible disaster, but a realistic attitude to the future made possible by faith in God. . . . Realizing the future is uncertain not only teaches us trust in God, it helps us properly to value the present. To be obsessed with future plans may mark our failure to appreciate present blessings or our evasion of present duties.'' Literature is full of references to the brevity of life: e.g., Bede's parable of the sparrow;[81] Sir Walter Scott's ''Till foam-globes on her eddies ride . . .'';[82] Herrick's ''Gather ye rosebuds.'' For Bible references, see, e.g., Prov. 27:1; Sir. 11:8f.; Luke 12:16ff.[83]

The Greek[84] has its common tinge of generic meaning, ''since you are such as can know nothing of tomorrow,'' i.e., not because they are conceited but simply because, like the rest of us, they are only human.[85] The qualitative force is further expounded in ''For what is. . . ?'' literally ''Of what nature is. . . ?''

The Greek[86] can mean either vapor or smoke; but it seems that here the term is used for mist, perhaps of the Mediterranean mountains especially familiar to the seafaring merchants.[87]

15 The thought of v. 13 is resumed. Over against such practical atheism James sets God and man's dependence on him. He has already spoken of submission to God's will (4:7); he now shows that this submission applies to all life.

If the Lord will,[88] *deo volente (D. V.),* the *condicio Jacobaea,* is essentially non-Jewish, being derived from earlier ''apotropaic'' pagan piety, e.g., *si deus dederit* (cf. also the Arabic *inshallah*), seeking to avoid suspicion of pride.[89] The formula was considered binding by some rabbis prior to any enterprise. In the earlier stages of Roman religion when nothing

---

[81]*Eccl. Hist.* ii.13.

[82]*Rokeby,* Canto Second vii.

[83]For striking word pictures of life's brevity, see Henry Drummond, *The Ideal Life* ([2]1898), p. 247.

[84]οἵτινες.

[85]On this adversative use, ''whereas actually'' (RV; RSV), see Moule, *Idiom Book,* p. 124.

[86]ἀτμίς.

[87]E. F. F. Bishop, *Apostles of Palestine,* p. 188.

[88]We prefer with B P, following Ropes, WH, to read θέλη rather than θελήσῃ (Mayor, Souter, Nestlé; see Sir. 30:6; 1 Cor. 4:19). We read ζήσομεν and ποιήσομεν, ℵ A B P minn. ff, and, *pace* Tasker, do not include ''live'' (in the subjunctive, of course, in texts where it is included) in the clause. On ἀντὶ τοῦ λέγειν, ''articular infinitive,'' cf. Moule, *Idiom Book,* p. 12; see Ps. 108(109):4 for the same construction.

[89]For a late secondhand Jewish formula, see the eleventh-century *Alphabet of Ben Sira;* and for the thought, if not the expression, see Prov. 19:21; *Pirqe Aboth* ii.4; b. *Ber.* 17a; elsewhere in the NT, e.g., Matt. 6:1; 26:39; Acts 18:21; Rom. 1:10; 1 Cor. 4:19; Heb. 6:3; see also Ignatius *Ad Eph.* 20:1; Justin Martyr *Apol.* 68; SB III, p. 758; Ropes, pp. 279f.

was done without first consulting the gods it had real meaning; later,[90] as today, the formula often degenerated into a perfunctory, "I hope so."[91] "If the Lord will" is a consideration no Christian, if he is wise, will ignore when he makes his decisions and plans his life.

16 You *should* say: "If the Lord will"; *as it is* (see Luke 19:42; 1 Cor. 5:11; 14:6), you boast in your braggings.[92] The vice of the braggart (*alazōn*) centers in self and is consummated in an absolute self-exaltation, while the *hyperēphanos* ("haughty") shows his character in his overweening treatment of others; the *alazōn* sins against the truth, while the *hyperēphanos* sins most against love. See 1 John 2:16 for the only other NT occurrence of *alazōn*.[93] All such "vaunting" (see v. 13) is certainly presumptuous pretense and also, since God only ordains the future, arrogantly *corrupt*.[94] The noun[95] plus the emphatic verb[96] here stresses the manner rather than the particular content of their boasts.[97] This exhortation is specific rather than general (Dibelius) in nature, addressed as it is to the heedless merchants of James's day; nevertheless its message, timely and timeless, must be plain to all.

17 James concludes this chapter, like each of the others, with a pointed sententious maxim: "Not to do what you know to be right is sin." The phrase *does not do it* does *not* merely signify a sin of omission; the omission of "good" is necessarily a doing of "evil" (de Wette).[98] Unlike Paul, James is silent on man's moral depravity, teaching (3:9) that he is made in God's image and morally independent; compare also the teaching of the Pastorals and the Parables (1 Tim. 6:9; 2 Tim. 2:24ff.; Luke 12:47; Tasker, pp. 107ff.). This verse, sometimes taken (without good reason) as an independent quotation (Spitta), a lost *verbum Christi* (Resch), or even as an attack on Paul,[99] clinches the thought of the previous verses.

---

[90]E.g., Minucius Felix *Octavius* xvii.11.

[91]See Mayor, pp. 222f.; Dibelius, p. 125, n. 2; Deissmann, *Bible Studies* (E.T. ²1909), p. 252.

[92]ἐν ταῖς ἀλαζονείαις ὑμῶν.

[93]AG, *s.v.; TDNT* I, *s.v.* (G. Delling), p. 227.

[94]πονηρόν—see Jas. 2:4; 4:2; Matt. 15:19; W. F. Lofthouse, *art. cit., ExT* 60 (1948–49), p. 264.

[95]καύχησις.

[96]καυχᾶσθαι.

[97]καύχημα would express the particular content of their boasting, but it is καύχησις that is used here.

[98]On intentional and unintentional sin in Judaism, see Lev. R. 25 (123a); SB III, pp. 541, 758; on Jewish casuistry, see Oesterley.

[99]W. L. Knox, *St. Paul and the Church of Jerusalem,* p. 100.

CHAPTER 5

The subject of speech, so prominent in ch. 3 and 4:11–12, recurs in ch. 5. In ch. 5 the main topics of the previous chapters obviously do recur, for example, faith (in general, and in prayer), endurance, the imminent end and reward, the rich, and guarding your tongue in the evil of this world (and in its good, 5:13; contrast 4:9, on the laughter, and 4:13–16, on the boastful pride, of worldly men). 5:7–18 sums up James's "essentials" of Christian conduct (and Christian hope, of apocalyptic imminence). It is not surprising that here, no less than in chs. 3 and 4, on the topic of Christian conduct the right or wrong use of the tongue, in wisdom or in sin, looms large in James's mind.

VIII. CONCLUSION (5:1–18)

a. The judgment of the faithless rich (5:1–6)

1 *Come now, you rich, weep and howl over your coming miseries.*

2 *Your wealth has rotted, your clothes are moth-eaten:*

3 *Your gold and silver is corroded, and the corrosion shall be for evidence against you, and shall devour your flesh like fire; you have laid up treasure in days that are coming to an end.*

4 *See, the wages of the workers that have mowed your fields, which you have withheld from them, cry aloud; and the outcry of the reapers has reached the ears of the Lord of Hosts.*

5 *You have lived on the earth in luxury and wantonness; you have fattened your hearts for the slaughtering-day.*

6 *You have condemned and murdered the just man; he does not resist you.*

After sharing the hardships of the poor, a pastor thus comments on this passage: "Luther might have appreciated James more had he been

182

rescued by peasants rather than princes.''[1] 5:1–6, on the damnation of the impenitent heathen rich, whether or not they professed Christianity, is a fitting climax to the appeals of ch. 3 and especially ch. 4, which try to bring to repentance some (we may say, many) professing and trifling Christians who are trying to combine God and Mammon in their lives. In this section the diatribe against the rich renews those of 2:1–13 and 1:9–11. We think it is characteristic of James that he begins and ends his chapters of censure (and indeed invective), 2:1 to 5:6, with the same theme, the rich, balanced round the intervening unity of the allied chapters 3 and 4.

It also seems characteristic that the Epistle ends, as it began, with sympathetic encouragement of the truly faithful to endure.[2]

1 *Come now,*[3] as in Latin (*age, agedum*) an interjection of encouragement, here obviously sarcastic, introduces the dramatic charge and sentence against the rich, as if calling their attention with the same forceful emphasis as in its three similar OT occurrences: Judg. 19:6, on a change of plan from that suggested in v. 5; 2 K. 4:24, where the Shunammite is urgent to reach Elisha after the sudden death of her child; and Isa. 43:6, in the joyous transformation heralded in chs. 40ff. Besides the present instance the only similar use of "come now" in the NT is also in the Epistle of James, at 4:13, in expressing overconfidence in the pursuit of wealth. In 5:1 it arrests attention to what James and his fellows believed to be imminent, the day of sudden and sad judgment for these sinners.

Like Paul (see 1 Cor. *passim*, e.g., 1:10–16), James often finds fault with his fellow Christians (as in 1:26f.; 3:13–17, and the whole of ch. 4); and the scene in 2:1–9 suggests that both poorer Christians and their fellow worshippers thought too much of wealth.[4] 5:1–6, however, is of a separate category: it does not exclude the (obviously scarcer) rich Christians, the "double-minded" of 1:8 and 4:8, whose prayers are in vain (4:3 and 1:7; see Zahn, Chaine), but its main purpose here is for a sort of climax, of comfort for the mostly poor Christians, on their release—imminent, as James believes, and assures them—from their miseries in this life. For that reason we think that here, though not generally in the Epistle, James is deliberately embracing the non-Christian as well as any Christian selfish rich in his curse (see Ropes, Dibelius, Meinertz, Feuillet, Plummer). The direct mode of address, vocative with article, shows that the rich are apostrophized as an

---

[1]*The Reformed and Presbyterian World* 29 (1970), p. 108.
[2]For a most colorful rendering of this section (5:1–6) see Clarence L. Jordan, *Practical Religion, or, The Sermon on the Mount and the Epistle of James. Koinonia "Cotton Patch" Version* (1964), pp. 10f. Cf. Menninger, *op. cit.*, pp. 141f.
[3]ἄγε is here used (as in 4:13) rather as an interjection than as a verb (hence not a plural imperative) in this apostrophe to the rich.
[4]See the Introduction, "Rich and Poor" (pp. 29ff.), for James's view of the rich.

(ungodly) social caste. That is why, too, 5:1–6 has no word of repentance but only of damnation, "weep and howl":[5] the tears are not of the penitent, but of the damned, the sorrow of whose world works death (2 Cor. 4:9). In tone and import, especially for its onomatopoeia, this passage should be compared with the prophets (e.g., Joel 1:5 warns the drunkards of Zion of their impending doom; see also Rev. 6:15ff.). Isaiah, we venture to guess, did not chiefly care what the Babylonians thought of his "Burden of Babylon" (ch. 13), or the Moabites of theirs (ch. 15), or the Tyrians of theirs (ch. 23), beginning, "Howl, ye ships of Tarshish." We may cite a modern secular parallel: Winston Churchill's wartime speeches. While directed at the enemy, his invective served to brace his people in their dark days. James, with like intent, "Come now, you rich, weep and howl over your coming miseries," is apostrophizing the rich, but really, like Isaiah, he is addressing his own people, that is, in his case, the Christian congregations to whom this letter was primarily written to be read aloud. Ps. 58 is a striking parallel; there an indictment of the ungodly is followed by a prayer for their damnation, and the end of the psalm turns to the same thought as that to which James turns when he has done with the rich: "The righteous shall rejoice when he seeth the vengeance: he shall wash his footsteps in the blood of the ungodly. So that a man shall say, Verily there is a reward for the righteous: doubtless there is a God that judgeth the earth" (vv. 9, 10, Prayer Book Version). So also James (5:7–11) tells his brothers to take courage from that prophecy (it is no less) of vengeance on the wicked rich, and to wait with patient endurance for their sure reward from the Lord of Mercy. As compared with the rest of the Epistle, this part of the chapter (vv. 7 ff.) addressed to sincere Christians is indeed monitory, but not harsh; and in vv. 13–19 James closes with comfort.

The earliest Christians firmly believed that Christ was soon to come for Judgment Day (vv. 7, 8, 9) and that this would be heralded by a series of disasters of a nature not yet forecast in detail; but James holds that they are imminent, "your coming miseries." They do not specifically indicate the agonies of the fall of Jerusalem (see Mark 13); the thought of *post mortem* punishments is not here impossible (see vv. 7, 9; Rev. 18:7f.; 1 Enoch 63:10; 99:15; 103:7), nor the messianic "birth pangs" preceding the apocalyptic Day of the Lord.

2–3 *Wealth* is collective for abundance of possessions; more detail follows. The earliest forms of wealth were food, clothing, and precious

---

[5]In older Greek both ὀλολύζω and ἀλαλάζω can signify either joyful or sorrowful cries as the case may be. In the OT ἀλαλάζω is used four times, never of mourning, and ὀλολύζω not infrequently, but only in cases of violent cries of grief, e.g., Isa. 13:6, in a context which (cf. v. 11) is like the present in James. Imperative plus participle, reminiscent of the Hebrew infinitive absolute, stresses the *continual* lamentation.

metal. The Bible often mentions the ravages of the moth (Job 3:28; Ps. 29:11; Isa. 1:9; 51:8).[6] There may be an echo here of a saying of Jesus (Matt. 6:19). The whole purpose of James's words is to bring out the great gulf in the society of that day and place, and the general callous failure of the rich to do anything serious for the poor: in the Judgment their wealth will not be an asset but *evidence against* them (on this Semitic phrase, meaning "witness," "pledge," "symbol," see Gen. 21:30; 31:44; Deut. 31:19, 26). The perfect tenses are of prophetic anticipation rather than "historical record" (so Bassett; Tasker), and the corruption of *gold,* etc., is supernatural in a supernatural calamity. Like Chaucer, James knows that gold does not rust: "If golde ruste, what shal iren do?" (Prologue to the *Canterbury Tales,* line 504).

The textual problem we approach with the conviction that here James is keeping "riches" as the avenger and only making a simile of "fire": against (i) Ropes, who removes the colon after "fire," assumes a pause in the sense after "your flesh," and prefers "since" for "like":[7] "since you have stored up fire which shall be in the last days" (p. 287); and (ii) C. C. Torrey, putting a colon after "shall be" and inserting "which" before "you have laid up treasures": "There will devour your flesh the likeness of fire,[8] which[9] you have stored up in the last days."[10] These conjectures are in Greek that James could not have written; and we think an equally serious objection is that Torrey certainly, and Ropes apparently, are introducing a vengeance, fire, as separate from the vengeance proceeding from the riches. James, we feel sure, had fire only as a simile here (*like fire*), and kept riches as the avenging witness (see also v. 4).[11] We have to choose, in effect, between "all your hoarding is (presently to be) for nothing," and "What you have accumulated is (to be) 'wrath.' " We prefer the latter; the former emphasizes their futility: "wrath" matches the "miseries" prominent in v. 1. The suggestion that "You have laid up treasures in days that are coming to an end" is misplaced from the end of v. 1 is unlikely: James (characteristically) rounds off the passage (vv. 1–3) with this sentence, before vv. 4–6 give some of the specific charges on which that sentence is based.

4 "The Epistle of James," wrote Deissmann, "will be best understood in the open air beside the piled sheaves of the harvest field."[12] This rural background is seen here. The commination of the rich in 5:1–6 includes

[6]Also Sib. Or. fragm. iii.26.
[7]ὡς.
[8]ὡς πῦρ as a Semitism.
[9]ὅ omitted.
[10]*The Apocryphal Literature* (1945), p. 20.
[11]The reading *thesaurizastis iram* of Codex Amiatinus and several other Latin mss. (compare Rom. 2:5) is not without merit (Calvin, Estius, Laurentius, Windisch).
[12]*Light from the Ancient East* (E.T. 1927), p. 248.

(v. 4) some farmers, who do not promptly and punctually pay the wages of men who have been working for them in the fields. As Mayor points out (p. 153), this charge goes deeper than that of 4:13–16, which concerns the illusion of self-confidence and self-sufficiency that rules the mind of godless men whose main interest is naturally in the pursuit of wealth.

On unattached workers hired by the day,[13] see 3:14; Matt. 20:1ff. The greedy rich do not pay them at the end of the day, and there was then no practical way of enforcing the law of Lev. 19:13 and Deut. 24:14. Oppression of laborers is often denounced from early times onward (e.g., Isa. 58:9; Jer. 22:13; Mal. 3:5; Sir. 34:22; Tobit 4:14). Prompt payment of wages is also enjoined by the rabbis.[14] Unlike the slave, who had someone who might protect his interests, the free laborer[15] had none. The scene is deliberately set after harvest: the owners of these large Galilean "estates"[16] were well able to pay wages. The compound *withheld*[17] indicates not just delay but complete default. Some would connect "by you" (see 1:13) with "cry aloud" and render "cry aloud from you," i.e., the place where the wages are wrongfully retained (see Gen. 4:10; Exod. 2:23 [22]); but this seems rather fanciful. We would hazard a reason for *from* in this phrase, viz., that the dominant notion is the employers' failure to pay the wages when due. The money itself is said to appeal for justice. *Cry aloud,* a wild, incoherent cry, often of animals in Classical Greek, is used in the LXX of protests, especially against wrong and injustice (e.g., Exod. 2:23; Deut. 24:15; Gen. 18:20, Sodom and Gomorrah's cry; cf. Luke 19:40). On at least one occasion the laborer himself is said to cry to the Lord (see Deut. 24:15). *The ears of the Lord* is simply a vivid "anthropomorphic" way of saying God listens and responds to his people.

The title "Lord of Sabaoth"[18] combines majesty and transcendence and emphasizes that the cause of the poor is to come before the supreme Sovereign, whose justice is now to be visited upon the rich: "it is the same God, who created the sun, moon and stars, and who orders their courses, who is also deeply concerned about the just treatment of the poor and insignificant" (Mitton, p. 180). The primary reference is to Yahweh as the God of the hosts or the armies of Israel and later of the hosts of heaven. The

---

[13]ἐριθεία (cf. 3:14, 16).

[14]E.g., M. *Baba Mezia* ix.11f. On the Sumerian farming laws see S. A. Cook, *The Law of Moses and the Laws of Hammurabi* (1903), pp. 171, 189f.

[15]ἐργάτης.

[16]χώρας; cf. Luke 12:16; Ropes, *ad loc.*

[17]ἀφυστερημένος (from ἀφυστερέω); inferior mss. substitute the commoner ἀπεστερημένος (from ἀποστερέω).

[18]Heb. *ts^ebā'ot*, LXX παντοκράτωρ in Jeremiah, Minor Prophets (cf. 2 Cor. 6:18), τῶν δυνάμεων in Psalms and elsewhere.

rabbis rarely use the title, but on Exod. 3:6 connect it with Yahweh's war against injustice.

"Sabaoth" has become familiar to us through the *Te Deum*; though strangely some writers, like Spenser, Bacon, and Sir Walter Scott, confused it with "Sabbath."

5–6   Verses 5 and 6 continue the account of the sins of the rich, coupling their oppression of the poor (v. 4) with their uninhibited luxury (v. 5), and injustice (v. 6). Even if the better reading in v. 5 omits "as" (*hōs*), we think the *slaughtering-day* is a day of feasting; and v. 6 ends with their unresisted sin.

5   Like an OT prophet James denounces the wanton luxury of the rich, warning of their coming doom. Like their Roman masters, rich Jews indulged in extravagant banquets.[19]

You have lived . . . in luxury—this verb[20] occurs here only in the NT. It is related to a classical form[21] meaning "break" "enfeeble" (cf. Latin *fastidire,* "grow slack"), usually, but not necessarily, in a bad sense (e.g., Sir. 14:4; contrast Isa. 46:11; Neh. 9:25). Underlying the words *on the earth* is a sinister hint on their future.

You have lived . . . in . . . wantonness—this verb[22] too is rare in the Bible but is less literary and also contains a more positive notion, that of vice and luxury, not merely of weakness and enervation. The meaning, here and elsewhere in Biblical Greek, is not in dispute; the etymology of the word is unknown, and there is no plausibility in any of the connections suggested.[23]

They have indulged themselves, as it were "fattening their hearts," like warriors in a feast after a victory (so Blackman, Mitton). We prefer this interpretation to Luther's: he compared the rich to cattle whose wealth was merely "pasturing their hearts" for the day of slaughter. But this involves taking the preposition to mean *for* rather than "in," and assuming a direct connection with the Day of Judgment. Our view gives the best connection of

---

[19]J. Jeremias, *Jerusalem in the Time of Jesus* (E.T. 1969), pp. 92f.

[20]ἐτρυφήσατε, from τρυφάω.

[21]θρύπτω.

[22]ἐσπαταλήσατε.

[23]E.g., Hort, pp. 107–109, collected passages illustrating the more general use of the word: he preferred to link it with σπάω, "to suck down," e.g., of men who live like swine, Ep. Barn. 10:3; Clem. Alex. *Strom.* iii.7, rather than with σπαθάω, "to contrive" (Mayor). E. Boisacq, *Dict. Étymolog. de langue Grecque* (1923), *s.v.* σπάταλος, has: "sensuel, débauché; luxuriant (Anth.); σπατάλη f. mollesse, luxe; parure (Anth.); σπαταλοῦν vivre dans les délices (Spt.). Etym. obscure." The only suggestion he quotes is that of Prellwitz, who connects the word with German *spildan,* "dissipate; to waste, destroy": this, for lack of semantic plausibility, is not accepted by Boisacq. "Taken your pleasure" (RV) hardly preserves the force of the original; and "have been wanton" (KJV) is decidedly more adequate. Though the expression may seem obsolete, we have preferred to translate "lived in wantonness."

thought with the first half of v. 5 and with v. 6. This gives vv. 1–3 to the punishment, and 4–6 to the offense. Rendall's view (p. 30, n. 1) is somewhat similar, but he takes the metaphor as from gloating over deeds of blood rather than from gorging their appetites. The former, or even the second, seems better than the usual interpretation, with the emphasis on "slaughter" as if it rang the knell for the sufferings of the siege of Jerusalem (Plummer); we do not think that James would have interrupted the mounting climax of his indictment in vv. 4–6 with such an interjected mention of doomsday. We think it is more in keeping with his characteristic style if we take this truly ironical and vigorous comparison to mean: "You have gratified your hearts' desires like victors in a bloody battle, and you have not even had to fight in order to get your way: you have condemned and murdered the just man; he does not resist you." The metaphor of war and battle is used as in 4:1–3, with this difference, that there it is applied to futile competition between rivals in greed, competing with one another, but here it is used of worldly success by the rich in their exploitation, and even judicial murder, of the underdog.

6 Ropes, very rightly seeking to avoid making a "triumphant denunciation" end in what he calls "anticlimax," supplies a mark of interrogation at the end of this verse—"Does he not stand to your condemnation?"—and interprets *condemned* as referring, like "cries" in v. 4, to the accusations made by the poor in the Day of Judgment (p. 292). We suggest, however, that the same point can be made without changing the text and with the usual meaning of this verb, indicating "formidable resistance," as in 4:6 (and as in 1 Pet. 5:5; Rom. 13:7; 18:6), a resistance negatived here in Jas. 5:6. *He does not resist you.* Why? Because he *cannot*. If poor men have not been able even to begin resistance it is not less but—if anything—more outrageous to have killed them. The (very effective) point of this climax plainly is that the helplessness of their victims increases the damnation of these rich: "You have condemned and killed the righteous: he is your defenseless prey." In "he does not resist you" there is a tinge of that conative, inchoate force which we found in 2:1: he does not begin . . . he cannot even try . . . to resist these magnates of wealth and power. See Mitton (p. 182), and Tasker: "It brings the section to an end on a note of majestic pathos." The rich are represented, not as bold and fearless champions, defending a cause against dangerous enemies, but as brutal bullies, picking as the victims of their outrages those who either cannot or will not resist. The idea of *Christian* nonresistance here is misconceived: Jas. 5:1–6 is denouncing not only Christian rich nor feeling only for Christian Jewish victims, and no question of Christian forbearance ("or will not") arises in v. 6 any more than in v. 4. The "righteous" or *just man* has been taken to mean James himself, who, says Bishop, "has come down to history with the *nisba* of 'the

Righteous'."[24] But it is hardly likely that James would have referred to his own martyrdom before it happened. Equally unlikely is the equation of "righteous" with Christ. Notwithstanding Bentley's emending "Lord" for "not" (Dibelius, p. 221, n. 2), the allusion would remain hopelessly cryptic and out of character with the rest of the passage. The "righteous" must be taken as a generic term often, and perhaps especially, used of prophets and teachers. In his Epistle James takes a special interest in both these groups (3:1; 5:6). Many of them, like the "quiet in the land" (Ps. 35:20), would be poor and, like Simeon the Just, Stephen, and James himself, shared the fate of "the righteous poor" described in Wisd. 2:10ff.: "Let us oppress the righteous poor; let us not spare the widow . . . ; let us lie in wait for the righteous man." Nobody denies that in Jas. 5:6 "the righteous" is apt to include Christian martyrs, but these were not the first so to suffer: see "the monuments of the righteous" (Matt. 23:29–32), on which it is to be remembered that the Jewish religious magnates of these times were tarred with the same brush as the secular magnates of wealth and power. Annas, high priest A.D. 6–15, retained much power even after he was deposed in A.D. 15, and was very wealthy. Five of his sons and one grandson became high priests, besides Caiaphas, his son-in-law. We note how Matt. 23:29–32 strikes the same note as Jas. 5:1–6, in its v. 32: "How can you escape the damnation of hell?"[25]

The thought here is not of specific cases but of a general social evil of the time among the Jews, viz., oppression of the poor and weak, by judicial process and otherwise (see again Wisd. 2:10f.). It is an evil from which our modern world can scarcely claim to be free.

b. Patience, a little: for the coming of the Lord draws near (5:7–11)

7 *Hold out then, brothers, in patience till the coming of the Lord. See, the farmer waits for the precious fruit of the earth, with persevering patience over it, until it shall have had the winter and spring rains;*

8 *You, too, must persevere with patience, and fortify your hearts; for the coming of the Lord is near.*

9 *Do not grumble against one another, brothers, lest you be condemned; see, the Judge stands at the door.*

10 *Take the prophets who have spoken in the name of the Lord, my brothers, as a model of endurance in affliction and of persevering patience.*

11 *See, we count them happy who have endured. You have heard of the patience of Job, and you have seen the consummation the Lord gave it: for the Lord is very pitiful and compassionate.*

---

[24]*Apostles of Palestine*, p. 182.
[25]See David Hill, "*Dikaioi* as a Quasi-Technical Term," *NTS* 11 (1964–65), pp. 206ff.

This section may fairly be regarded as expanding the ideas of the first chapter, the fatherhood of God, the brotherhood of Christians, faith, prayer, and salvation not with upbraiding but with forgiveness. The injunction "Confess your faults . . ." in v. 16 (again characteristically) balances the opposite example with which the first parenetic section closes, of the man who thinks he is religious, boasts, and deceives himself—almost in the language of "The pride of your heart has deceived you" (Obad. 3) or the familiar: "If we say that we have no sin, we deceive ourselves, and the truth is not in us; but if we confess our sins, he is faithful and just to forgive us our sins, and to cleanse us from all unrighteousness" (1 John 1:8f.).

Here it is relevant to observe the value of comprehending the unity of the concept of the "rich" in the Epistle of James, not least in the business of comprehending the plan of 5:1–11; as we have shown above, the prophecy in vv. 1–6 is the basis of the comfort of vv. 7–11 in the same way as is exemplified in the analogous Ps. 58.

However vv. 7–11 may be paragraphed in print, they form a unity, compacted by (*inter alia*) the last sentence of vv. 8 and 9, and by the theme of "patience" (vv. 7 [*bis*], 8, and 10) and the practically synonymous "so do not grumble" (v. 9), "suffering" (10), "those who endured," "endurance" (11), and the prophets (10) and Job (11), as examples of patient endurance to the end.

7 After 5:1–6 (vehement enough for anything) James wants to speak encouragement to the faithful, not in any cloud of vague verbiage, but with a bracing imperative: *makrothymēsate*. In the NT, of the nearly synonymous verbs *hypomenō* and *makrothymeō*, only the latter is used in the imperative; and moreover, patient waiting for delivery, in *makrothymeō*, is more prominent here than the fortitude which we show, e.g., against temptations, as in 1:2–4. So *makrothymeō* is used in Jas. 5:7 (*bis*), 8; the cognate noun *makrothymia* in v. 10; but in 5:11 (*bis*), James uses the other word, *hypomenō, hypomonē*: this meets the distinction between patiently *waiting* for the Day of the Lord, or the growth of the seed, or the fulfilment of prophecies, as contrasted with, say, *enduring* the boils of Job. *Makrothymia,* the spirit that keeps *hypomonē* alive, was recognized by the Jews as a gift from God (Isa. 57:15) to be used for all our good: "So should you display longsuffering to one another for good."[26] God's apparent indifference had led to grumbling. As an incentive to patience James appeals to the prospect of God's speedy intervention and bids his readers to look for the coming of Christ: unless we question the Epistle's Christian origin, *Lord,* in our opinion, must refer to Christ and not to God, "Lord of Sabaoth" (so

---

[26]Seder Eliyyahu R. xxiv (135); *TDNT* IV, *s.v.* μακροθυμία (J. Horst), p. 379; SB III, p. 78.

Spitta, Meyer, Windisch). The imminence of the Parousia is another strong argument for the Epistle's early date.

The farmer awaiting the harvest is a familiar Jewish picture of salvation[27] and the Last Judgment.[28] Like the farmer the Christian must be patient and depend on God to consummate his purpose.

On *the winter and spring rains* in Palestine, see Ropes, p. 296.[29]

8 Like the farmer, Christians must be patient and strengthen their hearts (compare Luke 9:51; 22:32; 1 Thess. 3:13). In both instances such confidence is based on hope: the farmer is sure that the rains will fall, and the Christian that the Lord will come. The tense of the verb[30] indicates that the coming is near.[31]

9 4:11, like the rest of 4:1–12, deals with aggressive ill-will, i.e., vv. 1–10 with jealousy and envy and the results, and vv. 11–13 with malicious slander and defamation. Now 5:7–11 turns to patience, *makrothymia* and *hypomonē*, and impatience: *grumble*[32] signifies the complaints that sometimes flow from the protracted trial of our patience. KJV "grudge" has the usual seventeenth-century connotation of some suppressed dissatisfaction which at least breaks out in muttered complaint: in Matt. 7:34 "groaning" and in Rom. 8:26, "groanings which cannot be uttered."[33]

Against one another—in this passage James is thinking not of our personal afflictions like pain, disease, or old age, but of malicious, inconsiderate, or unintended vexations such as we sometimes suffer from our friends, enemies, or others.

Here let us insert a kindred comment on 4:11, where "judge," in the present, signifies an adverse, but of course not conclusive, human judgment: similarly "speak ill of the law"[34] and "pass judgment on the law"[35] are almost synonymous: contrast the finality of the aorist infinitives in 4:12, "he who has power *to save* and *to destroy*."[36] So here the tense, "lest you be condemned" (so also KJV based on TR),[37] indicates the finality of judg-

---

[27] Midr. Cant. viii.14.

[28] E.g., Joel 3:13; Matt. 4:29; SB IV, p. 980.

[29] Cf. SB III, p. 758.

[30] ἤγγικεν, perfect of ἐγγίζω.

[31] See further A. Feuillet, "Le sens du mot Parousie dans l'Évangile de Matthieu: Comparaison entre Matth. xxiv et Jac. v. 1–11," in W. D. Davies and D. Daube, eds., *The Background of the NT and Its Eschatology* (1954), pp. 261–280.

[32] στενάζετε, present imperative of στενάζω.

[33] Cf. Shakespeare's *Much Ado About Nothing*, III.iv.90, "he eats his meat without grudging"; also *Henry IV*, Part 1, III.i.177.

[34] καταλαλεῖ νόμου.

[35] κρίνει νόμον.

[36] σῶσαι καὶ ἀπολέσαι.

[37] κατακριθῆτε ("be condemned") rather than κριθῆτε ("be judged").

ment, which here must mean *adverse* judgment: "who accuses his neighbor will himself be punished."[38] Judgment in the inchoate sense of consideration or trial by God on Judgment Day is not to be escaped by any man; and favorable judgment is not a thing to avoid.

At the door (see Mark 13:29; Acts 5:9, 23; Rev. 3:20) is a picture of imminent judgment, and an incentive to patience.

10 There was already a cult of Jewish martyrs[39] (Matt. 23:29–31; cf. Dibelius, p. 226); and the extensive list of examples of patience and faith under difficulties in Heb. 11 illustrates the importance of such virtues in Christianity. James names Job for his patience, and Ezekiel (14:14, 20) also names Noah for his righteousness, together with Job and Daniel before either of these two had a book bearing his name in the OT.

J. B. Lightfoot distinguishes between *hypomonē*, "the temper which does not easily succumb to suffering," and *makrothymia*, "the self-restraint which does not easily retaliate."[40] The latter, not a pagan virtue, is seldom found in the classics, but is frequent in the LXX and NT, of God (e.g., Exod. 34:6) and of man (e.g., Prov. 19:11, and often in Paul's Epistles, 2 Cor. 6:6, etc.). James (5:10, 11) is thinking mainly of patient endurance rather than of its collateral quality, abstinence from retaliation. In 5:10 the noun[41] means not merely "being afflicted" but "not succumbing to affliction," like the verb[42] in 2 Tim. 2:3 and elsewhere.

Whether James, in mentioning "the prophets who have spoken in the name of the Lord" and "the end of the Lord: that the Lord is very pitiful and of tender mercy," is referring primarily to the Father or the Son, we can understand why here he does not cite the case of Jesus; James evidently felt that Christ was in a class by himself. Similarly Peter (1 Pet. 2:18–25) cites Christ (under that name) not with any of the prophets or monumental patriarchs, but as a sole paramount example of endurance without succumbing and (v. 23) without retaliation or regard for the judgment of men. Also, as examples of what faith can *do* in a man, Heb. 12:2 clearly distinguishes, as outside their class, the case of Jesus, *the author and finisher* of faith, "on whom faith depends from start to finish" (NEB). For James, as for Peter (1 Pet. 1:7) and the author of Hebrews, Jesus is the Lord of glory.

11 The aorist of this macarism is deliberate—not men who are still enduring,[43] but men who have endured and have now completed their test (1:2, 12), as Job finished his, and wins the Christian envy of us all.[44] As

---

[38]*Rosh Hashana* 16b.
[39]Cf. C. C. Torrey, ed., *Lives of the Prophets* (1946).
[40]*The Epistle to the Colossians and Philemon* (1900), p. 138.
[41]κακοπαθεία.
[42]κακοπαθεῖν.
[43]K L 048 and minor mss.
[44]The better text omits the article before κύριος, as it is omitted with κυρίου, vv. 10 and 11.

Ropes says (p. 299), *telos* indicates *consummation*; but for the Christian, trial will not quite be over till the Parousia. Job is not cited as an example of *makrothymia* proper, but, like Elijah, of not altogether perfectly patient *hypomonē*, "that gallant spirit which can breast the tides of doubt and sorrow and disaster, and still hold on, and come out with faith still stronger on the other side";[44a] his lapse in patience proper did not exclude him from the Lord's pity and mercy.[45] The example of Job therefore would have a special appeal for those in trial.

Obviously the idea of *telos* must be connected in some way with the story of Job. If this is kept in mind, fruitless speculation on its meaning and integrity will be avoided. *Telos* is correct:[46] it refers not to Christ, his sufferings, death, or resurrection (Augustine, Bede, Wettstein; see Ropes), but to Job and the joyful consummation that crowned his sorrows (Job 42:10ff.). Though *telos* can mean "purpose" (RSV), it is best taken here as "outcome," "issue," "result" (Latin *effectus*): similarly the Syriac version, "the end which the Lord made for him" (*exitum quem ei fecit dominus*).[47] So James urges the same spirit in endurance to win a no less merciful award.

Instead of a noun, such as "mercy" or "pity," James uses a "that" clause—"that the Lord is merciful," with two adjectives recalling Ps. 103:8. *Very pitiful*[48] occurs nowhere else in the Bible: it is borrowed from a Hebrew locution,[49] literally "many bowels of compassion," i.e., "very kind"; *compassionate* illustrates[50] both James's force and his Hebraic affinities. James began this section (vv. 7–11) with an assurance of the quality of that reward.

c. Swear no oaths (5:12)

> 12 *But above all things, my brothers, do not swear oaths, either by heaven or by earth or any other oath; but let your yes be yes, and your no, no, lest you fall under condemnation.*

12 In his discussion of the structure of the Epistle of James, P. B. R. Forbes notes James's way of going back to where he began and also his comprehensive aim, to present an epitome of all the essentials of the

---

[44a]W. Barclay, *The Letter of James* (1957), p. 108; see Jas. 1:3, 4 with comment.
[45]Cf. A. Buechler, *Studies in Sin and Atonement*, p. 173, n. 3; H. A. Fine, "The Tradition of a Patient Job," *JBL* 74 (1955), pp. 28ff.
[46]In spite of emendations like ἔλεος (Torrey); θεωροῦντες, cf. Heb. 13:7 (Preuschen); αὐτοῦ for κυρίου (Könnecke).
[47]Cf. the rabbinic idea of the divinely given end, *sôphô shel YHWH* (Hauck, *ad loc.*, n. 77).
[48]πυλύσπλαγχνος.
[49]Heb. *raḥ^amîm*; cf. LXX πολυέλεος.
[50]οἰκτίρμων.

Christian life.[50a] James obviously feels that avoidance of oaths is one of those essentials.

Bridling the tongue is one of the duties stressed in the opening chapter of the Epistle, and in its third chapter, which opens the second half of the composition. In the final chapter James characteristically harks back to the subjects of both, i.e., prayer with faith (1:5f. and 5:13–18), the rich (1:10 and 5:1–6), "endurance," and the tongue (1:3 and 13, 19, 26; 5:7, 8 and 9, 12; see 4:11). There is here an express warning against grumbling at one another in our troubles, and the mention of Job at least ought to remind us (as James certainly did not forget [1:13] about Job 1:22 and 2:9–10) how Job in his afflictions did not sin with his lips nor charged God foolishly.

The introductory *pro pantōn, above all things,* is said to be (i) hyperbole (Augustine); an "elative" superlative (A. T. Robertson); (ii) an allusion to Zebulon (*Sebulonspruch*) (A. Meyer); (iii) a signal for a *verbum Christi* (A. Resch); (iv) equivalent to a letter's P.S., an addendum, or appendix (Knowling, Plummer, Ropes). We submit that, far from interrupting the general sense (Mitton, p. 190), "above all" links this passage with the previous passages on the discipline of the tongue, not only in 5:7–11 but also in 1:19 and 26. We see here not divorce but a strong bond of unity: reverence for the name of God may well be called paramount in the discipline of the tongue. 5:9 and 12 illustrate very well James's habit of opening and closing a paragraph on the same note: so *pro pantōn* comes "into focus." This does not mean that abstention from oaths is more important than the avoidance of other sins. The immediate reference is to sins of speech. Both formal and informal oaths were loaded with danger, which with the utmost temperance the best of men can scarcely avoid (3:2). Apart from any question of lying—possibly the ancient Jews and Greeks were easy liars—the habitual use of oaths could verge on blasphemy. The invocation of God's name in common speech is a practice which even if sincere at first can only lead to irreverence; from this failing even the rabbis were not exempt.[51] The temptation to make rash vows (Sir. 18:23) was one to which the Galileans apparently were particularly prone. Paradoxically, swearing not only increases the untruthfulness which oaths are supposed to prevent but also as inevitably leads to blasphemy. The oath is the commonest and most serious moral fault in speech, and James is hardly to be blamed for ranking it *pro pantōn,* above all errors of the tongue, e.g., boasting, grumbling, and backbiting. Like "above all" in English, so *pro pantōn* means "above all

---

[50a]*Art. cit., Evangelical Quarterly,* 44/3 (1972), pp. 147ff.; also F. O. Francis, *art. cit.,* pp. 124ff.

[51]M. *Ned.* v.5; see H. Danby's note, *The Mishnah* (1933), p. 271.

else.'' Thus the phrase can be related to the "other things," i.e., the other kindred faults of speech in v. 9, and (we think, but do not wish to press this) in other parts of the Epistle (4:13–16; 5:9; 4:11).

5:9 condemns grumbling, and 5:13 swearing. James could not approve the use by Christians of the pagan challenge to an oath in court, a process not abolished in England until the Civil Act, 1833 (see Prov. 30:9); the teaching on oaths may reflect "the outlook of a persecuted minority" whom the rich haul into court (2:6).[52] Neither could he be silent against Christian use of oaths in other transactions or relations in daily life; he knew the dangers involved: "lest you fall under condemnation"[53] (see Prov. 30:8, 9). It is hard for us to see the problem of the conclusive and promissory oath in true perspective; the old pagan, the Jew, and the early Christians believed in God in a way in which most of our present world does not.

It is possible that here, and in Christ's prohibition, the point is pride and presumptuousness, as in 4:11–12: there a man condemns his fellows as if he were God; so to swear falsely by God is obviously impious. Even an honest man can rarely be sure that he is infallibly telling the truth even of the past, much less of the future; and even if he is within the truth in the particular case, there is the danger of error and, especially in freely swearing in antiquity, of presumptuousness, in (as it were) taking God as a man's partner, not to say accomplice.

But we think James here is chiefly concerned with what was a sort of idiomatic and not always consciously profane swearing in conversational extravagance, as, like the Greeks and the Romans, we often say or at least hear, "By Jove." James, surely, is not against honest legal oaths; he did not require a Christian Jew to repudiate the Mosaic law, though he advised him to rely rather on the law of liberty, as supplementing, not cancelling, the old law (see 2:8–13). The Epistle of James is not given to paradox or extremism, but to basic essentials; these, quite properly and indeed inevitably, include the discipline of the tongue in relation to God and our fellows. The judgment of 5:9 and 12 refers not to human judgment but to God's: so "under condemnation" must be interpreted eschatologically. Here is yet further proof that the Epistle of James is permeated and dominated by an urgent sense of imminent judgment in the end of the present world (5:9).

The point of this command and its parallel in Matt. 5:34 is that the Christian does not need to swear, for his word is his bond:[54] swearing is necessary only in a society where the truth is not reverenced. Whether he

---

[52]See F. C. Grant, in S. J. Case, ed., *Studies in Early Christianity*, p. 275.
[53]ὑπὸ κρίσιν, *pace* Erasmus, Tyndale, *et al.*, who read εἰς ὑπόκρισιν following K L M and other inferior mss.
[54]See Paul S. Minear, *Commands of Christ*, p. 37.

swears or not, the Christian ought always to speak the truth, and this will mean that a simple unadorned "Yes" or "No" is sufficient. James's target is the sort of thing exemplified today in the use of the name of Christ as a mere expletive.

d. Individual occasions for the services or exercises of the church or congregation (5:13–18)

13 *Is one of you in affliction? let him pray. Does one feel happy? Let him sing praises.*

14 *Is one ill? Let him send for the elders of the church, and let them pray over him, anointing him with oil in the name of the Lord.*

15 *And the prayer of faith shall save the sick, and the Lord shall raise him up: and if he has committed sins, they shall be forgiven him.*

16 *Confess your sins to one another, and pray for one another, in order that you may be healed. The prayer of a righteous man is very powerful in its operation.*

17 *Elijah was a man of the same limitations as ourselves, and he prayed earnestly that it might not rain: and there was no rain on the earth for three years and six months.*

18 *And he prayed again, and the sky gave rain and the earth produced its fruit.*

From the stern rebukes of others in 4:1–5:6, James turns to words of sympathy and counsel for his sincerely striving brothers. In 5:7–12, he urges patience in conduct and restraint in speech; in v. 13, prayer in hard spells, and sacred song in moments of joy; then (vv. 14–16), with the unity of his characteristic coherence of thought and exposition, he continues to counsel prayer, and includes (in v. 16) confession.

Among sincere but divergent followers of Christ there is not yet complete agreement in the interpretation of all the points in this section. We approach the problems in our declared belief that the Epistle is by James, the Lord's brother: his observed care in structure suggests that throughout there is one dominant theme, *prayer*.

13 In the end of his Epistle, James comes round to where he began. He had begun with trials; and now having spoken of various afflictions and adversities, including "hardship of the poor," he continues the same theme: in affliction, do not grumble at others (as in v. 9), but pray; in joy, prosperity, and the like, do not boast (as in 3:13–16), but "sing psalms" to God.

Affliction is comprehensive, "calamity of every sort" (Ropes). Grumbling is the natural response to trouble; but the Christian is exhorted to pray. "Praise and prayer are great comforters," wrote Bishop Chavasse;[54a]

[54a]*Great Christians*, ed. R. S. Forman (1933), p. 111.

and so after prayer James goes on to speak about praise. He knows the value of doxology. For the Jew singing psalms characterized, and was required of, the righteous man.[55] "It seems natural," Mitton writes (p. 196), "to give expression to high spirits in singing, but it is characteristic of Christians that their singing takes the form of praises to God." *Sing praises*[56] is found frequently in the LXX, and is, strictly, to twang the harp or similar instrument; it is used also for singing to the harp, or even for singing without any instrument (Ropes, p. 303). This passage in James shows that from the earliest days the Church possessed a rich treasury of praise.[57]

14 Visiting the sick, often with a helpful gift, probably goes back to prehistoric times. It was, of course, common among the Jews; see Matt. 25:43, with the verb (*episkeptesthai*) used in James's penetrating definition (1:27). "Follow the attributes of the Holy One," the rabbis taught; "as he visited the sick (Gen. 18:1), so do you visit the sick."[58] In Jerusalem there were societies of pious men which attended weddings, engagement parties, and the bereaved, even of the Gentiles.[59] The visit of the Jewish elders was already a Jewish custom (Ropes; see 5:15); here also "elder"[60] signifies not, as sometimes, simply age,[61] but office, like the Jewish "elder."[62] *Church* seems to point to a rudimentary organization like that in the early chapters of Acts; this occurrence of the word is possibly earlier than that in Acts 5:11.

Anointing[63] (Ropes, p. 305) is the quite regular "contemporaneous aorist," which is used to express not precedence in time to the main verb but completeness of the process of anointing. Oil was used as a curative by the ancients generally, including the rabbis.[64] The Jews, however, were scrupulous in their use of it; and James, by thus setting it within the purveyance of the Church, seems to be guarding against pagan and other attributions of mystical properties to the oils.[65] It has been well suggested (Ropes, p. 305) that James includes oil in this Christian ceremonial in order to reduce the temptation to use charms, incantations, and other such pagan devices.[66] K.

---

[55]Test. Tenj. 4:4; Ps. Sol. 3:2; 15:3ff.

[56]ψάλλειν, Heb. *niggēn, zimmēr*.

[57]See, e.g., *The Odes of Solomon*, ed. J. H. Charlesworth (1973). For fragments of primitive Christian hymns, see Phil. 2:1ff.; Eph. 5:14; 1 Tim. 1:17; 3:16; 6:16; 2 Tim. 4:18; cf. A. M. Hunter, *Paul and His Predecessors* (²1961), pp. 41ff.

[58]b. *Soṭah* 14a; Gen. R. vii *ad fin.*; see Deut. 13:4; A. Cohen, *Everyman's Talmud*, pp. 225f.

[59]Tos. *Megillah* iii.15; b. *Giṭ.* 61a.

[60]πρεσβύτερος.

[61]So F. W. Puller, *The Anointing of the Sick in Scripture and Tradition* (1904), p. 14, n. 1.

[62]Heb. *zāqēn*. See H. Danby, *Tractate Sanhedrin: Mishnah and Tosefta* (1919).

[63]ἀλείψαντες (from ἀλείφω).

[64]*TDNT* I, *s.v.* ἀλείφω (H. Schlier), pp. 229ff.; *SB* I, pp. 428ff.; II, pp. 11f.; III, p. 759.

[65]Schlier, *art. cit.*, p. 230.

[66]On rabbinic use of magic formula, incantation, and gesture, see b. *Shab.* 67a; b. *Ber.* 55b; SB II, pp. 17, 174; IV, pp. 533f.

Kohler, therefore, overstates when he says that in Judaism the person anointing pronounced "incantations over the sore spots (*loḥesh 'al ha-makkah*) *exactly as* stated in the Epistle of James 5:14."[67] The invocation of the power of the Lord's name makes the proceedings indisputably Christian.[68] As Mitton indicates (p. 199), the use of the oil would itself have a valuable psychological effect in the ritual.[69]

15 The origin of sickness from sin, from Adam downward, was a commonplace of Jewish thought,[70] recurring in the NT (Mark 2:5ff.; John 9:2; Ropes, p. 308; Mitton, p. 201) and the patristic period,[71] and still, though not widely, among us today. It must be admitted that there are today no fewer or less difficulties in the identification of sin with disease.

On the meaning we agree with most commentators, including Estius, who remarks: "By the word 'shall save' is signified bodily health, according to the exposition of nearly all the interpreters. For since the Apostle is speaking of *corporal* sickness, it is natural to understand the word 'shall save', which follows, of a deliverance wrought in the same order of things." James does not hold that the sickness is bound to be due to sin—*and if* (not "since") *he has committed sins*—but the service, except in cases of paralysis, stupor, mental incapacity, or the like, would obviously include at least the patient's confession of sin; and in vv. 14f. James is concerned not with such exceptional cases but with sick persons able to send for their Christian brothers. The prayer of faith in connection with healing was a Jewish custom,[72] though not to the exclusion of physicians; faith was the secret of the Lord's earthly life and gospel: its value, even outside religion, is recognized in some modern psychosomatic medicine.[73] The faith James here has in mind is, of course, both that of the patient and that of the elders, shown in his calling for them and their response to his call.

16 Some think vv. 16–18 are meant to be quite disjunct from 14 and 15, and are concerned not with illness but with miscellaneous neighbors' quarrels and offenses. We cannot believe that after vv. 14 and 15 a stylist like James would here have invited misunderstanding by using "heal" in any but its medical sense. The well-documented association of sickness, sin, and confession in Jewish thought and ministrations seems to us to confirm (against, e.g., Dibelius; see Mitton, pp. 202ff.) the unity of the whole

---

[67]*JE* I, p. 612 (emphasis added).
[68]Acts 5:41; 3 John 7; Ignatius *Eph.* iii.1; vii.1; S. New in F. J. Foakes Jackson and K. Lake, eds., *Beginnings of Christianity* V, pp. 121ff.
[69]See Excursus H, pp. 204f.
[70]E.g., Gen. 3:14ff.; Test. Reub. 1:7; "No sick man is healed until all his sins are forgiven him," b. *Ned.* 41a; SB IV, pp. 525ff.
[71]B. Frost, *Christian Healing* (1960), pp. 206ff.
[72]Mek. *Mishpaṭim,* ch. vi *ad fin.*
[73]See, e.g., A. Graham Ikin, *New Concepts of Healing* (1956), pp. 46f.

passage in question (vv. 13–18, esp. 14–18, including the connective *oun,* "therefore," found at the beginning of v. 16 in all the great manuscripts, though missing in a few others). But our case does not stand or fall on that reading: we hold that exactly as 5:12 belongs to the whole passage 5:7–12, so there is no break between vv. 15 and 16. Confession and prayer were already implicit in Jewish thought of the sickbed; and the elaborate passage from "The prayer of a righteous man is very powerful in its operation" to the end of v. 18 is climactic not merely to the first ten or eleven words of v. 16 but to the whole passage, certainly from the beginning of v. 14.

In the ancient mind sin and sickness went together, and so confession of sin was necessary if prayer for the sick was to be effective. The confession is to be not only to the elders (or other ministers) but *to one another,* that is, probably to those they have wronged. But the OT speaks much of the necessity of confession for those who are well, as a private or as a public or national act of repentance, and the rabbis developed quite elaborate formulas for the purpose.[74] The texts cited by the authorities show how the sick man's visitors, the Jewish "guild for visiting the sick,"[75] swept his room, reminded him to make a will, prayed for him, and habitually exhorted him to confess his sins in the belief that he would be cured: "Great is the power of repentance. . . . It brings healing."[76] The NT Church, as is shown by 1 John 1:9 and this passage in James, continued the practice: its subsequent history we need not here explore.[77]

On the Greek words rendered "is very powerful in its operation,"[78] Mayor thinks (p. 173) that the interpretation of De Wette and Alford, "the prayer of a righteous man avails much in its working," is "irrefragably correct," giving the sense that is apt, necessary, and lucid. Westcott saw that the word *energoumenē* is middle, not passive, and got it so translated in RV, "availeth much in its working"; but, with the notable exception of Ropes (pp. 309f.), critics have not generally accepted his view. The word does not here signify fervor (as in KJV, "the effectual fervent prayer").[79] Ps. 29:4 shows the Hebrew idiom: the voice of Yahweh "is with power" (where KJV, RV, and RSV quite correctly say, "is powerful"; cf. the Anglican Prayer Book Version, "is mighty in operation"). We join the participle and main verb in 5:16 in a way not unusual in Greek, as in, for example, "I have sinned in betraying" (Matt. 27:4).

This aphoristic form, without any connective, typical of James's

[74]See *JE* IV, *s.v.* "Confession" (S. Mendelssohn and K. Kohler), pp. 217ff.
[75]*bikkur ḥolim.*
[76]b. *Yoma* 86a.
[77]See Ropes, pp. 305ff.; S. Schechter, *Rabbinic Theology,* p. 336.
[78]πολὺ ἰσχύει ἐνεργουμένη.
[79]See J. B. Lightfoot, *On A Fresh Revision of the NT* (³1891), p. 182.

style, pithily expresses the effectiveness of prayer. "Prayer," declared P. T. Forsyth, "is not mere wishing. It is asking—with a will. . . . It is energy. *Orare est laborare.* We turn to an active Giver; therefore we go into action."[80] Prayer is an act of faith (Jas. 1:6), and so *energoumenē* is apt enough for a "principle" or "power" from above at work. See further Excursus I, pp. 205ff.

17 To illustrate the truth he has just stated James cites the case of Elijah—his fourth and final OT figure—and the indisputably impressive working of his prayers. With Moses, Abraham, and David, Elijah is the most often named character in the NT: "no Biblical figure so exercised the religious thinking of post-Biblical Judaism";[81] and James begins with a reminder that Elijah was nevertheless only human: *of the same limitations,*[82] a classical word, in the NT here and in Acts 14:15, and in the LXX twice (Wisd. 7:3; 4 Macc. 12:13), is aptly translated "of like passions" or "nature" (RV mg., RSV). James is stressing the common bond between his readers and Elijah, "the grandest and most romantic character that Israel ever produced," the precursor of the Messiah, and above all "a righteous man" whose prayer on this and other notable occasions was answered by God (1 K. 17:17–24).[83] "Such a potency of prayer is not out of our reach, for Elijah possessed it, though he was partaker of human weakness" (Mayor).

The duration of the drought is not constant in all the recorded traditions: (i) "these years," "in the third year" (1 K. 17:1; 18:1); (ii) "three years and six months," as here,[84] half of the perfect number seven and sometimes interpreted as a period of disaster, as in Dan. 12:7; Rev. 11:2 (W. H. Bennett; Moffatt); (iii) eighteen months, e.g., R. Berachiah and R. Chelbo in the name of Jochanan said: "three months before and three months after, and twelve in the middle made eighteen months, and because they were days of suffering he called them many days."[85]

But if, as is probable, these arose from an actual drought, it need not have lasted long in all parts of the land and also its length may have been calculated in different ways; and it is possible that long before James the discrepancies in the traditions were already irreconcilable. Perhaps James is

---

[80]*The Soul of Prayer* (1916), p. 12.
[81]*TDNT* II, *s.v.* Ἠλ(ε)ιας (J. Jeremias), p. 928; SB IV, pp. 781ff.; *JE* V, *s.v.* "Elijah" (L. Ginzberg), p. 122.
[82]ὁμοιοπαθής.
[83]See R. Young, *Analytical Concordance*, p. 295; J. Klausner, *The Messianic Idea in Israel* (E.T. 1956), pp. 451ff.; Jeremias, *art. cit.,* pp. 931ff.
[84]Cf. Luke 4:25; Yalquṭ Shimoni 32, col. 2, cited by G. Surenhusius, *Biblos Katallagēs* (1713), pp. 680ff.
[85]Lev. R. xix (118d); SB III, pp. 760f.; G. Kittel, *Rabbinica* (1920), pp. 31ff.; *Die Probleme des palästinischen Spätjudentums,* p. 53; Dibelius, p. 237, n. 1.

using "three and a half years" very loosely like our "half a dozen" to mean a long time or "many days" (1 K. 18:1).[86]

Prayed earnestly—literally "prayed with prayer."[87] Tautology like this is not rare in the NT, in some extra effort by the author of the discourse to get more attention for his words than he fears they might otherwise receive, or to express the grandeur, power, or other magnitude manifested in his subject. C. F. D. Moule points out that it reflects the OT absolute infinitive, which is used in Hebrew "to express emphasis or frequency."[88] It occurs several times in NT quotations from the OT, but it is rare in passages that are not OT quotations. In Hebrew the idiom is said to express not emphasis in the speaker's mouth but intensification in the fact or activity he is describing; in Greek the case is the opposite. Here the point is not that Elijah put up a particularly fervent prayer but that praying was precisely what he did.

The question at issue is whether we are to assume that here James is following the example of LXX translations of Hebrew phrases or is following the normal habit of Greek. We see no ground for assuming that here James saw any need to adopt Septuagintal style. Though his Christianity is the most Hebraic in the NT, his Greek is among the least subservient to Semitic influence.

To encourage frequent use of prayer, we will not naturally urge how hard, but how manageable, is the effect we must emulate. Verse 16 is not calling for "fervent" prayer: but that mistaken notion is probably part of the reason for the common translation "prayed earnestly" in v. 17. We submit the true force of these verses is as follows: "When a righteous man prays, it is very powerful in operation. That is precisely what Elijah did, and that, let me tell you, is how it worked." We see no difference between the praying in vv. 17f. (apart, of course, from the contents) except in James's effort for emphasis.[89]

18 In the other biblical occurrences of "to give rain"[90] (1 Sam. 12:17; 1 K. 18:1; Acts 14:17) the pronoun that is the subject stands for God. The use of "sky" or "heaven" here does not imply any deification of "heaven"; we may compare our Lord's reference to the occasion "when the

[86]See E. F. F. Bishop, "Three and a Half Years," *ExT* 61 (1949–50), pp. 126f.; Plummer, p. 344; G. Fohrer, *Elia* (1957), p. 57.

[87]προσευχῇ προσηύξατο.

[88]*Idiom Book*, pp. 177f.

[89]As in Luke 4:25 and Gen. 7:12, here in τοῦ μὴ βρέξαι ἐπὶ τῆς γῆς, after the previous simple τοῦ μὴ βρέξαι, and 1 K. 18:1 in ἐπὶ πρόσωπον τῆς γῆς after the simple, "There shall not be dew nor rain," the elaboration is for emphasis. See Ropes, p. 312, last paragraph.

[90]ὑετὸν διδόναι. ἐβλάστησεν, "(the earth) produced its fruit"—this verb is usually intransitive, as in Matt. 13:26; but the aorist is used a few times as transitive, e.g., Gen. 1:11; so also, in later Greek, the present.

heaven was shut up three years and six months'' (Luke 4:25). If, however, James is thinking of *God* as the giver of rain, his language provides us with a further example of the well-known reverential replacement of ''God'' by ''heaven'' in later Judaism (cf. ''Heaven rules'' in Dan. 4:26 alongside ''the Most High rules'' in vv. 17, 25, 32, and Matthew's preference for ''the kingdom of heaven'' as against ''the kingdom of God'' in the other Gospels).

RESPONSIVE VERSE:

e. The saving of human souls earns a great reward (5:19f.)

19 *Brothers, if one among you strays from the truth, and someone brings him back to it,*
20 *let him realize that a man who brings back a sinner from the way of error will save a soul from death—and will wipe out a host of sins [of his own].*

19 All our NT Epistles end with a direct message to the hearers, of greeting, blessing, warning (as 1 John) or, as the Epistle of James, of encouragement and reward. Since most of them are by Paul, it was only to be expected that they should nearly all end in much the same way, as Paul's also do in their opening, except that to the Galatians, in whom he could find nothing to be thankful for, and Ephesians, which was probably not addressed to one particular groups of readers. The close of the Epistle of James is supremely characteristic of its author, and his way of coming round to where he began. As he began (1:3, 4) and ended (2:14–26) the first half of his Epistle with faith and the necessity for corresponding conduct in the Christian life, so he began the second half with the teacher's responsibility, and now ends it with the teacher's reward: it is precisely the sort of end that the discerning reader should have learned to expect, and this is just about the point in length at which we should reasonably have expected the letter to end.

In 5:19, therefore, the ''wandering brother'' emerges not from the immediately preceding context (e.g., v. 16) but from the content of the Epistle as a whole. The deadly peril of sin, mentioned in its very last verse, harks back to the same thought in 1:15, as the warning against erring, wandering, or straying in the figurative moral sense (1:16) recurs, in effect, in *if one among you strays* (5:19); and *the truth* (5:19) repeats the thought, and the word, of 1:18, for the Christian gospel.

The Church is a redemptive brotherhood; through its efforts the wandering brother can be restored: ''turned'' from error to righteousness.

Only later the word acquired the technical KJV meaning "convert."[91] The indefinite "someone" shows that this is the responsibility not only of both teachers and elders but also of every Christian.

20   The letter closes (5:20) with James's characteristically fraternal thought of the teachers—not only the professional teachers—striving to rescue the straying brother from the way of death, and of the reward of their success in any such rescue.[92]

In 5:19, *if one among you* . . . , James is speaking, not comprehensively of the population among whom his hearers are living, but of "one of you" Christians, who has fallen (inceptive aorist) into some habit of false doctrine or, probably more often, of sinful practice. As instances of "saving" in this sense with a human subject Ropes cites Rom. 11:14; 1 Cor. 7:16; and 1 Tim. 4:16. The soul is that of the erring brother; see 1:21. Death, from which he is saved, is the penalty of sin, as in 1:15, and under the covenant "final exclusion from the Divine Society" (1 John 5:16; so Westcott).

If the soul to be saved and the sins to be covered are taken to be of the same person (adding "his" before "soul"),[93] this produces a kind of tautology which we fear is intolerable in James, quite different from examples such as "wars and battles" (4:1) or "cleanse your hands, and purify your hearts, be afflicted and mourn and weep" (4:8f.). Further, in our discussion of "Faith and Works" (pp. 34ff., 120ff.), we have shown that scruples such as those of Mayor, quoted by Mitton (p. 214, line 7), are unfounded. James would never have believed, nor preached in this context, that the rescue of a sinner (or, for that matter, of a drowning man) could be good for the soul of only the person rescued. Dibelius (p. 239) cites many passages that reveal a similar pattern: e.g., "Great is the reward of him that leads sinners back to the way of the Lord."[94] Finally, "cover a multitude of sins," which may echo Prov. 10:12[95] or a *verbum Christi*,[96] seems peculiarly apt in a conclusion characteristically designed by James to hark back to the opening of this second part of the Epistle. Why does love "cover" sins? Not because it is blind or refuses to see faults. "Hide"[97] here is like the Hebrew[98] and suggests a kindred, though different, aspect of the thought not

[91]Matt. 13:15; Luke 1:16; 22:32; Acts 3:19; 14:15; 1 Thess. 1:9; Polycarp *ad Phil*. 6:1; *Apost*. 2:6.
[92]γινωσκέτω ("let him know") is the better reading; it is more likely to have been ousted by γινώσκετε ("you know") than vice versa.
[93]So RSV, WH, von Soden, Nestlé. αὐτοῦ is added after ψυχήν by ℵ A *al*. lat syr. (it is omitted by K L and the majority of later mss.).
[94]*Zohar* xcii.18; cf. Ezek. 3:19; *Aboth* v.18.
[95]1 Pet. 4:8; 1 Clem. 49:5; 2 Clem. 16:4.
[96]Clement of Alexandria *Paed*. iii.12.91; cf. *Didascalia* ii.3.
[97]καλύψει, future of καλύπτω.
[98]Heb. *kissāh 'al*.

uncommon in such as: "Hide ('Turn,' Prayer Book Version) thy face from my sins, and blot ('put,' PBV) out all mine inquities ('my misdeeds,' PBV)" (Ps. 51:9; 32:1f.; 85:2), i.e., "cause them to be forgiven and forgotten." To hide or cover sin is, in effect, for God in his charity (1 Cor. 13:6) not to look at it—in short, to get it remitted. These sins are obviously the sins of the reclaimer, not the reclaimed. The magnitude of the reclaimer's reward, not the multitude of the sins of the reclaimed, is, as it were, of the essence of the covenant. The multitude of sins in 5:20 repeats the thought of the greater damnation and the many offenses of 3:1, 2 (on the comprehensive use of "multitude," *host,* for sins of both teacher and sinner, see Mayor, p. 180 with references); at the end of ch. 5, as at the beginning of ch. 3 (vv. 1–6), James is deeply conscious of his infirmities, the characteristic infirmities and special responsibilities of the teacher; but to that thought the last eight exquisitely balanced words of the Epistle add the triumphant inspiration of the reward of the teacher's work, to the rescued sinner and his rescuer.

EXCURSUS H
ANOINTING WITH OIL IN LATER TRADITION
(JAS. 5:14)

The service of Jas. 5:14 and 15 and 16–18 is one of intercession only, not of absolution: that, like the recovery of the sick, is the Lord's response to the prayer of faith. The story of how Severus showed his gratitude to Christian Proculus for having once cured him by anointing (Tertullian *Ad Scapulam* 4) and the cases collected by F. W. Puller (*The Anointing of the Sick in Scripture and Tradition* [1904]), dating from the third to the seventh century A.D., show no sign that in that period this therapeutic use of consecrated oil was generally thought of as also having spiritual efficacy. Conversely, Origen (*Hom. ii in Lev.* 4) quotes this text in James to teach the forgiveness of sins through penitence, but apparently ignores James's mention of oil. Similarly, Chrysostom (*De sacerd.* iii.6) employs James to support the belief that a priest has power to grant absolution, but he, too, apparently ignores the reference to oil.

The importance of this use of consecrated oil in countering the strong menace of pagan magic is well attested in the literature of this period: see Ropes (p. 306) on Cyril of Alexandria, Caesarius of Arles, and the Venerable Bede.

From the fourth century there are Greek and other oriental formularies for the consecration of the holy oil, and likewise others in Latin. A letter of Pope Innocent I, dated 19 March, A.D. 416, mentions "the holy oil which, being consecrated by the bishop, it is lawful not for the priests only, but for all Christians to use for anointing in case of their own need or that of members of their household." Before the end of the eighth century the Church in the West transformed the use of the holy oil into "extreme unction" (*extrema unctio* or *sacramentum exeuntium*), first named as one of the seven sacraments in the twelfth century, and officially defined by the Council of Trent—not intended to be therapeutic but sacramental, administered by a priest to the dying by way of remission of sins. It may well have been intended to remedy abuses by which the older custom was increasingly menaced, and to concentrate attention on the spiritual aspects of the patient's danger and of the rite. Unction for the dying seems first to be mentioned in connection with the Gnostics; see Irenaeus i.21.5 (Harvey xix.4).[1] In the Greek Orthodox Church the anointing[2] can be administered to the sick while there is still hope of recovery, which, according to Ropes (p. 307), is the main point in the Russian use, whereas the Greeks concentrated on the remission of sins.

We may conclude, therefore, that the rite of extreme unction has no obvious connection with the practice first described in Jas. 5:14ff., which was intended to heal the sick man, not to prepare him for his last journey. Significantly, however, the Second Vatican Council (1962–65) revised this interpretation, declaring that "Extreme Unction" may "more fittingly be called 'anointing of the sick.' "[3]

EXCURSUS I
"THE PRAYER OF A RIGHTEOUS MAN"
Energoumenē: Middle or Passive? (Jas. 5:16)

Middle or passive? This is, understandably, apt to be the first question asked about a verbal form that may be either middle or passive. Yet it cannot be answered unless we have first reached some decision, however provisional, about the meaning of the sentence in which it occurs—and then perhaps it does not need to be answered at all!

---

[1] On the whole subject see *ERE* V, *s.v.* "Extreme Unction" (H. Thurston), p. 671; XII, *s.v.* "Unction" (A. J. Maclean), pp. 511f.; F. Fenner, *Die Krankheit im NT* (1930); M. Goguel, *The Primitive Church* (E.T. 1964), pp. 369ff.; *TDNT* I, *s.v.* ἀλείφω (H. Schlier), p. 229. On the rite of Extreme Unction itself, see H. B. Porter, "The Origin of the Mediaeval Rite for Anointing the Sick," *JTS* N.S. 7 (1956), pp. 211ff.
[2] εὐχέλαιον.
[3] *Study Text II: Anointing and Pastoral Care of the Sick* (1973), p. 4, *et passim*.

Until then all we can say is that in the writer concerned the ambiguous form is usually (or perhaps always, or never) used in the middle, or in the passive, sense. In this instance, which is the only one in James, we cannot do even that. In the rest of the NT, however, middle forms of ἐνεργεῖν occur eight times altogether, and in seven of these it seems to have an active sense, while in the eighth (Gal. 5:6) most scholars think the active sense more probable, while admitting that the passive sense is possible. So, if Paul's usage is any guide to that of James, ἐνεργουμένη in our text probably should be taken in the active sense. It is this which we propose to investigate more fully in the present note.[1] We shall base our investigation on Mayor's classic and almost definitive discussion (pp. 171–73). Can we summarize him effectually?

First, Mayor gives about a score of instances of this verb in the *passive*, thus first, in the order in which he prints them: 1 Esdras 2:16 (LXX), "the works of the temple are being pushed on." In the KJV (and Bagster's edition of the Greek LXX) it is v. 20, and it is translated, "the things pertaining to the temple are now in hand." Our point is that the verb does not necessarily always mean, in the passive, "to be pressed or pushed on with vigor," though that is right enough, we think, in this verse. Sometimes it may mean "is being done." Five lines later, Mayor quotes Barn. 1:7 and gives, quite correctly, "seeing the several prophecies being accomplished." Then follow many examples with the meaning "activated" or "inspired," often in a sinister sense, e.g., by the devil or demons, and so "possessed," but not always so: e.g., line 15 of his note (p. 171), from Clem. Alex. *Strom.* iv.615, which we translate: "the same action admits of a distinction of quality, according as on the one hand it comes through fear or on the other hand it is performed through love, or is executed on the one hand in faith or on the other hand in knowledge"; so, about line 20, "many not knowing the source of the power by which they are activated, conjecture that it is by the evil designs of the devils" (Clem. *Hom.* ix.12); line 22, ". . . that the bodies of the dead continue to survive for three days, being animated or energized by the mere life of nature" (Arethas *In Apoc.* v. 6, so Mayor). Thereupon at once he cites a statement by Stephanus: ". . . but ἐνεργεῖσθαι is found in the NT also with *active* meaning"; and Mayor then adds, "which [statement by Stephanus] the latest editor corrects in the words, 'Nay rather, always passive'." Mayor continues: "so Dr. Hort[2] . . . writes . . . ἡ ἀκοὴ ἐνεργουμένη, 'passive as always.' "

---

[1]Before plunging into this let us look at some of the various translations. To be sure, translators, ancient and modern, give little help. It seems that Luther was at first content to render it quite literally: "Wenn es tätig ist." But could anyone suppose that prayer had much strength except when it was *tätig*? In later editions this became: "Wenn es ernstlich ist"; this is more meaningful, but is it a meaning that ἐνεργουμένη naturally has? The Vulgate had already rendered it *assidua*, to which the same objection applies. Michaelis (1935) has much the same sense: "wenn es (anhaltend) geübt wird," but indicates by the brackets that "anhaltend" is not really in the Greek. Where the KJV gets "fervent" from ("the effectual fervent prayer") we do not know (it would be interesting to investigate this point), but we notice with interest that it is retained by Ronald Knox (1945), who drops "effectual"—"when a just man prays fervently." But we need not continue this investigation of the efforts of translators, for we do not think any of the translations we have seen is really very satisfactory or convincing.
[2]In his edition of Clem. Alex. *Strom.* vii (1902), p. 852.

Thus Mayor has dealt with the passive meaning of the verb. Now he expressly admits that some of the commentators state that the passive of ἐνεργέω is never used in the NT (Alford) or at least never in the writings of Paul (cf. Gal. 5:6, which Lightfoot takes as middle with active sense: so translated by KJV, RV, RSV, NEB, Vulg.).

The use of the active is, of course, quoted by Lightfoot;[3] but he makes the following distinctions: "The Spirit of God or the Spirit of Evil" has the *active*, ἐνεργεῖ, in its predicate, the human agent or the human mind ἐνεργεῖται (middle, with the active sense common to a host of middle verbs in Greek).[4]

Then (p. 172, lines 8ff.), Mayor makes an observation more relevant to Jas. 5:16 than perhaps he realizes: "It is however not quite correct to say that [it is] the human agent [that] ἐνεργεῖται; the word [in the *middle*, in various moods, tenses, and persons] in the N.T. is always used of some principle or power at work, whether in the soul or elsewhere. . . ." As examples he cites Rom. 7:5; 2 Cor. 1:6; 4:12; Eph. 3:20; Col. 1:29; 1 Thess. 2:13 (λόγος θεοῦ); 2 Thess. 2:7; we would add *prayer*, Jas. 5:16.

After thus correcting the scope of Lightfoot's dictum in one direction, Mayor increases its scope in another, pointing out another modification of Lightfoot's dictum that the Spirit of God or the Spirit of Evil ἐνεργεῖ, in the active: "the active is not exclusively confined in the Hellenistic writers to the immediate action of a good or evil spirit" (p. 172, line 18), by which he means that there may be some *intermediate* steps or links in the chain of causation between the originating action of the good or evil spirit and the ultimate result. He then gives his examples.[5] Next he cites instances of the transitive use of the active,[6] and the use of the passive noun ἐνέργημα (which comes in 1 Cor. 12:6 KJV, "diversities of operations," and v. 10 KJV, "working of miracles"), and continues to the effect that in view of these instances "it *seems more natural* to understand ἐνεργεῖσθαι here [i.e. in Jas. 5:16] with a passive force, of prayer *actuated or inspired by the Spirit*, as in Rom. 8:26," where, we may point out, the verb ἐνεργεῖν does not even occur (*q.v.*); rather the verse says that the Spirit "helpeth our infirmities . . ." (KJV), and he is *not* said (and here we translate Bull's Latin) "to actuate or inspire our prayers with divine ardor of force," but does his own praying for us, and in our infirmities.[7] Is that any ground for Mayor's statement that in Jas. 5:16 ἐνεργεῖσθαι, naked and unidentified, can mean either Macknight's meaningless "unwrought prayer" or Bassett's "when energized by the Spirit of God"? Benson's "inspired" is either too vague or, if definite in intention, too near Bassett's version.

Next, on Rom. 7:5, Mayor holds that Chrysostom, like himself, took

---

[3]Cf. (*inter alia*) 1 Cor. 12:6; Gal. 2:8; Eph. 1:20; Phil. 2:13; Eph. 2:2.

[4]See Mayor, p. 171, last 3 lines, and p. 172, lines 7 and 8.

[5]Prov. 21:6; Matt. 14:2 (with which, says Mayor, compare ἐνεργουμένη used in Eph. 3:20; Col. 1:29); Wisd. 15:11; Prov. 31:13; cf. Josephus *Jewish War* iv.6 (ἐνήργουν, "put in practice," Mayor); Justin *Dial. with Trypho* 7, δυνάμεις τινὰς ἐνεργεῖν, "to work."

[6]Gal. 3:5; Phil. 2:13; Eph. 1:20.

[7]"Itself maketh intercession for us," as likewise in the next verse, Rom. 8:27, "because (NEB) he pleads for God's own people in God's own way."

ἐνηργεῖτο there as passive: but we submit that Chrysostom appears to take it not as passive but middle (in active sense), for he paraphrases or presents Paul's τὰ παθήματα... ἐνηργεῖτο ἐν τοῖς μέλεσιν ἡμῶν thus: "indicating that the origin of the evil was from elsewhere, viz., from the operating (operative, active, working) considerations, not from the affected members," i.e., affected by the operative causes. Then Mayor says that Abbott, "after a careful examination of all the Pauline passages," "is convinced that the passive meaning is not only possible but in every case superior to the middle." Here we observe only that even he calls the passive in these texts possible, and *superior,* not absolutely certain. Mayor's statement before his quotation of Abbott may repay consideration:

> The passive interpretation being thus supported by the early Greek and Latin commentators, as well as by the constant usage in non-Biblical Greek, we are naturally led to ask whether there is any necessity for a different explanation in the nine passages of the NT in which the word occurs, viz. eight times in St. Paul and once here [i.e., Jas. 5:16].

We suggest that there is an obvious and cogent reason for differentiating between the NT passages and the others quoted by Mayor. In all the passages with the verb ἐνεργεῖν in the passive (p. 171), we cannot find a single example that is not indisputably, transparently, and unambiguously a genuine passive in meaning: in the nine NT texts there is not more than one[8] that is not at least as plausibly to be considered middle as passive in meaning.[9] The evidence seems to suggest the following conclusions.

> The instances quoted on p. 171, in the first 23 lines of Mayor's note, are all genuine passives of normally transitive verbs.

> In the NT the active of ἐνεργέω occurs in Matt. 14:2 (Mark 6:14), "that is why these miraculous powers are at work in him," NEB, and as follows in Paul:
> 1 Cor. 12:6: (God) works all things in all.
> 1 Cor. 12:11: That one and the same Spirit (of God) works in all these things.
> Gal. 2:8: (God, who) wrought effectually in Peter to the apostleship of the Jews, wrought also in me for the Gentiles.
> Gal. 3:5: (God) that... worketh miracles among you (KJV).
> Eph. 1:20: (According to the working of his mighty power) which he wrought in Christ, when he raised him from the dead (KJV).
> Eph. 2:2: the (evil) spirit that now worketh in the children of disobedience (KJV).
> Phil. 2:13: (God) worketh in you both to will and to do (KJV).

> In the NT, then, apart from the exceptional dictum attributed to Herod the tetrarch (Matt. 14:2), the active of ἐνεργέω is predicated only of God seven times, and of the devil once; and the verb—apart from Matt. 14:2—is

---

[8] The textually uncertain 2 Cor. 1:6.
[9] The eight in Paul are Rom. 7:5; 2 Cor. 1:6; 4:12; Gal. 5:6; Eph. 3:20; Col. 1:29; 1 Thess. 2:13; 2 Thess. 2:7.

transitive, with an expressed object in the accusative, except in Gal. 2:8 (for the apostleships of Peter and Paul) and in Eph. 2:2, where the context shows what the devil's works are—trespasses and sins. *None* of the other examples of this verb in the NT is *active*.

Jas. 5:16: The prayer of a righteous man is mighty in operation. The other eight examples are from Paul.

Rom. 7:5: the passions which worked in our members.

2 Cor. 1:6: text uncertain.

2 Cor. 4:12: death worketh in us (KJV).

Gal. 5:6: faith active in love (NEB).

Eph. 3:20: the power that worketh in us (KJV).

Col. 1:29: his working, which worketh in me mightily (KJV).

1 Thess. 2:13: the word of God, which effectually worketh also in you (KJV).

2 Thess. 2:7: the mystery of iniquity doth already work (KJV).

Apart from the textually uncertain 2 Cor. 1:6, all these have a form *not active*, with an intransitive meaning.

We see, then, that in Paul only God, seven times, or the devil once, ἐνεργεῖ in the active, and of these eight instances, six, all referring to God, are transitive, with an object in the accusative. We have seen, too, that all the nonbiblical or biblical (e.g., 1 Esdras) passives noted by Mayor (p. 171) are indisputably passives. Let us now suggest a reason why learned and estimable men, such as Lightfoot and Mayor, are in complete disagreement about the voice (middle or passive?) of ἐνεργεῖσθαι in the NT.

In Greek it is usually clear in a particular instance whether an ambivalent voice in a sentence is being used in middle or passive meaning.[10] Mayor and Abbott and some others maintain that in all our nine examples (one in James, eight in Paul) of that verb in a *prima facie* ambivalent potentiality, "the passive meaning is not only possible but superior." We saw that of Mayor's quoted passives not one is, in the Greek quoted, anything but unquestionably passive; and so far as we can determine, Greek scholars generally agree that the context normally precludes any doubt whether the given form is used with middle or with passive meaning: as we have emphasized, there are some cases where the question can reasonably be raised, but they are far from numerous. If, then, Mayor and those others are so sure that all the nine examples in the NT are passive, how is it that, if the passive is thus so

---

[10]Thus, to give a few examples, the context usually shows whether λύομαι is middle (henceforth designated M), "I ransom, get someone released," or passive (designated P), "I am released"; μισθοῦμαι M, "I hire," e.g., take a house for rent, or P, "I am hired," e.g., a lawyer at an appropriate fee; διδάσκομαι M, "I get someone else (or even myself) taught," or P, "I am taught"; M, "I am cautious, am on my guard," or P, "I am under guard, am in custody." Sometimes, however, there is not a really crucial difference. Thus it may happen that παύομαι may plausibly be translated either as M, "I stop, I cease," or P, "I am stopped," whether I am resigning or being dismissed; if it is said that the maidens κινοῦνται it may be unclear whether this means that, M, they are dancing, are moving, or, P, are having fits, are being convulsed. Indeed, at the end of the *Phaedo* some scholars debate whether, at the very moment of death, ἐκινήθη means, as a genuine P, that Socrates was convulsed, or, virtually as M, that at the end of his dying coma his body gave a slight momentary quiver, "moved."

standardized in the use of this verb in the NT, it never there appears in even one single *indisputable* example? The answer is plain: all those nine verbs are not passive but *middle*, intended by the authors, James and Paul, to be so understood by their readers. If these authors were so devoted as is alleged to using only the passive (and the active) of this verb, but never the middle, we do not believe that they would *never* have produced that passive in even one indisputable example. We submit that nobody who had not already had his mind made up could tolerate passive in those nine texts. Apart from everything else, ἐνεργουμένη in Jas. 5:16 is better taken to mean "in operation" than taken as a passive: this prayer is mighty in what it is *able* to do, not in what it is *enabled* to do. This latter is not without any indication of the source from which the power is alleged to be derived. We know that all strength does come from God; but there is a natural feeling that a righteous man's prayer, like Elijah's prayer (it was a curse), carries a mighty punch.[11] So we translate: "the prayer of a righteous man is very powerful in its operation."

[11]If, however, after all we have said, there are still those who insist on making ἐνεργουμένη passive in Jas. 5:16, context and common sense allow only one interpretation: the prayer . . . is mighty, very powerful, very potent, in its *fulfilment,* in being fulfilled, effectuated, made to work—by God. On consideration, we will allow that God's concern in the prayer to him may be assumed without mention. We do not retract one word of our main argument for the middle; and in point of style, we prefer to keep the prayer and the petitioner in front of our mind, in keeping with the vivid πολὺ ἰσχύει: a thing ἰσχύει, is potent (at least to our mind's eye), rather as *working* than as *being worked.* Mayor criticizes Alford and others (p. 173, line 26) for translating "the prayer of a righteous man avails much in its working," which is virtually our "in operation." When he says that this gives "a poor force," he fails to see that here ἐνεργουμένη, at the end, shares the force of πολὺ ἰσχύει at the beginning and they together are meant to be a most powerful "wedded pair." On the broad question of idiom, ἐνεργ- is like ἀρχ-: ἀρχή is "beginning" or initiative, rule, government. Thus God, the Ruler, ἄρχει (active), rules, governs, makes men and things start and ἐνεργεῖ, initiates activity. Man, the subordinate, "begins," ἄρχεται M (*intransitive,* like the "nine NT texts" of ἐνεργεῖσθαι), "bestirs himself."

210

INDEX OF PRINCIPAL SUBJECTS

INDEX OF AUTHORS

INDEX OF SCRIPTURE REFERENCES